Community Leadership 4.0

Several people have graciously granted interviews for this book. These interviewees have expressed their own viewpoints and opinions. Their positions, perspectives, beliefs, and opinions are distinctively their own and do not necessarily reflect the positions, perspectives, beliefs, and opinions of the author or publisher.

This book presents authoritative information on the subject of community leadership. In no manner is the information in this book to be construed to be a source of legal, financial, or economic advice. Please seek expert counsel from competent professionals if advice is necessary.

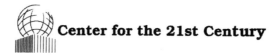 **Center for the 21st Century**

ISBN: 1439252882
ISBN-13: 9781439252888
LCCN: 2009907975
Printed by CreateSpace, an Amazon.com company

Center for the 21st Century
www.c21c.com
214.802.5212

Community Leadership 4.0

Impacting a World Gone Wiki

Carolyn Corbin

 Center for the 21st Century

DEDICATION

Gratefully dedicated to the McKinney (Texas) Chamber of Commerce
Jodi Ann LaFreniere, CCE, President and CEO
Deb Fitzgerald, Director of Membership and Leadership Development

The McKinney Chamber of Commerce is a true champion of community leadership. Under the forward-thinking, dynamic direction of President Jodi Ann LaFreniere, CCE, the chamber is committed to producing highly capable 21st century leaders through unique and innovative initiatives.

While directing the chamber's leadership programs, Deb Fitzgerald manages and influences Leadership McKinney and the Northern Collin County Leadership Program. Because of her energy, expertise, and efforts, these programs are among the best in America. Thanks to Deb, these highly-rated classes became the living lab for this book. Working with her is delightful. She is my role model, teacher, friend, and collegial team leader.

Jodi, Deb, and the entire McKinney Chamber of Commerce staff, along with the McKinney Chamber's Leadership Committee, Curriculum Committee, Leadership McKinney and Northern Collin County Leadership Program class members and alumni, have furnished vital input, feedback, lively debates, and valuable suggestions. They've made this book possible.

Heartfelt thanks and blessings to all.

OTHER BOOKS BY CAROLYN CORBIN

Strategies 2000

Conquering Corporate Codependence

Great Leaders See the Future First

A Promise to America

CONTENTS

Section Four   Putting It All Together

ACKNOWLEDGMENTS

THIS PROJECT HAPPENED because of the contributions of many important people. Their encouragement and support in so many ways made the writing of this book possible over the past year.

Terri Ricketts had the vision. She envisaged a course for Leadership McKinney using the principles from my book, *Great Leaders See the Future First,* published in the year 2000. Seven years ago, she suggested that I specifically target the leadership skills necessary to move communities forward in the new global paradigm. After experimenting, assessing feedback, researching, and drawing conclusions from testing the material in classes concerning 21st century community leadership, this book became a reality.

Ray Corbin, my husband, is my inspiration. He was invaluable in the research and production of this work and was always on the lookout for articles and relevant material to enhance the quality of the book for the reader. He reviewed, edited, provided feedback, and spent a great number of hours lending his expertise to the financial and economic topics. And he understood the long days and weekends that were required to get this job done. His patience, genuine interest, positive attitude, and love spurred this project to completion.

Sylvia Odenwald was the motivator who kept me on track daily. She edited, clarified, questioned, and helped me find thoughts I was searching for when writer's block overtook me at various times. She was always available, constantly cheerful, and worked intensely over the past year. She is both my editor and my special friend.

Edie Dunavan affected this project by editing, helping clarify my viewpoints, and offering thoughtful insight into applications for various communities. Her suggestions were especially valuable.

Nelson Wilkerson was so conscientious. As a design consultant, he worked with graphics, furnished ideas, and took a personal interest in the book from beginning to end. Working with him was a joy. He was always available for meetings or electronic communication—and was a role model for diligence and persistence.

Garden Graphics produced the images for this project. The expertise and talent found at Garden Graphics were unsurpassed. Working with Georgene Wood and Leslie Larson was such a pleasant experience. Their artistic eye was a welcome addition to our design team.

Frank Roma, McKinney's assistant fire chief, and Julie Smith, McKinney's manager of the Office of Environmental Stewardship, took special interest in this project. When they heard about the subject of this work, they both suggested that I study Greensburg, Kansas, for its courage after a devastating tornado and its goal to rebuild as the greenest city in America. Because of them, I was motivated to research and visit Greensburg—and you will read about this experience in the book.

The McKinney Chamber of Commerce nurtured this book from beginning to completion. For that reason, this work is dedicated to them. Please see the dedication page for their role in this project.

Many people gave generously of their time in interviews. Their stories and comments add vitality and real-life experiences. You will meet them throughout this book as you encounter their quotes, narratives, and accounts of life in their communities.

I have worked with various topics relating to conflict since the early 1980s. That experience helped to develop my material for Chapter Nine of this book. However, in 2004, I interviewed four practitioners in conflict management for an unpublished white paper I was writing for credit toward my doctor's degree. They left footprints on my mind. Dr. Marty Farahat, with the Lombard Mennonite Peace Center (Lombard, Illinois), caused me to explore more deeply and conduct additional research on forgiveness and healing in all types of conflict. Dr. Jan Daehnert of the

Baptist General Convention of Texas introduced me to options for handling discord that go beyond the traditional approaches. My takeaway from him was that it is sometimes justifiable to walk away from a dispute. Rev. George "Sonny" Spurger of the Baptist General Convention of Texas emphasized the strong motives of power and control in many conflict situations. After that, I noticed how many people constantly struggle to be the one who is definitely right in a dispute. And Dr. James Puckett, my former pastor, mentor, and friend—who is now deceased—constantly demonstrated compassion and peace in the midst of conflict. He taught me to be careful to allow other people to save face. These four interviewees made an indelible impression on my thinking.

Jennifer Beck of JBeck Photography created my professional photo for this project. She is highly proficient, very patient, dedicated to her work, and offers acute attention to details.

Numerous friends, professional colleagues, and family members provided much-needed nurturing as this project took a life of its own. Uplifting words, emails, hand-written notes, telephone calls, acknowledgments, visits, invitations to lunch for dialoguing sessions, and the sending of helpful articles, references, and ideas—all these were gestures of support and encouragement for which I am profoundly grateful.

INTRODUCTION

THERE ARE MANY great leadership books available. I have read a large number of them and have referred to them often in working with my clients over the past four decades. However, when I searched for a leadership book that dealt directly with the skills I felt were necessary for leading communities forward in contemporary global society, I didn't find the exact book that I was searching for. So I decided to write one that addresses subjects that I feel are necessary in today's socioeconomic climate.

The world is experiencing chaos. Uncertainty abounds. As technological innovation intersects globalization, conditions are occurring and opportunities are arising that most of us wouldn't have considered 30 years ago. Now is the time for leaders to prepare their communities for sustainability in the competitive global arena. It's important for them to know what's happening and how to take advantage of the tremendous prospects that lie ahead. In the socioeconomic venue now extant on Planet Earth, there are specific leadership skills that will be required.

Communities now exist in one of four stages. Most of them are concentrated in the third stage, Community 3.0. To move to the sharply competitive fourth stage, Community 4.0, most communities must take giant leaps forward. And add to that the fact that the global culture is patterning after the contemporary mores percolating on the Internet, we find a world gone wiki (i.e., open-source, chaotic, dynamic, and vital).

Leaders who understand how to take their communities to 4.0 status and lead in a wiki culture will be heroes in the 21st century.

Please join me on the journey of becoming an accomplished Community Leader 4.0. There are exciting adventures ahead for those who choose to navigate the socio-politico-economic whitewater that will be encountered, avail themselves of the gold-mine of opportunities along the way, and doggedly climb the rugged, obstacle-laden mountain of the global marketplace to experience the exhilaration of breathlessly reaching the top and shouting: "Mission accomplished!"

May your journey be rich, abundant, and fulfilling.

SECTION ONE

A World Gone Wiki

CHAPTER ONE

Leading a World Gone Wiki

E X-CONVICTS. FORMER GANG members. Drug addicts. Tough guys who've bullied entire neighborhoods. Many of them are repeat offenders. Often they seem to be incorrigible. But are they?

Various programs are available to them as they seek a second, third, fourth, or fifth chance. After trying and failing multiple times, occasionally something magnificent happens. As a result of program participation, society's offenders turn around and move forward to lead productive lives. Some middle school dropouts eventually earn college degrees. They go on to create successful careers for themselves.

Why are some programs more successful than others? What triggers personal change? Although there are countless reasons for experiencing such dramatic transformation, there is one that stands out. These organizations have something in common. They are applying social principles that have been practiced since the beginning of time. They are equipping people to quest for a better life.

My personal conclusion stems from an observation of the obvious: these programs have found a way to create a winning environment in which people successfully do life together. I believe these organizations—among other things—masterfully create relationships in three areas: individuals to themselves, to one another, and to something greater than themselves.

Whether the point of reference is a non-profit organization rehabilitating society's offenders as we have just discussed, social or civic group, committee, board, commission, business, religious organization, city, town, or village—when people do life together, they form a community. And that's what this book is about—cutting-edge skills for leading communities to success in the 21st century. Specifically, communities formed by residents of cities, towns, and villages who are doing life together.

A democratic community is quite open. Both independent activity and civil unrest can simultaneously exist, yet the community is usually unified at a certain level. In some ways, a democratic community is similar to a wiki website. It is open-source, vital, chaotic, dynamic, and typically emerges as a cohesive unit. Leading this world gone wiki demands special skills.

I formed the idea of a wiki community from the many uses of the word *wiki* on the Internet. The inventor of the original wiki software over 15 years ago was Ward Cunningham (Wikipedia 2009). Today, a proliferation of websites with open environments allows people to enter and edit material. Instead of being finite, the content is dynamic. Today's communities must work in a similar way if they intend to survive in the globally competitive environment.

For over 30 years I have worked with organizations by providing speeches, executive briefings, think tanks, research, and training. During that time, I have experienced many organizational types and models. I have always found it exciting when my work contracts take me to cities and towns as well as local government associations and schools of public affairs. Each one has a different personality. From my experiences with several community leadership programs, I have collected information on communities that aspire to world-class status. I have found that there are definite differentiators between average and world-class communities. Through the years, I have shared this information with participants in various community leadership training programs.

The definition for the word *community* that I use in these classes is people doing life together. Obviously, during the last several years, the word *community* has assumed a definition much broader than merely a physical place where people connect. With the introduction of the Internet and the availability of online communities, social networks, and virtual societies, a variety of communities exists in cyberspace. In this book, however, I will refer to a community as a physical place. The communities in cyberspace can then be used to enhance the value of the physical community.

Another word that begs definition is *citizen*. The Constitution of the United States, Amendment 14, provides a formal definition: "All persons born or naturalized in the United States, and subject to the jurisdiction thereof, are citizens of the United States and of the State wherein they reside." Technically, a citizen of a specific city or town must reside within the legal boundaries of that city or town. My definition, however, of a citizen is a viable community participant. Please note that I am using the word *community* instead of *town* or *city*. It seems that towns, villages, and cities have a more legal definition than the word *community*, which is about people. A community is more intangible and soulful. The qualities that comprise a community reach beyond physical boundaries, laws, and infrastructure. A community may be comprised of people from several towns, cities, suburbs, exurbs, and villages. In fact, Planet Earth is a global community.

Throughout history, the community model has gone through three phases and is now in its fourth phase—hence the title of this book—*Community Leadership 4.0*. The first phase of community began thousands of years ago during the period of history when people were nomadic. The community actually moved to a place where living conditions and food could be found for the community's survival. The community itself was mobile. That was Community 1.0.

In Community 2.0, the community stabilized. It was likely an independent unit surrounded by miles of agricultural and/or mining properties from which people extracted a living. Most people who were born into Community 2.0 lived there throughout their lives. The citizens rarely, if ever, traveled very far from home except for those few brave souls who explored new territories.

When the railroads and, much later, airplanes and interstate highways began to connect communities, then Community 3.0 emerged and became a more dynamic entity. People moved in and out. Citizens traveled hundreds, and even thousands, of miles from home on work assignments or adventurous vacations. Mobility became common. However, most people lived within a comfortable commuting distance of their workplaces. Yes, they may have traveled on work assignments, but the home base was normally near or in their community.

Beginning in the late 1980s, it was evident that Community 4.0 was forming. In this community paradigm, the availability of global technology relating to the Internet provided the capability for people to live in a community chosen for quality of life and place rather than for the aspect of being close to the organization that employed them. And now, that concept is being lived out fully as many people live in places of their choice and work for organizations halfway around the world. Their projects sometimes require travel, but they can also use technology to produce work any time and anywhere. The ideas of outsourcing and off-shoring are becoming commonplace. Thus, Community 4.0 has the capability of high social and intellectual capital, intelligent technology, and an elevated quality of life and place. The unique nature of Community 4.0 demands a different leadership dynamic than in Communities 1.0, 2.0, and 3.0.

Leaders in Community 4.0 come from many different walks of life. They may be elected officials; business people; national, state, and local government employees; nonprofit executive directors and board members; citizen volunteers; members of the educational and religious arenas; and grassroots activists—to name a few. In Community 4.0, a leader is anyone who makes a positive impact. And in a wiki community, there may be no formal leader for a particular project. A grassroots effort might begin because of the interest of a concerned group of citizens. They will move the project forward to success while working with the formal community leaders and other stake holders. In Community 4.0, leaders emerge as needs are perceived. And these leaders can step forward from many community groups.

ﾟﾟ

Are You a Community Leader 4.0?

Here is an exercise that will help you determine whether you are a Community Leader 4.0. Please answer the following questions with either *yes* or *no*. Be honest with yourself.

1. Considering all aspects of your community including people, education, religious institutions, infrastructure, size, businesses involved, and other such community-based initiatives as resources, energy, and transportation, do you have a big-picture vision of your community 30 years from now?

2. Have you defined your purpose in the community?

3. Do you propose ideas that you are willing to alter (if your conscience allows you to do so) in order to compromise with the ideas of others—all for the good of the community?

4. Are you willing to stand alone while backing an issue that you feel strongly about?

5. Are you willing to do the right thing regardless of the consequences?

6. Do you serve your community in a selfless way without consideration for your own agenda?

7. Are you flexible in the center of rapid change?

8. Are you willing to share power in order to cause a project to succeed?

9. Do you know yourself to the point that you can identify triggers of your anger, stress, happiness, satisfaction, temper, and feelings of peace and wellbeing?

10. Do you have a clear definition in mind of right versus wrong?

11. Can you adequately define consequences that might occur if you take specific actions?

12. Can you think objectively without prejudice?

13. Are you good at "reading" people and applying empathy for the thoughts and actions of others?

14. Are you adept at creating new paths to follow, combining current processes to establish new ideas, or finding multiple ways to apply a process currently in use?

15. Can you look at seemingly disconnected events and establish a pattern of connections?

16. Are you open to wide ranges of diversity in all categories?

17. Can you find clarity and a sense of order in constant chaos?

18. Are you comfortable using such technological tools as telepresence, social and business networks, web software, wiki applications, and virtual techniques that literally connect the world?

19. Can you work simultaneously with multiple sources of community power, i.e., wiki power structure and/or grassroots movements as opposed to top-down vertical lines of power?

20. Are you willing to drive change even though it is necessary but unpopular?

Give yourself 5 points for each *yes* answer. Now add up your score.

Total Score _____

Below are explanations of your score.

95-100	You are a Community Leader (CL) 4.0. Congratulations!
85-94	You are almost to CL 4.0. If you set your goals and make the necessary changes, you can get there soon.
70-84	You are more involved in CL 3.0 than CL 4.0. During the next six months, you may wish to set a goal to reach CL 4.0 status.

Below 70   You face challenges in developing Community Leadership 4.0 skills. It is possible to acquire these skills in a 12-to-24-month period of time if you identify your needs and work hard.

❧

Community Leadership 3.0
Versus Community Leadership 4.0

I purposefully introduced you to the previous Community Leader 4.0 instrument and asked you to evaluate yourself by answering the questions before I discussed Communities 3.0 and 4.0 further. I didn't want your answers to be skewed. However, I now wish to depart from considering Community 4.0 leadership skills in order to discuss the profiles of Communities 3.0 and 4.0. Then we will return to a discussion of Community Leader 4.0 qualities.

In a large part, the United States (sometimes referred to as U.S. in the remainder of this book) initiated its 3.0 communities in the mid-1800s, and those communities have been maturing since then. It was not until the latter 1980s that American community leaders began to realize that 4.0 communities were beginning to emerge. However, many communities are mired as 3.0 communities without leadership knowledgeable of the changes necessary to move their communities to 4.0 status. Most communities find themselves at a puzzling juncture of what to do next. Having researched both 3.0 and 4.0 communities, I have discovered some interesting patterns. In this section, I want to contrast the profiles that I have observed in 3.0 and 4.0 communities. I don't claim that these lists are exhaustive, and you may want to add to or argue some of these points. However, I do believe that these are accurately reflective of each community.

Community 3.0 Profile

Tradition-mindedness. For over 30 years as a futurist, I have traveled extensively, especially in the United States, addressing topics concerning necessary changes required for organizational competitiveness. I have worked with many communities during that time and have had the opportunity to meet many community leaders while watching the progress or the retreat of many places. One of the noticeable characteristics of 3.0 communities stuck in their growth process is that of tradition-minded community members. Although I highly advise that communities honor their culture and heritage—and, in fact, work hard to preserve them—it is recommended that communities not concentrate totally on preserving their traditions to the point that change is not invited. The idea of "we've always done it this way" does not bode well for progress.

Concentrated power. There are a few people who rule the community either by exercise of authority or manipulation. There is also a firm belief that a small number of influential people have most of the good ideas. These individuals tell the remainder of the community members what and how to think as well as pointing out the direction in which the community is to go. The other members of the community loyally follow, often without questioning the wisdom of the leaders. Frequently, community members compete for the few existing power positions. The friction can escalate to such a degree that the community's progress is blocked.

Homogeneity. Most community members adhere to a similar set of values, traits, and customs. There is little diversity. Often differences are rejected rather than embraced. Outsiders are not necessarily welcome. Ideas departing from the status quo stand little chance of being accepted. There are pockets of exclusivity in the community to the point that class, philosophical, ethnic, or other differences threaten the community's advancement.

Local perspective. There is little recognition that local communities must necessarily take on a global outlook. There continues to be an attitude of self-containment and independence. Little insight exists concerning the need for preparing the community's business and private subgroups for global interaction, education, trade, and reception of people from all parts of the world.

Low risk mentality. Fear is prevalent. The ideas of global competitiveness and innovation are frightening. Resources are viewed as finite. The community members operate with a scarcity mentality. There appears to be lack of vision and knowledge of how to calculate risk for the factors that would produce sustainability. Community 3.0 is in a constant mode of reactivity instead of proactivity.

Emphasis on order. Members find it bothersome to have chaos and conflict. They spend a great deal of energy trying to maintain the status quo. If innovative ideas upset the community's equilibrium, then those ideas are rejected or sabotaged in order to maintain balance. Often, new ideas are refuted because they might be a threat to the power structure presently in place.

Shortsightedness. The community has no long-term vision for its sustainability or strategic plan for the future. They may have had a prominent consulting firm prepare a comprehensive master plan, and that plan is mistaken for a long-term visionary design for the community's future. Because of leadership myopia, and even blindness toward the soulful aspects of the community's future, the community will be struggling for identity in the global marketplace in the not-too-distant future.

Belief that leadership and management are synonymous. If I am serving on a nonprofit board or a search committee for a new organizational executive, I often pose the question: what is the difference between a leader and a manager? It is amazing how people answer that question. The answers range from never having thought about it to, perhaps, they are one and the same to giving answers such as: a leader is a master visionary, influencer, and innovator whereas a manager plans and executes the details. Mostly, people give thoughtful answers, and I am impressed—but not always. In Community 3.0, leaders have a hard time understanding their role and truly believe that their job is to micromanage projects and dictate the direction of the community.

Pre-smart. A community wherein there is social connectedness ranging from below average to high and where there are people holding bachelor's and advanced degrees at or below the national average, but considered a candidate for increasing its intellectual capital, would be considered pre-smart. Perhaps there is a community college in the community or in the region where it can be easily accessed. The infrastructure needs to be updated, and that fact is recognized by community leaders. There is little recognition of the need for a tie to a research university.

Community 4.0 Profile

Innovation and tradition. Honoring traditions and fostering innovation are both important aspects of Community 4.0. Preserving historical sites, establishing museums, sustaining downtown vitality, valuing its heritage, and continuing to tell the stories about the people and events that brought the community to its present position are considered exciting adventures. Yet the value of moving forward is a part of the current culture. The leaders and community members continually strive for uniqueness. They realize that to be globally competitive, innovation must thrive. The workforce and organizations that the community attracts are state-of-the-art and understand the need to invent new products and processes. They are well aware that innovation is the trump card in global competitiveness.

Distributed power. There is a listening culture because those who are elected and appointed to power positions realize that much wisdom and knowledge are dispersed throughout the network of community members. Face-to-face and/or electronic focus groups and town hall meetings are frequent. People are asked to help solve problems and provide input for innovative programs and projects that will move the community forward. Grassroots groups come forth with ideas and create a dynamic environment. Leadership can happen both formally and informally. Influencers exist at all levels of the community.

Diversity. Diversity is honored as the root of creativity. As people introduce various values, interests, traits, customs, and cultures to Community 4.0, it expands in the quality of life offered to its citizens and in its attractiveness to organizations and people who wish to locate there.

Tolerance is valued. I define the word *tolerance* as peaceful coexistence. There are various definitions used in contemporary culture. Often *tolerance* is conceptualized as *approval*. But, in a highly diverse population, it is rarely possible for all people to approve of the philosophies, behaviors, and traits of others who practice differing, yet legal, approaches. The idea of tolerance is that people of conflicting philosophies concerning how to do life together can have their disparities; yet they can peacefully coexist, and their behaviors can remain within the law. They do not have to agree. In fact, they may simply agree to disagree. But just because someone has a differing philosophy, or is dissimilar in some other way, does not justify the right for physical or personal attack, hateful words, and detestable actions toward a person or group. Healthy dialogue is a valuable part of a democracy. The discussion and argument are about the issues—not the person or group debating the topic.

Global viewpoint. Community 4.0 is constantly finding ways to integrate with other countries through trade, communication, partnering, idea exchange, and visitation to one another's cities. There is openness to the relocation of people and organizations from other countries to the community. The values are flexible in that they easily recognize the uniqueness of other cultures living there and work hard to accommodate their customs. The schools, institutions of higher education, religious organizations, merchants, and local government reach out to various groups to invite them to community activities and celebrations. In considering the kinds of festivals and gatherings provided, the planners include activities that will be enjoyed by all cultures. In many communities, various activities are specifically held to honor particular groups holding membership in the community. There is a concerted effort to attract people from all parts of the globe and to provide an inclusive atmosphere where recognition of uniqueness, as well as blending of creative ideas, can flourish.

Community 4.0 leaders realize that their competition for labor force and company relocations to their community does not lie merely within the regional area, but that major competition for recruitment of global resources exists among communities throughout the world. In his book, *The World is Flat*, Thomas Friedman (2005) suggests that local communities must be open to outside influences and mutual collaboration. Harvard Business School Professor Rosabeth Moss Kanter (2003) advocates that local communities must function with a global marketing strategy if they are to thrive in the future.

Calculated risk approach. By having a willingness to step beyond its comfort zone, Community 4.0 works outside its presumed safety boundaries. This community paradigm presupposes that new discoveries will breed prosperity. It operates from a viewpoint of abundance rather than scarcity. Community 4.0, however, does not exercise risk with reckless abandon. It does its homework and calculates the costs involved in taking the envisioned chances. Rather than be a tree hugger, however, this community is willing to experiment and try new ideas, programs, and processes. Community 4.0 realizes that to give itself permission to win, it must first give itself permission to fail. Rather than regarding failure as a negative, Community 4.0 tags it as a learning opportunity and perhaps a serendipitous break for better things to come.

There is a philosophical nuance penetrating the culture that to remain vital, the community must take calculated chances. The community leaders know that sustainability depends on exploring the unknown, making unique discoveries, and having the courage to take calculated risks. Community 4.0 has the courage to move beyond that which is easy and do that which is hard. In other words, Community 4.0 will do things that Community 3.0 is afraid to do.

Acceptance of chaos. In the 1980s, when social and business chaos became prevalent, people were taught to react to the chaos. The idea was to fight the whitewater, as it was called in those days. Many books written about business chaos carried a depiction of a boat in treacherous waters on the cover. Whitewater became a metaphor for the confusion, bedlam, and disorder that resulted from constant change. Amid the angst of community endurance three decades ago, people adopted a survival mentality. To a large extent, that mental set continues to prevail. People truly believe the world will slow down and reach a state of equilibrium in the near future. It was not until recently that I came to the conclusion that disequilibrium—not equilibrium—is the status quo. And, for many years into the future, we will be operating in daily whitewater. There will be short periods of balance, but mostly imbalance will prevail. Community 4.0 realizes that the ability to thrive in chaos will be a great stimulator of its success.

Long-term vision. Communities with vision have existed from the beginning of time. Nomadic 1.0 communities saw better survival conditions in new locations and moved to those sites. In 2.0 communities, new tools were conceptualized and invented for increased productivity. As 3.0 communities were linked by transportation lines, people perceived the value of economic development. There are so many positive results of community visions echoing down through history that they are too numerous to mention.

However, there is one major difference between visions in earlier phases and in Community 4.0. In this fourth phase, visions must be projected forward for at least 30 years, and it is good to envisage even a century ahead. Obviously, things are changing so rapidly that the long-term future will never end up as it was first imagined. But it is important to project and then revisit the visions every six months to a year in order to make the proper adjustments. The ability to "see" the future for a long timeline is a great predictor of a community's success. Shortsightedness worked in Community 3.0, and the community could experience success by planning for 20 or fewer years ahead. But in today's global economy, sustainability into the distant future must be taken into consideration as both a survival technique and an economic competitiveness strategy.

Awareness that leadership differs from management. Leadership—the ability to drive change resulting in positive impact—is a necessary quality for Community 4.0. Good management—planning, organizing, analyzing, managing details, and executing goal-directed tactics—is also necessary for success of Community 4.0. The unique feature of Community 4.0 is that it differentiates the roles. Leaders work with strategies while managers affect tactics. Each role demands distinctly different skills and the proper people allocated to the role for which they are best suited.

Smart. Both social and intellectual capital are important to the success of Community 4.0. A smart community will exceed the national average of people who have earned bachelor's and graduate degrees. This type of community will employ sophisticated technology to monitor and maximize the efficiency of its infrastructure. Innovative businesses and institutions will be located there and will attract a labor force that specializes in high-level knowledge work involving such professions as science, engineering, math, health care, and computer technology. Its education system is highly rated, and there is access to higher education in the community or in close proximity to the community. There is a respected university nearby. The community also has access to at least one esteemed research institution in its region.

Additionally, a smart community has social connectedness ranging from average to high. If not, then the Community 4.0 has recognized its needs and is designing plans to increase its social capital. More about the necessity of social capital for making a community smart can be found in Chapter Three.

Skills and Traits of a Community Leader 4.0

Now let's return to "Are You a Community Leader 4.0?" for a discussion of the exercise. The foregoing instrument is an indicator of your readiness for community leadership at the 4.0 level. There are primary traits that are necessary for a Community Leader 4.0. As you read through these qualities, you may think to yourself that great leaders have always possessed these skills and abilities. You may feel that nothing new is being discussed. And indeed many leaders in the past have had a great number of these skills. The difference in Community Leaders 4.0 from leaders in other phases of community development is that 4.0 leaders must either possess all these skills themselves or have available sources for all these skills to be effective. I will list and discuss these qualities briefly in the sections that follow. However, throughout the book, these traits and skills will be developed more thoroughly.

Vision

A big-picture view of the future is not a new concept. Throughout history, leaders have looked ahead. Christopher Columbus saw a world that was round rather than flat and dared test that vision by searching for new trade routes. President John F. Kennedy envisioned the United States landing humans on the moon before the decade of the 1960s ended. Dr. Martin Luther King, Jr. visualized a society that honored people's civil rights. Even in ancient times, wise King Solomon claimed in the King James Version of the *Holy Bible,* Proverbs 29:18: "Where there is no vision, the people perish." The importance of vision to sustainability cannot be denied. I am sure that you can name several leaders whose visions, combined with actions on those visions, have changed the world.

As I mentioned in the Community 4.0 profile, long-term vision is a necessary ingredient for moving forward. And leaders of those communities must exercise that type of vision. They have the ability to assess key trends and name the possible conditions that might prevail when the trends converge. Community 4.0 leaders design a process for evaluating the trends so that they can detect changes in trend directions and speed thereby observing emerging patterns. As a result of their vision, they can construct actions and interventions for their community's advantage.

Purpose

There is a clear sense of mission. Leaders who have attained 4.0 status know the roles they are to play. Their strategies are outlined. They have lucid goals. They have defined outcomes and know how they will measure their ultimate successes. These leaders have distinct progress markers. Focus is a key skill imbedded in purpose. In the 21st century, success demands focus.

For many years, organizations have developed mission statements. It has become both an art and a science to have a statement of purpose that is clear and easily understandable. However, in 4.0 communities, leaders themselves have personally developed their own clear mission statements concerning how they will lead their communities. In thinking through their purposes, 4.0 leaders need to keep their statements short. For example, Colonel Theodore Roosevelt knew that he was destined to charge San Juan Hill in the Spanish American War of 1898. With that information in mind, he did just that.

In contemporary America, a Community Leader 4.0 might decide to devise strategies for doubling a community's innovative labor force over the next seven years. Another key Community Leader 4.0 might claim the mission of organizing groups of volunteers who will work with underperforming groups in the local school system. In any community, there are thousands of personal missions being carried out on a daily basis. If a leader can clearly define her mission, then the techniques for accomplishing that mission will fall into place.

Team Orientation

When the team wins, everyone on the team wins. When people do life together, there is an interconnectedness that causes the community to rise or fall together. Leaders who possess 4.0 level skills understand this phenomenon. They realize that their own selfishness will diminish the community's chances for long-term sustainability. When leaders are continually vying for visibility and credit for great ideas, the community will eventually take a back seat in competitiveness. Leaders set the tone for the community's culture. If greed is expressed among the community's leaders, then the whole community will suffer.

Community Leaders 4.0 realize the "power of one." They understand that strength for growth, quality of life, and prosperity are realized when everyone pulls together in unity—hence the concept of the power of one. In other words, a community is a group of people operating together. It takes great skill in diverse environments to reach unity at some level.

Courage

Community Leadership 4.0 is tough. It should only be practiced by the brave. Leaders in 4.0 communities will experience criticism, chaos, conflict, intense demands for dialogue, and many stressful moments. Additionally, these same leaders will feel richly rewarded when problems are solved, prosperity is experienced, quality of life is complimented, and citizens are closely connected. Courage is demanded for navigating the ever-bubbling whitewater in order to transport the community through change to a world-class global position.

Anytime that a person is a change agent, he can expect to meet resistance—often fierce resistance. However, Community Leader 4.0 has assessed the possible consequences of his role and has decided to lead the community forward anyway. Sacrifice on the part of the leader will sometimes be necessitated for the ultimate community good.

Ethical Character

Ethics can be defined in multiple ways. We will discuss more about this subject in later chapters. However, in this context, I use *ethical* to describe a person who has the best interests of the community in mind. An ethical person is known for her fairness, choosing the honorable route in spite of the consequences, and placing heavy consideration on the rights of others in a conflict situation. An ethical leader never intends to do harm. In solving problems, his goal is a double win. He puts quality of community above personal gain. He seeks input from all sides in the decision-making process. An ethical leader has an unambiguous philosophy by which he governs both his life and his work.

Selflessness

This characteristic can best be described by what it is not. Selflessness is not narcissism. In fact, it is the opposite of narcissism, which is self-absorption. Society in the United States is often characterized by its overabundance of narcissistic leaders. As I mentioned earlier, leaders set the culture of the community. If narcissism reigns, then the citizens have permission to become self-absorbed. Greed and envy prevail. The community eventually turns against itself and implodes. History is replete with accounts of leaders who destined their communities to ruin due to their narcissistic behaviors. Dictators and top-down-management-style leaders doom their communities to mediocrity at best and bankruptcy and/or destruction at the worst.

Selfless leaders achieve opposite results of those depicted in the preceding paragraph. They are willing to provide constructive ideas and create an innovative community without concern for who gets the credit for the ensuing success. Community 4.0 leaders realize that selflessness must be both a personal quality and a sustainability strategy. They exercise self-discipline while sacrificing their need for personal recognition in order to achieve community progress. By encouraging the achievements of others and acknowledging the successes of those who are also making a difference, the 4.0 leader guides the community to peak quality of life and competitiveness.

Flexibility

In my book, *Great Leaders See the Future First* (Corbin 2000), I told the story about the discovery I made relating to the willow tree. While watching the video, *Texas*, which is named for the book by the same name (Michener 1985), I discovered that the willow tree is stronger than the oak tree. I had always been taught that the oak tree was the strongest of all trees. Often strong leaders have been compared to mighty oaks. Michener claimed that the willow tree is stronger than the oak tree because it is more flexible. Its branches are agile and supple, blowing with the wind, not against it. They flow rather than resist. In Charles Darwin's theoretical work (Augustine 1997), Darwin accounts for survival of the fittest by defining the fittest as being "the most flexible and adaptable."

In the current wiki community, change happens at an alarming pace, a swiftness sometimes too rapid to comprehend until the change has already occurred. For example, the events of September 11, 2001 (which I sometimes will refer to as 9/11 throughout this book), came as a surprise on a beautiful fall morning. In the blink of an eye, terror interrupted a relatively peaceful day and changed many people's lives forever. The rapidity of change will only increase in the future as nations continue to globalize. Communities will follow suit, and leaders will be expected to move at warp speed in a highly aggressive global setting. The ability to respond to, and even plan in advance for, the flow of events will be a rare talent among contemporary leaders. However, 4.0 leaders will by necessity possess this ability.

Responsibility

It is refreshing to hear a leader say: "I take responsibility for that mistake." Or "I was wrong. I want to apologize to you." We are increasingly living in a world wherein leaders feel that there is too much risk in taking responsibility for actions. It is easier to blame others or particular events and/or philosophies for the outcomes being experienced. It takes great courage for a leader to bear responsibility for her errors in judgment. Assumption of responsibility is required for the fostering of community trust, and 4.0 leaders understand that this trait is a prerequisite for commanding respect in the community.

Self-Knowledge

Carved into the beam at Delphi's Temple of Apollo are the Greek words meaning "know thyself" (Hart 1985). For many centuries, this adage has been espoused as a source of personal wisdom. This maxim is so important that we will invest in more discussion of it later in this book. Modern educators refer to this concept in several ways. Some call it intrapersonal intelligence. Others may mention personal introspection. And some people simply call it self-knowledge.

Unfortunately, this skill is not often considered highly significant in leading a community. However, to the contrary, this skill is one of the most important proficiencies that a leader can possess. Community 4.0 leaders are highly adept at self-knowledge. They understand the triggers for various emotions they exhibit. Leaders on the 4.0 level have internalized a clear philosophy by which they live their lives. They know their strengths and weaknesses while continually searching out learning opportunities for growth and development.

Judgment

When leaders' legacies are reviewed by historians, they are often evaluated by the outcomes of decisions they made. An insightful book by leadership experts Dr. Noel M. Tichy and Dr. Warren G. Bennis entitled *Judgment* (2007) goes so far as to claim that one's success in life is calculated by his judgment calls. Many of the skills of the Community Leader 4.0 combine to produce quality of judgment. How a leader thinks is important to the value of judgment outcomes. Later in this book, I will discuss in more detail five thinking skills that are necessary for sound judgment: consequential, contrarian, critical, creative, and connectional. Creativity, a valuable thinking skill, is a process that produces innovation, which is a key component of community competitiveness. With change moving at warp speed in our world gone wiki, Community 4.0 leaders will be called on to make intelligent decisions at a rapid pace.

Interpersonal Insight

Relationship-building has always been important. In the 21st century, however, with chaos becoming a social norm, the ability to master interpersonal relationships is a necessity. In Communities 3.0 or below, often the leaders possessed judgment acumen and several other technical skills but were short on such "soft" skills as self-knowledge and social astuteness. Community Leaders 4.0 will necessarily possess relationship-building skills. These skills embrace the idea of including all types of people in the community system because their ideas and presence are valued. Interpersonal insight grants the Community Leader 4.0 the ability to use a network form of leadership, i.e., listening to ideas of all people before important community decisions are made. This contrasts with the top-down traditional type of leadership. Relationship-building expertise restores some degree of order to chaos and manages conflict for the community's advantage.

Dr. Daniel Goleman has conducted extensive research and published widely on this concept in his books and articles. Two suggestions for acquiring further knowledge in this area are his books *Emotional Intelligence* (1995) and *Social Intelligence* (2006). I will survey this topic later in the book.

Comfort with Connective Technology

During the next decade, technology will be introduced at mind-boggling speed. As I mentioned earlier in this chapter, this book will concentrate on community as a physical place, but it is important to be familiar with the technological tools that can enhance community connectivity. For larger communities, it may not always be productive to hold meetings with board members in attendance at a physical place. Occasionally, it may be helpful to call on telepresence technology as a method of conducting meetings—i.e., the meeting place is virtual. This technology is available virtually worldwide so that committee members can visually interact while the meeting is being conducted.

Teleconferencing, a simpler form of gathering by telephone, has been in use for several years and also works well for increasing productivity. Community Leaders 4.0 are familiar with various tools for making connections other than the standard traditional connecting mechanism of personal meetings. Of course, Community Leaders 4.0 practice good judgment concerning whether to have personal meetings versus using technology. Use of various methodologies should be balanced.

Transformational Mindset

Community Leaders 4.0 impact their world. They have influence as is so often descriptive of leaders at all levels. However, Community Leaders 4.0 go beyond influence to produce outcomes that are robust. Impact is more powerful than influence. Change happens due to the actions of these leaders. Community Leaders 4.0 intend to make a distinct difference. Therefore, Community 4.0 is transformed because of its leaders.

⁓

Dialogue with Community Leader 4.0 Don Paschal: Practical Advice for Leading Your Community Forward

Listing the characteristics of Community Leaders 4.0 is important. However, observing how these skills work in the real world is even more valuable. With this thought in mind, I dialogued with Don Paschal, who deals with communities every day and knows from many years of experience what works and what doesn't.

Paschal, owner of Paschal Consulting, works with cities, the private sector, and developers to create a win/win situation—between the city as regulator and the developer's vision—in order to establish value for the business side of the equation. In the past, Paschal, who holds his master's degree in public administration from the University of North Texas, has served as city manager of McKinney, Texas, my hometown. McKinney is one of the fastest-growing cities in the United States and was named in 2010 by *Money Magazine* as #5 in its list of "100 Best Places to Live in America" (for cities with a population between 50,000 and 300,000 people). Paschal is currently active in international, national, state, and local city management associations. I respect his professionalism and proven credibility. Furthermore, he has a broad perspective of community happenings from a global worldview.

Paschal spent two decades taking McKinney from a small town of approximately 16,000 people to a competitive, larger city—which today boasts approximately 130,000 people and will build out at more than 350,000 people. The city, nestled in the Dallas-Fort Worth metroplex, is an important contributor to the Texas Triangle, a 60,000 square-mile mega-region (Butler et al 2009), which will be an important global megalopolis in the future. The assistant city manager, Pat Doyle, who worked with Paschal to execute the community's vision, talks about Paschal's courage in making the tough decisions necessary for making things happen during the community's transformation. "Don laid the groundwork for growth," Doyle said. "He had a vision of what McKinney could be. Recognizing the importance of specific elements of a successful community, he expanded the airport, instituted a long-range plan for McKinney, was instrumental in developing a regional water and wastewater supply system, and worked with innovative developers—which totally changed the community's personality dynamics and the future direction of the city. Don is excellent in establishing collaborative partnerships. And he is definitely a visionary."

When I asked Paschal about the greatest problems facing communities today, Paschal replied without hesitation that lack of visionary community leaders coupled with the inability to maintain adequate community focus were the two greatest challenges. He commented that many people know how to *manage*, but there are few people who know how to *lead* in a community environment that has a rapidly shifting paradigm. Paschal stated that the ability to construct and carry out a vision for at least 30 years into the future will be a necessity for Community Leaders 4.0. He perceives that so many changes are happening in communities today that strong leaders must have the ability to say "no" to things that are not relevant in order to focus on the important factors that will sustain the community well into the future.

Paschal comments: "Great community visionaries have the ability to leap-frog to new paradigms rather than continue to think sequentially. So many changes are taking place that there will be a new normal—which creates new opportunities. Astute leaders will see these opportunities and act on them for the sake of community sustainability."

In contrasting leaders and managers, Paschal articulates that managers deal mostly with technique whereas leaders require more passion.

Leaders must translate abstractions into practical initiatives that can be embraced and applied whereas managers deal with visible data which they organize and control. Leaders envision the big picture whereas managers work with details, he espouses. In today's financial, political, and social environment, Paschal believes that there are more great managers than great leaders.

When I queried him about the effect of global and national influences on local communities, Paschal expressed the following point of view. "Communities with only a local perspective will miss the big picture concerning how they fit into the global economy. Events in other countries affect us locally. Federal action also influences the way communities perform in almost every aspect. If the national economy doesn't grow, local revenues are lost. Global and national environmental issues (e.g., the volcanic eruption in Iceland or an oil spill in the Gulf of Mexico) can also trickle down to local communities. If an overwhelming load is cast on one area of a state's budget—for example, health care—then money might be taken from transportation budget allocations. This can hold highly negative consequences for local communities. Additionally, local communities can be in danger if the federal government overspends."

I asked Paschal how 4.0 communities can become globally competitive. He cited five ways: (1) renewable intelligence base through education and technology; (2) ability to communicate efficiently and quickly on a global basis—i.e., quick information and transaction exchange; (3) smart transportation network ranging from mass transit, air, automobiles, and cargo logistics; (4) vision at least 30 years ahead for wise use of natural or human-constructed resources—e.g., wastewater treatment, drinking water distribution, recycling, and alternative energy; (5) strong will of leaders and members of the community to be competitive in the global arena.

And finally, Paschal believes that leaders can allow differences to overwhelm the community. He feels that too many differences disallow the formation of a critical mass necessary to get things accomplished. That factor can ultimately damage community sustainability (Paschal 2010).

ϩ

The Process of Becoming a 4.0 Leader

Very few communities have entered the 4.0 level. They may have a few factors necessary to be classified at that phase of development; however, no community is totally 4.0. The majority is either in the process of attainment or has never even contemplated moving beyond Community 3.0. Those with Community Leaders 4.0 have the best chance of reaching 4.0 status.

It is possible to become a world-class community. It will take development of special 21st century skills coupled with hard work. The remainder of this book will provide the context in which our communities will evolve and the steps necessary for exercising Community Leadership 4.0.

How to Use the Community 4.0 Leadership Strategies And Questions for Contemplation in This Book

At the end of each chapter are two sections: Community Leadership 4.0 Strategies and Questions for Contemplation. Although many tactics are discussed in the chapter text, the Community Leadership 4.0 section offers suggestions for implementing some of the principles discussed throughout the chapter.

In the Questions for Contemplation section, I list questions aimed at promoting thinking skills most useful when used in a think tank setting. In forming a think tank, call together a diverse group of people from different disciplines to gather a broad view of an issue. The disciplines involved will depend on the issues at hand.

Meet on a regular basis for a specific amount of time (one to four hours) to address issues and provide suggestions for problem solutions. As dialogue takes place, interesting results will emerge. After the goals have been achieved, the same group can either disband or become involved in implementing solutions.

Only your imagination will limit how these questions can be used.

৵

Community Leadership 4.0 Strategies

The major thrust in this chapter has been to introduce you to the four community levels and to emphasize the necessity for leading your community to the 4.0 level. To boost your community to the 4.0 level, you must be a Community Leader 4.0. Here are some steps for discovering your present status and for determining movement to Community Leader 4.0.

1. Review the profiles of Communities 3.0 and 4.0.
2. Determine where your community falls in these profiles.
3. Review your answers to the "Are You a Community Leader 4.0?" instrument. Analyze your responses and determine how you can move forward.
4. Set a goal to be operating at Community Leader 4.0 level within 24 months. List the steps you must take to meet that goal.

Questions for Contemplation

1. On which level is your community operating today?
2. What community characteristics caused you to answer Question 1 as you did?
3. If your community is not at the 4.0 level, what does it need to do to move to that status?
4. Are you a Community Leader 4.0?
5. If you answered *yes* to Question 4, how are you using your strengths to move your community forward?
6. If you answered *no* to Question 4, what steps do you need to take to become a Community Leader 4.0?
7. How does your community foster innovation?
8. How does your community honor diversity as a root of its creativity?
9. What calculated risks have leaders in your community taken in the past five years?
10. What is the 30-year vision of your community?
11. What judgment calls have you had to make in your community during the past five years?
12. Have you had to publicly demonstrate ethical character in your community during the past five years? If so, how did you do that?

Leading Community 4.0—The Context

CHAPTER TWO

The Future Is Not a Continuation of the Present

L EADERS OFTEN LOOK into the future and envision it as an extension of today. Circulating on the Internet is a picture of a model of the home computer for 2004 supposedly created by scientists in 1954 and published in *Popular Mechanics*. You may have received it in your inbox during the past several years. The picture is a hoax but, surprisingly, it is a fairly accurate depiction (minus the huge submarine console) of the home computer as was envisioned four to five decades ago. The hoax model depicts a huge submarine control unit with a 1950s era television somehow hooked to a teletype machine (Saelinger 2004). Viewing this apparatus today elicits laughter and disbelief that anyone could conceive of anything so ridiculous. But, even if this picture weren't a hoax, it would have seemed logical in 1954 to assume that future technology would be an extension of the technology of that age.

The reason I know that this model could have some merit, even though it is a hoax, is that my first job as a futurist in the early 1970s was to work on the design of the home and school computer. Strange as it might seem, the contraption I had in mind was much like that hoax picture floating around the Internet. I didn't use the submarine control unit as depicted. However, in a computer room remote from the school or home computer, there would have been a control console somewhere. I use this example to illustrate a point: the future is not a continuation of the present. It's difficult to project the future based on what is happening today unless you do very detailed homework and have flawless future vision. That is impossible.

Of course, now we know the rest of the story because we can see with our own eyes how the personal computer looks today. Through technological innovations, computers have greatly shrunk in size, and technology has converged to a point not conceptualized 50 years ago.

As I mentioned earlier, I was part of a team working with computer models for the public schools and the home in the early 1970s. My idea of how computers in the schools would look and function was based on the computer systems in use at the time. I envisioned a teletype machine, over which instruction would be delivered, being online through a telephone receiver immersed in a coupler. All this was hooked to a cathode ray tube for visual applications. Our technology team actually designed and built such a device and tested it at conventions for educators. On one occasion, a severe thunderstorm outside the convention center brought down the whole system. Educators walked off in disgust saying that all this new technology could not even withstand a cloudburst. Most people told me this concept had no future.

Again, we know the rest of the story. The "school" computer and the "home" computer are now one and the same, and much beyond anything that could have been conceived by anyone four to five decades ago.

In Figure 2.1 I have drawn a present-to-future timeline beginning after World War II.

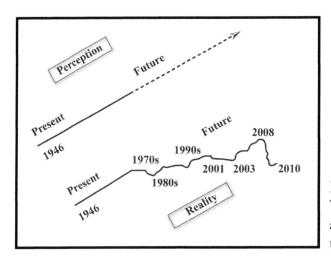

Figure 2.1
The Future: Not
a Continuation of
the Present

Immediately after World War II ended, life became predictable to a great extent in the United States. There continued to be building and expansion, involvement in international conflicts, economic booms and busts, and recurring economic cycles. People could expect to go to work for a stable corporation, and if they demonstrated a good work ethic, they could anticipate retirement from that organization after many years on the job. In the 1980s, as the United States began to globalize to a greater degree than ever before, the prospect of socioeconomic predictability and stability in the workplace forever changed.

For those people who grew up in the 1950s, 1960s, and 1970s, the expectation was that life would always move cyclically as it did during those decades. When the socioeconomic cycles changed, it was difficult for Baby Boomers (born 1946 to 1964) and Generation X (born 1965-1976) to make the transition to a different mindset concerning how the world works. Since Generation Y (born 1977-1997) has had very different experiences, the global changes are not as shocking to them.

The phenomenon happening today is this: structural changes are increasing. To set the stage for understanding the context of Community Leadership 4.0, it is important to understand the difference between cyclical and structural change. When structural change happens, things change to the degree that they will never be as they were. For example, the terrorist attack on New York City in 2001 changed the way national and international security is enforced. Life is not the same today as it was before that horrible September 11, 2001 event. After structural change happens, then the cycles of change will also be different.

Just as earthquakes cause physical structural changes, socioeconomic structural changes alter the way the economy performs and/or the way various social subsystems work. And, like an earthquake, socioeconomic structural changes have varying degrees of intensity. Highly intense structural changes cause radical socioeconomic changes whereas less intense structural changes have lighter effects.

Consider the economy as an illustration. After September 11, 2001, the economic cycles for the following decade differed from those of the former decade. All this, of course, was not entirely due to the 9/11 event, but can be attributable to such related effects as resources being tapped for war efforts following 9/11—whereas those resources might have been used by other agencies to put into effect more watchful enforcement of investment laws had 9/11 never occurred. In other words, cycles between structural changes are repetitive, but the rhythms and content of the cycles alter after another structural change takes place. If one envisions the future based on economic cycles, for example, predictions will be largely off course after a structural change, especially if leaders are using data from cycles occurring before the last structural change.

With structural changes happening more rapidly, Community Leaders 4.0 must be able to call the results of changes that are taking place without having had experience in solving the problems that arise. They are asked to make judgment calls in areas where they have had no previous experience. Today's problems cannot necessarily be solved with yesterday's solutions. Thinking skills, in today's brave new world, are often more important than past experience.

In Figure 2.1, the first line depicts the general public's perception of life: the future is an extension of the present. The second line indicates the reality that exists: significant events have caused structural changes which have forever changed how the world works. You will notice that the line runs rather predictably from 1946 until the early 1970s, then the line becomes jagged, never again to form a straight path. In the 1960s, there was civil unrest. Tragedies such as the assassinations of President John F. Kennedy, Dr. Martin Luther King, Jr., and Senator Robert F. Kennedy took place. Pressure was on the U.S. government by an increasing number of people to end the Vietnam conflict. On the diplomatic front, the U.S. and the Soviet Union struggled in the grip of the Cold War. In general, the pattern signaled domestic rebellion against former American assumptions. These trends fed into the ensuing decade.

In the 1970s, events began to drive the United States in a different direction. The end of the Vietnam conflict, two energy crises, and Japan's entry into the automobile market along with double-digit inflation converged to produce structural change. Oil prices began to rise, and tension increased in the Middle East. With U.S. oil imports escalating, the United States became more dependent on OPEC (Organization of the Petroleum Exporting Countries) for its energy needs. At the same time, Japan entered the U.S. auto market and triggered competition that would be a great factor in the problems that American automobile companies would suffer in 2009. By the end of the 1970s, structural change had impacted the U.S. to a degree that it would never be the same.

In Figure 2.1, you will note that the 1980s brought more structural change. There was a savings and loan crisis that reduced real estate values tremendously. And there was a global drop in oil prices that sent many states into a deep economic recession. This oil price reduction was the beginning of the end for the Union of Soviet Socialist Republics (USSR). By 1989, the Cold War between the United States and the Soviet Union had ended. The Soviet Union was dissolved in 1991. It could not sustain its economy with the sharp drop in energy prices. The convergence of these events coupled with a change in economic philosophy in the United States caused the United States to enter a period of unprecedented prosperity. Credit became easier to obtain in the following decades. The U.S. adopted a credit economy, and consumers had easy purchasing ability. This structural change seeded the eventual economic collapse that happened in the last half of the first decade of the 21st century.

The 1990s brought the commercialization of the Internet and produced an economic bubble that kept the economy exuberant until the dot-com bubble burst in the early 2000s. However, many strong companies survived the economic downturn, and the Internet introduced one of the strongest global structural changes that has ever happened. This phenomenon changed the way the world lives, works, and communicates. Still in its infancy, the Internet has many years of mutations ahead and will drive the world into a totally new cultural experience.

In 2001 a great tragedy hit the United States. Multiple terrorist attacks on American soil forever changed America's homeland security philosophy. The events of this day triggered an American reaction heard and felt around the world. The effects of America's responses will continue to foster global responses and internal socioeconomic conflict for many years hence. America's view of global safety and security will never be the same as it was the day before the terrorist attacks.

On March 19, 2003, the history of the United States intersected its future. The mix of global alliances altered as the United States and an international coalition of a few willing nations entered Iraq to remove the existing regime. This move provoked a storm of global controversy.

Polarization strengthened over this pre-emptive strike and set the tone for politics for many years to follow.

In 2008 the oil markets became erratic. America's dependence on foreign energy imports became painfully obvious. The escalating price of energy ignited the push for energy independence coupled with the exploration for energy alternatives in America. Added to this was the realization that the United States and most countries around the world were economically affected by the huge recession in the United States. Triggered by problems with multiple financial instruments and too much credit having been unwisely extended to individuals and businesses, the United States entered the worst recession since the Great Depression of the 1930s. The philosophy concerning the role of government in the socioeconomic lives of individuals and businesses shifted from its previous position held over the past two decades. It will take several years for America to work its way out of this debacle. Recovery will be slow. The global economy was affected. Again, structural change happened. The socioeconomic culture in America will never return to the way it was previous to the midpoint of the first decade of the 21st century.

The year 2010 saw many structural changes. The Health Care Reform Bill (and other highly controversial legislation) passed by the U.S. Congress, as well as the shaky economy of Greece and the teetering position of many other countries and American states over social and financial issues, will cause permanent socioeconomic shifts. Things will never be as they were before 2010. The futures of these deeply affected areas will not be as once conceived even a few years ago. These areas can still have a positive tomorrow. However, the leaders of these cities, states, and nations must be innovative and think creatively in order to produce forthcoming prosperity.

Structural changes are happening so rapidly that it is difficult at best to lead Communities 4.0. In fact, many Communities 3.0 may find it difficult to survive the economic fiasco of the late years of the 21st century's first decade. One noticeable result of the socioeconomic shift taking place is that the recovery will be more jobless than other recoveries following a deep recession. After the recession that technically began in 2000 and intensified after the terrorist attacks on 9/11/2001, the recovery brought corporate growth—but did not restore as many jobs as people had hoped. Many people were able to find work—but under different conditions and at less salary and benefit replacement values.

After the protracted recession experienced in the latter part of the first decade of the 21st century, the job climate may be more of the same as happened after the 2000 (into 2002) recession. Corporations will be reeling for a while trying to get back to secure footing. The global workforce will be available for outsourcing jobs to them. The climate in the United States may not be as business-friendly as in past years. Thus, thinner profit margins, global competition, and the need to make up for lost time during the recession will cause businesses to keep their costs as low as possible. Hiring freelance workers (part-time workers and contract labor) will be a welcome opportunity. This will allow businesses to control the numbers of people on their payroll at any one time depending on market conditions and will allow them to ask their workers to negotiate their own independent worker contracts.

The economic crash in financial markets in 2008 triggered a shift in dominant political philosophy in America. This shift has thrown the culture into conflict over the amount of control the U.S. government should have in the socioeconomic milieu. Vast change is occurring in all American institutions. As this shift happens, many people in the labor force will not be prepared for the jobs that will be created in the future. This situation will further fan the flames of debate over how these unprepared people are to be reintroduced into the workforce and/or compensated while out of work. Conflict will escalate between those prepared for 21st century work and those who are unprepared to work in the future.

Trends Drive Structural Change

To envision the future, there are at least 13 major trends at this point that Community Leaders 4.0 should understand. You may be able to cite others. Later in the book, I will point to a model for assessing trends and looking ahead to possible resulting conditions. However, I will concentrate on the following trends at this time.

Science and technology are producing massive changes.

Just in the consumer category alone, technology is making it possible to form social networks worldwide, acquire college degrees online, download music, movies, and books at lightning speed, and tune in on global conflicts as they happen. In the medical field, a doctor can administer advice to a patient at virtually any place on Planet Earth that is set up to receive Internet services. It is also possible to direct a robot to perform surgery thousands of miles away. Scientists are beginning to ask the question: is it possible to replace enough mandatory body parts through use of new technology and conquer enough serious diseases so that humans can live on this earth forever (Myers, 2009)? Due to Internet capabilities, workers can do jobs at worksites thousands of miles from where they live without leaving home. I could continue endlessly with this list of innovations that will change our lives within the next two decades.

However, the point I wish to make about this trend is that because of innovations in science and technology, massive changes will take place very rapidly. In *The Wall Street Journal* article entitled "The Ten-Year Century," authors Tom Hayes and Michael S. Malone (2009) identify forces causing the compression of events into a timeline approximately 10 percent of what it would have been just a few short years ago. Community Leaders 4.0 must be prepared to contend with this brisk rate of change in order to sustain their community's competitiveness and quality of life.

Structural changes are accelerating.

As I have mentioned earlier, the speed of structural change will continue to quicken. As discussed previously, structural change causes an environment to be as it never was before. Thus, if structural changes increase in occurrence, then a new operating environment will be appearing before people have had time to adapt to the former setting. Constant chaos will prevail. Smart leaders will realize that they, working alone, cannot possibly access enough information to make necessary decisions for adaptation to the rapidly changing environment. Community Leaders 4.0 will build a team of advisors to help with the judgment calls necessary for efficiency in this warp-speed world.

Globalization is increasingly becoming the norm.

Since the 1970s, globalization has escalated. You will probably observe that Planet Earth, however, has always been in a globalization mode. Explorers have moved farther from their homelands to foreign places since the beginning of time. Each century has brought expanded exploration throughout the world and even beyond Planet Earth. International businesses exist in multiple locations all over the globe. With the introduction of the Internet, globalization became a reality for individuals as they realized they could live in one place and work in another place while never leaving home. Technology has changed the way work is done and how we communicate. Worldwide social and business networking will continue to take place with people we have never seen personally. The Internet has introduced a shrinking global community. This trend will cause leaders to think globally while leading the local community to expand its business and social horizons for inclusion of diverse populations.

Fast is morphing into warp speed.

Speed with which data is accessed and the velocity with which transactions happen will grow incrementally until the human mind cannot embrace the available intelligence for accurate decisions. Artificially intelligent technology will become the tool for leadership. This expertise will also be accessed for judgment calls. When that happens, machines will be smarter than humans, and the results will be unpredictable.

Competition is getting stiffer.

As more nations emerge into the global marketplace, goods and services will flood the consumer with more purchasing choices. With supply increasing, cost of these goods and services will decrease. This will have a ripple effect on the economies of countries that are in the competitive economic race. Emerging economies will grow an educated middle class—which will consume more products and services—and enter the global workforce. Due to the increase in use of technology, the amount of total business income being spent on human labor in advanced countries will be cut to increase productivity for competitiveness reasons. Technology will replace human workers in positions wherein that replacement would succeed. Otherwise, jobs that can be outsourced and offshored will be sent to countries with lower labor costs. Community Leaders 4.0 must prepare for pockets of unemployment or low employment for workers who are not prepared to participate in the new nature of work. Leaders must keep this trend in mind when recruiting businesses and workers to their communities. Leaders must also understand the importance of partnering with educators for developing curriculum relative to their community's needs while keeping in mind preparation for a globalized workplace.

Profit margins are continuing to shrink.

Unless a business has an innovative product or service that is highly desired by the consumer and not yet reproduced in the marketplace, then competition will be heavy, thus causing profit margins to shrink. When profit margins shrink, companies must use all methods available to keep their costs low as we discussed in the former topic on stiff competition. This, of course, has a ripple effect on the community in that community revenues will be affected as a result of lower employment and perhaps lower revenues from local businesses.

Key labor markets are tightening.

There are great numbers of unemployed people in the United States, but many of them do not possess the skills for filling the jobs that exist. Special proficiencies in science, technology, engineering, and mathematics (STEM) are required for securing the well-paying positions open worldwide. There are not enough workers educated in these disciplines to fill the openings for these jobs today. In the future, there will be even more jobs that will be difficult to fill. According to Manpower's 2009 Talent Shortage Survey, 36 percent of employers in the American region—and 30 percent worldwide— are under pressure to fill positions due to lack of available talent (Manpower 2009). Through informal communications with small business owners and community college administrators, I've found that shortages are also being reported for occupations requiring licensing—such as plumbers and electricians—and technicians, especially in intelligent technology, requiring certifications beyond high school. According to Edward Gordon in his article "The Global Talent Crisis," unless we educate American students more appropriately, after 2020 there might be 12 million to 24 million jobs unfilled in the U.S. economy (2009). This trend indicates to Community Leaders 4.0 that an initiative on their agenda must be a matching of education to job preparation for the future.

Rightsizings are continuing.

Due to razor-thin profit margins, companies will continue to monitor talent flow. This process will become as important as cash flow to organizations around the world. People will be hired for projects, and then they will be terminated once the project is complete unless their skills match the needs for another contract being executed by the organization. Most labor will work on a contract basis. Perhaps up to 70 percent of the workforce in the United States will work via contract. Negotiation of agreements between organizations and their contractors will be an important skill in tomorrow's talent bank. In recruiting businesses to their area, Community Leaders 4.0 should be aware of the potential for itinerant workers who will move to the community temporarily for work then perhaps move away from the community once the contract is complete. One consideration in community planning is to chart related clusters of organizations so that the workers can have a pool of opportunities in the same community or region.

Conflicts are increasing.

As globalization causes more involved interaction, the diversity of cultures, ideas, philosophies, and goals for the future will continue to collide. Heterogeneous populations will be forced to relate to one another whereas, in the past, these populations lived independently. Increasing interdependence will cause conflict over desired directions for local communities, states, nations, and the world itself.

In 1995 I was asked to make a speech to a Leadership USA conference being held in California. While preparing for that presentation, I identified trends that would be happening as conflict continued to increase. That research resulted in five trends that I felt would intensify in the next decade—which is now the present decade. Those trends indicated conflicts would occur over (1) distribution of wealth; (2) racial and ethnic issues; (3) religious belief systems; (4) definition of "family;" and (5) solutions to high crime rates. As I write this book over a decade later, it seems as if all five of these areas are indeed experiencing intensification of conflict. I predict that the discord will escalate even more in the years following 2010. Community Leaders 4.0 must maintain an awareness of these conflicts and learn to manage them if their communities are to maintain a sense of unity.

Chaos is prevailing.

Chaos is a byproduct of change. When change is initiated, any system will be thrown into varying degrees of chaos. The ability to manage chaos is such an important marker of great Community 4.0 leadership that I will dedicate a chapter of this book to a discussion of community change and chaos—and another chapter to conflict. With structural change accelerating, then chaos will be unavoidable. Without leaders' ability to manage turmoil, then communities will experience dangerous gridlock. Progress will be impeded. Competitiveness and quality of life will suffer.

Institutions are changing.

Institutions are organizations that serve defined purposes in a society. Schools, governments, businesses, and religious organizations are examples of socioeconomic institutions. Historically, the roles of these institutions were predictable, and the community understood their missions. As we move deeper into the 21st century, the purposes of these organizations will continue to be redefined. For example, there is continuing debate in the United States over how much power the government should have in the personal lives of its citizens. In religious institutions, there is intense deliberation concerning acceptable social behaviors of their leaders. Schools, once defined as learning organizations, will be further expected to fill such other roles in the future as servicing responsibilities once reserved for the family. In the United States, businesses historically provided jobs and innovative marketplace solutions. They were located in the United States and employed most of their workers in the United States. That business model may be shifting.

Most of these changes have already begun and will intensify over the next decade. Community Leaders 4.0 must clarify their philosophy about the missions of the various institutions in their local communities as well as at all levels up to the highest echelons of their countries. Eventually, leaders will be called on to define global institutions and the roles they will play in the lives of all individuals on earth. It will be difficult to guide a community if a leader is not clear on her position about the roles various institutions should play in contemporary culture.

Intelligence is a growing source of capital.

Capital is a source of wealth or advantage. As we enter the new decade, intelligence will grow more important as a source of personal and community wealth coupled with competitive advantage. Intelligence, in my observation, is information converted into knowledge that is useful in making good decisions. For centuries, global governments and military organizations have gathered intelligence on perceived enemies. Centuries ago the methods were rudimentary. In contemporary society, very sophisticated technology is used to gather intelligence. Competitive intelligence-gathering is also common today. Businesses employ people who are specialists in accumulating information on competing companies and assessing potential new products and/or services that those companies are preparing to launch into the marketplace.

In the larger arena, gathering intelligence will be a required skill of Community Leaders 4.0. Without the ability to gather and assess information on future technology, demographics, economics, political directions, ecological issues, and social concerns, leaders cannot make accurate decisions for driving their communities' future successes. Gathering that information themselves, or asking others to do that task for them, is only the first step. The resulting information must be converted into applicable, helpful knowledge (intelligence) that will foster accurate decisions.

We are quickly moving to a workplace wherein a majority of the jobs will require the ability to convert information to intelligence. Today those people are known as knowledge (or creative) workers. As higher levels of intellect are required to do the jobs of tomorrow, the labor force will continue to be called on to tap their intelligence-gathering skills. Leaders must understand the importance of intelligence as a source of personal and community wealth building and work with businesses, educational institutions, social entities, and citizens to see that this skill is developed.

Success is increasingly demanding focus.

Because of the sophistication of technology, the speed of change, and the availability of virtually unlimited information, communities must narrow their focus. In other words, they must specialize in particular industries and worker preparation for those industries to be successful. Community Leaders 4.0 will focus their marketing efforts on recruiting and incubating particular company categories and will see that community workers are trained as experts in the fields on which their community has decided to focus. Further, Community Leaders 4.0 will direct the charge to target specific talent pools and encourage community stakeholders to partner in developing a milieu that will attract those talent pools to the community.

Special skills will be demanded of Community Leaders 4.0 as they seek to define the delicate balance between too much diversification for economic purposes and too much focus for marketplace competitiveness. Too much diversification can dilute the community's marketplace attractiveness whereas too much focus can endanger a community's revenues during economic downturns. In order to assure sustainability, communities must concentrate on finding the right balance between these two extremes.

What in the World is Happening?

The dozen and one trends previously discussed are introducing five conditions shaping the types of communities that will be in demand in the years ahead. These conditions are as follows:

1. Uncertainty even in previously stable civilizations
2. Globalization as a norm
3. Demand for increasing freedom
4. Life in virtual worlds due to sophistication of technology
5. Emotional poverty caused by extreme materialism

International chaos and conflict along with constant polarization on the domestic front are causing uncertainty to prevail. When this much discord is constantly taking place, people feel ill at ease and uncomfortable. Since globalization is becoming the norm, citizens are thinking broadly about life and careers and do not have as much local integration as was once the standard. People are pushing for more individual liberties, and citizens throughout the world are demanding more freedom from oppression. Often when the expression of individual freedoms becomes extreme, the freedoms of others are threatened. The assumption of broad freedoms often invades the boundaries of others. Conflict may result.

The digital revolution has launched the ability to communicate in a virtual world. Everything from email to social and business networking allows people to relate without experiencing face-to-face or voice-to-voice conversation. Technology is being perfected to allow visual interaction as well as verbal interchange. People can now choose to isolate themselves socially and continue to communicate via the Internet if that is their preference.

As far back as 1982, the Canadian Conference of Catholic Bishops released a report condemning corporations and governments for placing greater importance on profits than people. Bishops called for an emphasis on human needs and a de-emphasis on maximization of profits and growth. In his book, *The Poverty of Affluence,* Dr. Paul L. Wachtel (1983) underscored the concerns of the bishops. Wachtel argued that in America, at the time he wrote the work, there was a standard of living far superior to any other the world had ever known, yet more people were feeling psychologically deprived than ever before.

After becoming familiar with that premise, I began to follow America's social health through indices published by Fordham University. Dr. Marc L. Miringoff, now deceased, invented the The Index of Social Health at the Fordham Institute for Innovation in Social Policy to measure America's well-being. An analysis of his report cards on our nation over the years shows a sharp drop in America's social health from 1973 to 1993 (Porter 2004). Afterward, our social health rose but never reached 1973 levels. During the years after 2000, the social health again began to decline but never reached the lows of the 1980s (Institute for Innovation in Social Policy 2009). During the years when the American economy was performing well, America's social health was declining. This negative correlation caused me to believe that materialism increasing above a comfort level (defined differently by each individual) could possibly produce varying levels of spiritual poverty just as Wechtel had concluded in his book.

Counter Conditions Will Define
Qualities of Communities 4.0

Anytime conditions occur, there is natural pushback, or countering of those conditions. If there is peace, eventually discord will arise. Out of the discord will finally come peace. Then from peace will ultimately come chaos. The situations are cyclical—resulting in repetitively pushing forward and countering.

Communities are subject to the same conditional cycles. Considering the five prevailing conditions previously listed, people will seek counter conditions in choosing communities in which to live over the next decade. Uncertainty will lead to a search for certainty. Globalization will cause localization to be valued. Rugged individualism, a precursor of anarchy, will produce need for unity. Prevalence of virtual communities will motivate people to desire a sense of place. Excess materialism will promote the desire for cultivation of spiritual needs. These counter conditions will create the need for communities to offer the following qualities:

1. Sense of place
2. Essence of stability and permanency
3. High quality of life
4. Multiple choices
5. Citizen empowerment

Let's discuss these five qualities.

Sense of Place

People value a physical anchor, i.e., a place to call home. In a community, this entails a central point at which to gather, geographical capitalization, connectedness, sensitivity to heritage, stories of the past, and distinctive culture. Community Leaders 4.0 are highly visible and constantly communicate a message of expectation, exciting growth, and opportunity. A wonderful book to read for additional information concerning creation of a sense of place is *The Gift of Community*. The author, Dr. Gary McCaleb, takes a global perspective from both a citizen's viewpoint and also that of an elected official (2001, 2010).

Gathering space. Citizens enjoy gathering for social interchange. Communities should consciously provide a central place and multiple decentralized places, if the community is large, for assemblies and celebrations. Coming together promotes a feeling of connectedness. Some pundits challenge me on this idea in that they feel that people had rather stay at home and experience digital community experiences. I believe that preferences for specific community experiences differ by generation. Younger generations relate to digital communities well and have adopted that type of communication as a lifestyle. I believe, however, that people want both experiences—digital and personal. They also want to choose when and where to meet. The challenge in contemporary society is not necessarily that people do not want to assemble. It is that they want to congregate at the place and time of their choosing. Therein lies the challenge.

Geographical capitalization. Wherever a community is located, there will be geographical assets. Sometimes leaders must get creative and dig deeply to find those assets, but they are there. Location has historically been considered a major quality in drawing people to a community. Today, however, with technology becoming more sophisticated and accessible, location does not matter to some people (although they do not constitute a majority) as much as it once did. There must be other factors that attract people to a place. Community Leaders 4.0 will creatively develop the community assets in such a way that they will act as a magnet for those attracted to those things the community has to offer.

Whether something is considered beautiful is all in the perception of the person making the choice. Communities that take their natural positives and structure them into something beautiful lure people to their perceived beauty. Places in the desert can be extremely beautiful if carefully landscaped. Other natural areas from mountains to plains can be beautified through careful design. No place is exempt from attracting people if leaders are creative and have the ability to capitalize on their geographical assets.

Connectedness. Later in the book we will discuss the value of social capital in more detail. When people feel connected, the sense of being at home is intensified. Connectedness can bring feelings of comfort, peace, and a reduction of stress.

Unique heritage. The combination of inherited values and traditions are unique to each community. In a place that emphasizes its distinctive heritage and makes the most of its positives, citizens sense a special connection to the community.

Narratives of past events. Heroes exist in every community's history. Often the stories of people's hardships encountered and victories won in moving the community forward are a part of the lore that ties the citizens to the community. When these stories are purposefully communicated, citizens grow to admire and appreciate the courage demonstrated by their predecessors.

Additionally, if the community still has historic buildings, leaders should support their preservation. Museums, lecture series, commemoration of significant past events, and perhaps dramas about the community's history lend to the appreciation of earlier periods.

Distinctive culture. Every community (and each community inside the community) has a distinctive culture that is composed of the current values, beliefs, and behaviors of the citizens. When people select a community to join, they test the culture to see if it coincides with their approach to life. Often great numbers of new residents can change the community's culture. That is often a point of conflict in a growing community. Also, the culture can change the people who participate in it.

Ultimately there will be a blending of cultures to some degree. However, when people choose a community, they are often drawn to subgroups with whom they identify inside the community and wish to retain much of their original identity. When this happens, the community becomes more like a mosaic.

A mosaic offers challenges because unity happens only at higher levels rather than penetrating the community. Leading a mosaic requires a different skill set than leading a blended community. It is important to remember that when choosing a community, people often look for a cultural preference.

Essence of Stability and Permanency

In a world of conflict and confusion, people want to feel safe both environmentally and socially. I have taken multiple informal surveys in the community leadership classes I have taught, asking the participants to name the number one quality they desire in choosing a community. The answer is always safety. People want trustworthy leaders, a low crime rate, well-trained first responder units, a peaceful local government that is not constantly in verbal warfare, and a sense that their leaders exercise visionary planning for community sustainability.

Community Leaders 4.0 understand that they aid in sculpting the perception of stability and permanency. They are constantly visible in the community by attending many events and conducting town hall meetings and focus groups to gather input from the citizens. They are inclusive of all groups. Balance is a goal, and sustainability is a part of their mission. Community Leaders 4.0 are directing renewal opportunities and focusing on the community's future. They are constantly communicating progress, prosperity, and hope while consistently demonstrating personal and professional integrity.

High Quality of Life/Place

From ample green space to excellent educational opportunities, people desire a high quality of life in the place they call home. A majority of knowledge/creative workers want to be no more than an hour's drive from a major airport, their work, institutions of higher education, sources of good health care, shopping, and sophisticated arts and entertainment. In their community (if it is a suburb), people want local arts and entertainment, sports activities, grocery stores, highly rated schools, places of worship, state-of-the-art infrastructure, convenient modes of transportation, easily moving traffic patterns, and recreational opportunities. High air and water quality standards along with low noise pollution are prominent on their lists.

Multiple Choices

We live in a consumer society. Because people are attuned to choosing from several alternatives, they want that same framework in their community. Not only do they desire quality, but they also want choices of entertainment, worship, restaurants, educational opportunities, workplaces, arts, sports activities, health care, and many other things. They want diversity to be honored. In other words, citizens want to devise their own life plan and have alternatives available to accommodate that plan.

Citizen Empowerment

Community Leaders 4.0 ask people for input. They do not make decisions in isolation. Citizens prefer to be part of the solutions to community problems. In most communities, a small percentage of the registered voters elect officials. Likewise a small percentage of the population turns out for town hall meetings or focus group sessions. There are exceptions, of course. When there are emotional social issues being discussed or economic forces in play that will affect people's pocketbooks, then the response is much greater. Sometimes up to 75 to 80 percent of registered voters in the local community show interest.

However, leaders are not to be deceived by low turnout for elections and meetings. Citizens nonetheless want to be asked their opinions. Strangely enough, they may not participate, but citizens still want their leaders to be open to their ideas if and when they decide to offer them.

❧

Community Leadership 4.0 Strategies

The purpose of Chapter Two has been to demonstrate the speed with which structural change is happening. Because of this phenomenon, projecting the future based on the present is virtually impossible. To develop inviting communities, it is important to be aware of the specific trends driving the socioeconomic structural changes that we will experience in the next decade.

1. Draw your community's timeline from 1946 until today. Note the dates of specific structural changes that have occurred and the impact they have had on your community.
2. Review each of the trends driving structural change. Specifically analyze how each trend is affecting your community.
3. Evaluate each of the five conditions shaping the types of communities that will be in demand in the future. Assess whether your community is creating its future around the counter conditions such as sense of place and the four other factors mentioned.

Questions for Contemplation

1. Have you ever projected the future by assuming that the present would extend into the years ahead?
2. In considering Question 1, did structural changes intervene to change the direction of movement into the future?
3. What is the most impacting structural change that has happened in your lifetime? How did it affect your life?
4. What massive changes do you believe will happen during the next 30 years in the fields of science and technology? How could these changes affect your community's future?
5. How is your community preparing for the tight labor market that is predicted to occur not too many years hence?
6. How is your community creating a sense of place?
7. What factors in your community provide its citizens with an essence of stability and permanency?
8. In thinking about the quality of life offered in your community, what aspects stand out in your mind?

9. Do you feel that your community offers adequate choices for its citizens? In what categories do choices need to be extended?
10. List the techniques used in your community to empower its citizens. In your opinion, are there methods not being used that your community should be employing?
11. Do your community leaders have the trust and respect of community members?
12. How are your community's institutions changing?

CHAPTER THREE

Building Sustainable Community Systems

I N A BROAD sense, sustainability is the capacity of a system to maintain its vitality far into the future. As a Community Leader 4.0, it is helpful to envision your community a century ahead and plan for its continuing renewal. In the first phase of planning, leaders should make preparations for at least 30 years hence—then plan forward in 30-year segments. As we discussed in the last chapter: the future is not a continuation of the present. Therefore, it is impossible to make plans and then assume that those plans will be valid in the years ahead. That's why these ideas should be revisited, and perhaps revised, every year. If circumstances are changing rapidly, the strategies should be reconsidered more than once per year in order to redirect the community's course.

Often leaders use the rapidity of change as an excuse for making few plans or none at all. However, that is a sure way to nullify the community's sustainability. Even though your plans change, it is important to devise strategies anyway so that you, at least, possess a roughly-sketched roadmap to the future.

More Than Green

In this chapter, I will approach sustainability horizontally in that sustainability involves much more than the green movement that is gaining global prominence. Often, when people speak of sustainability, they take a vertical approach and think of sustainability only as pertaining to eco-friendly issues. However, I will take a systems approach and discuss the necessity of functional interface among interactive subsystems in order to sustain the community system's viability over a protracted length of time.

Definitely Includes Green

With the continuing global population increase and the escalating number of nations entering the worldwide marketplace, all people must be good stewards of our natural resources. We must use them efficiently and leave an abundance of these resources for ensuing generations. This involves seeking alternative energy choices, reducing the carbon footprint of communities, maintenance of clean air and safe water supplies, development and use of safe and economical renewable energy sources, protection of the earth's eco-systems, effective use of green building and manufacturing materials, installation of green information technology, development of new methods of water conservation and reuse, efficient and environmentally friendly land use, and innovative waste management systems. These items I have mentioned do not compose an exhaustive list but act as basic foundations of an eco-friendly (green) environment. Community Leaders 4.0 will be called on to address the balance of implementation versus the amount of investment capital necessary for execution of green programs. Achievement of green community status will be one of the major challenges facing Community Leaders 4.0 during the next decade.

Often sustainability is described with a three-pronged approach: ecological, social, and economic. My concentration in this book is on the social and economic aspects of the community, which I will emphasize as a combined word, *socioeconomic*. However, socioeconomic issues cannot be discussed in isolation from ecological issues in that these concerns both directly and indirectly interact with the social and economic aspects of a community.

The Community System

For the past several decades, many organizations have been using the systems thinking approach to analyze and improve performance. I feel that it is important for Community Leaders 4.0 to consider using this same approach in order for the community to continue to maintain its vitality.

In the first phase of my career path, I had the privilege of serving as a systems analyst. Therefore, I obtained a great deal of experience that has shaped my thinking process through the multiple decades of my career as a futurist. My view of a community as a system was initiated by my experiences with systems design and analysis.

A complex system is a whole entity composed of interrelating parts. In other words, a system has interacting subsystems that produce an outcome that is greater than any of the subsystems could produce alone. In fact, a complex system may also have subsystems within subsystems. Things can get rather complicated, and in turn, very difficult to manage. The human body is an example of a complex system. The major mission of the human body is to sustain life. Inside the body are many subsystems. Examples of the body's subsystems are respiratory, digestive, nervous, and circulatory. By doing their job correctly, these subsystems help the body in its major mission, i.e., to maintain the person's life. If any one of these subsystems malfunctions, the major mission of the human body is compromised or may even fail altogether. There is necessary interaction of the subsystems for producing a successful outcome for the total body. When one of the subsystems malfunctions, the whole body is endangered. Other subsystems may also be affected.

A community is similar to the human body. It has a major mission. When its subsystems (and subsystems within subsystems) are functional, the system as a whole performs well. If any one of the subsystems is dysfunctional, the community's mission is endangered, and the other community subsystems may be affected. To understand how a community functions as a complex system, we'll discuss more about system principles and how they apply to communities in the following paragraphs.

Elements of Open Complex Systems

In an open systems loop, it is important to consider four terms—input, process, output, and feedback. Input initiates a process in the system. The process then takes place. During the process, multiple subsystems may be called into play to produce the output that is expected to result from the process that has taken place. Feedback will indicate whether the output is the desired end product or if adjustments need to be made. Each subsystem also has these four elements acting on it. Again, the human body may be used as an example. Food (input) is eaten from the external environment. The body uses its multiple subsystems to process the food. Desired output of this process comes in the form of sustained life. If the food is tainted, the feedback translates into the person's becoming ill. The subsystems are affected and cannot produce the desired outcome. In serious situations, the person's life is endangered. If, on the other hand, the food performs as expected, feedback in the form of increased energy and sustained good health will result. Life continues.

In a community, the same principles can be applied. Picture a community on a beautiful spring afternoon. Children are walking home from school. People are scurrying to meetings. The highways are busy with traffic. Life seems to be going smoothly. All at once, there is an explosion in a major building located in the city. First responders immediately go into action. Hospitals are alerted. The streets are cleared. Parents are frantically looking for their children. Workers are eagerly awaiting directions concerning whether to stay at work or access their various means of transportation and start in the direction of their homes. Until they know the problem, the city lives in chaos.

After a two-hour wait, residents are then alerted that the explosion happened in a vacant building across town. The cause was escaping gas, and nobody was injured because of the building's vacancy. There had not been a terrorist attack as so many people had feared. Public safety officials provided instructions on how to move about the city to avoid problems in the danger zone. After that, people felt free to return to the afternoon's business in a more stable manner.

Let's look at the situation from a systems point of view. The input was the information (visual and auditory as well as newscasts and word of mouth) concerning the gas explosion. The process was the interaction of all the city's subsystems that were churning as a result of that information. In this process came chaos in several forms—first responder units rushing to the scene of the potential tragedy, fear, panic, people speeding on the streets in their cars to find their children, switching on radios, telephoning and texting family and friends, sending Twitter messages and using other social networking sites, and waiting anxiously for news of the source of the explosion. The system output came in the form of solving the problem and restoring balance to the city's life. Feedback came when the news was heard that the explosion was gas-induced and instructions were given for travel and going about life for the remainder of the day.

This was an indication that the process had worked, and the problem was solved by the successfully interacting functional subsystems.

Characteristics of Open Sustainable Complex Systems

In this discussion are seven characteristics that sustainable open complex systems will have in common. It is not my objective to have a deep discussion of these qualities. I merely wish to mention them so that it is easier to understand the community from a systems perspective.

- The whole system has a purpose. It exists for a reason. It has a defined mission toward which all the subsystems are designed to work. In our previous example of the human body, the major purpose of the body's system as a whole is to sustain life.

- When the process is engaged, each of the subsystem's loops in the process has a predictable outcome. Again, from the example of the human body, each time a person eats food, the process through which the human body goes engages the same subsystems. Each subsystem is designed to produce a similar predictable outcome each time it is involved. The circulatory system, when working normally, never tries to do the job of the digestive system. The circulatory system has its own predictable outcome each time it is engaged in the process.

- A healthy system is designed to absorb change. The human body can be injured and still continue to function. Some of the subsystems may be changed through surgery, yet the system as a whole adapts to the change and continues to deliver the purpose of the whole system, i.e., life continues. Because change continually happens to a system, chaos (a natural byproduct of change) prevails. If some chaos were not happening in the human body, the body would be flat-lined. In other words, without some degree of chaos, the person would be dead.

- A system naturally tries to take care of itself. It rejects those things identified as not belonging to the system. For example, in an organ transplant, the body naturally tries to reject the organ being transplanted into the person's body until drugs are administered to suppress the recipient's immune system in order to try to cause the body to accept the "foreign" organ.

- A complex system is capable of simultaneous activities. Multiple subsystems are at work at the same time with each subsystem performing the task for which it is designed. The activity loops happen on a timeline in a way that the ultimate purpose of the system is attained at just the right moment. Concerning the human body, this simply means that all the systems in the body are working on their specific tasks at relatively the same time and are designed in such a way that the results come together to maintain the definitive mission (to sustain life).

- All subsystems are interrelated. One dysfunctional subsystem damages the whole system. It is easy to see this example in the body. When the digestive system is damaged, the system's mission might be compromised. The other subsystems could possibly be affected and/or endangered.

- The subsystems are dependent on the viability of the whole system. If damage is done to the whole system either externally or internally and the system's mission is thwarted, the subsystems' results will not be achieved in the same capacity, or at all. If the system dies, then the subsystems die also.

A Glance At The Community System

Now let's apply these principles to a community. In Figure 3.1, you will see an example of a community socioeconomic system.

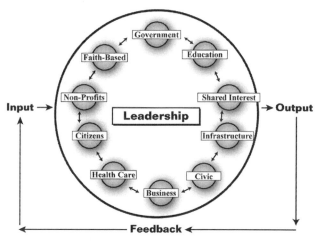

Figure 3.1 Community Socioeconomic System

In the small circles of the diagram are some of the socioeconomic subsystems that compose a community. I'm sure that you can think of many other subsystems that can be included. In my mind these are some of the major subsystems involved. In the circle where I have listed the words *Shared Interest*, I am intending this subsystem to mean all the groups not listed in the other circles and which are assembled because of a common interest of all the people in the group. For instance, a book club is composed of people who hold a common interest in reading books. A motorcycle club is formed because people in the group are all interested in motorcycles. There may be hundreds, or even thousands, of different groups in a community held together by a common thread. A community member may belong to multiple groups either in other circles or in separate shared-interest groups.

Please note that I have included a category for *Citizens* of the community. Each inhabitant is also a subsystem of the bigger community. Behaviors of the citizens affect the community as a whole.

I have also included *Infrastructure* as a socioeconomic category. This involves the physical support systems of the community. Some examples are transportation, communication, utility, and energy systems. If these systems are eco-friendly, the community will be better able to meet its socioeconomic sustainability goals. If the infrastructure is decaying, then the community will not be globally competitive in the 21st century and will lose the opportunity to attract a viable global workforce and state-of-the-art businesses. Rather than enjoy progress, the community will suffer decline.

Additionally, I have listed *Leadership* in the center of the system because it drives the process. Leaders orchestrate the activities of the subsystems. And there are several leaders in the community—including citizens in the grassroots category. Leadership is part of the process, yet it can also produce internal stimuli (for example, passing an ordinance which affects the whole system). There can also be external input which may come from people or the environment outside the community system. Examples include other governments, nature, and several other sources. The systemic output should be consistent with the community's mission. However, other output—perhaps unpredicted output—may happen. In a complex system, leadership decisions may be directed to one subsystem, yet there are unintended consequences on other subsystems. In that case, the feedback should be analyzed to determine how to adjust the external or internal input in order to regulate the ultimate systemic output.

Now let's discuss each of the seven characteristics of open sustainable complex systems in the context of community.

Systemic purpose. It is important that Community Leaders 4.0 come together to arrive at a common understanding of the community's purpose or mission. I will use *purpose* and *mission* interchangeably in this discussion. Included in this purpose should be community values and the means by which the mission is to be accomplished. In a true system, the mission is accomplished repeatedly. If the community's mission is to maintain a high quality of life for its citizens, then that must be achieved continually in order for the community to be sustainable. Sometimes imbedded in the big mission is a temporary mission. In the case of a disaster, the community's mission may be to almost totally renew itself (to maintain its quality of life) as in the case of New Orleans, Louisiana, after Hurricane Katrina.

In order to maintain quality of life as a community purpose, quality of life must be defined in detail. Various subsystems will espouse different definitions. To function with a lower degree of chaos, the definitions should be consolidated to arrive at a workable definition. This can only be accomplished through joint efforts, input, and cooperation of all community groups (subsystems).

Predictable systemic and subsystemic outcomes. Each entity in the community is designed to produce a specific result. These results are designed to work together to accomplish the big system's mission. It is important for Community Leaders 4.0 to collaborate in defining the purpose of each subsystem and the manner in which each entity is to function in order to help the other groups in producing the ultimate mega-purpose of the community system.

Here is an example. A grassroots effort has begun with the purpose of bringing a charter school to the community. A systems approach to this project would involve more than just the education system. The grassroots leaders would work with interested citizens, seek cooperation from the public school system and other educational institutions in the community, approach local government for zoning and infrastructure needs, seek out different interest groups who can help in the marketing of the charter school, contact businesses that can contribute supplies, scholarships, and informational sessions, and seek support and ideas from civic groups, health care institutions, and faith-based groups. And this paragraph may only contain the short list of how the subsystems can work together. There may be additional grassroots groups trying to bring other schools to the area. These groups should be consulted for cooperation. Each subsystem will be requested to define its contribution to the mission of establishing a charter school. By working this way, all involved systems will seek to produce predictable outcomes.

Change absorption. The introduction of a charter school will inflict change into the community. Some learners will chose to attend that school and withdraw from other schools thus changing school populations. Perhaps zoning will change. Infrastructure will be expanded. Possibly the school will house students who will come from outside the community. Additional groups will be asked for monetary and social support. In other words, change will happen in the system, and change always produces some degree of chaos. If the system is healthy and a proactive approach has been taken by the community's leaders, then the change will be easily absorbed. If proper planning has not taken place, and the system reacts rather than proacts, the degree of chaos may be more profound. Chaos to some degree is welcome and invigorating. If chaos happens to a great degree, however, it can destroy a healthy community.

Immunosuppressive approach. The natural desire of an organic system—and a community is organic because it is alive—is to reject major changes. The system is programmed to produce predictable outcomes based on predictable input and activities. When change is introduced into the system, chaos automatically takes place, and the system must be reprogrammed in order to accept the differences which have been introduced. Communities 3.0 might not possess enough flexibility to accept change whereas Communities 4.0 are designed for flexibility. In other words, Communities 4.0 have built into their community DNA (chemistry) the immunosuppressive capability to accept change. The citizens are flexible. Diversity is welcome. Community Leaders 4.0 are open to new ideas and innovation. They are not bound to traditional thinking and to doing things the way they have always done them.

Simultaneous subsystem activities. A healthy community is comfortable with different groups working on separate projects at the same time. Community Leaders 4.0 plan projects in such a way that the timeline for subsystem results will coordinate with the expectations of the community system as a whole. They depend on each group to understand the process that will bring desired results to help in accomplishing the community's mission.

Interrelated subsystems. In a truly integrated community, the subsystems are interconnected in such a way that if one subsystem succeeds or fails, the remainder of the subsystems are affected. For example, if the education system has one of the highest rankings in the state, other entities in the community are positively affected in that education is considered a major economic development tool of the community. A great education system causes people and corporations to choose that community over others when relocating. Businesses prosper by being able to attract high-quality workers. The local government experiences increased revenues. The infrastructure can be improved due to availability of funds. I could go on and on. But I'm sure you get the big picture of interrelatedness by now.

Subsystemic dependency. In a truly interconnected system, each subsystem is dependent on the functionality of the other subsystems. Each of the groups represented in the circles inside the community system in Figure 3.1 is dependent on the predictable functioning of all the other circles. If there are not enough productive businesses in the community, the tax base is affected. Citizens' taxes will be elevated more than if there were additional productive businesses in the community. If the health care system is limited, the community cannot attract as many citizens as a community with a strong health care structure. With diminished population, the other subsystems are affected. The idea here is to emphasize that Community Leaders 4.0 must recognize that one group is dependent on the other for its well-being. Moving a community forward requires the involvement of all subsystems. Each subsystem is important to the community's strength.

Total system vitality. If the community fails, the relationships of the groups in the community fade away also. Even though citizens may move to other communities, the former groups to which they belonged have disappeared. That group may move to a different system, but the DNA will never be the same as it was in the original system. Subsystems working together in one community cannot reproduce exactly when a subsystem moves to another community and must interact with a different set of subsystems. The change may be good for the subsystem or it may be harmful. However, one thing is certain: subsystem interaction after the whole system changes will cause an alteration in all the subsystems.

Evidence of this phenomenon can be seen in a television series. If the show is dropped from the network lineup, then the actors, producers, directors, writers, and all others involved must find other work. The system has died. The subsystems (workers on the show) must either quit their careers or find other means of expressing their talents in another series. Even if most of the people move on together to participate in a new series, the total system will still be different. When changing systems, subsystems do not replicate exactly. I have seen a situation where there was a hit TV series and one actor left the show. With the replacement of that one actor, the series was eventually cancelled. The DNA of the system changed. The new system wasn't a success. The same can be true of communities with the change of just one leader.

Of course, it is obvious that when a community suffers hard economic times, all the groups in the community suffer also. And the opposite is true. When communities prosper, the subsystems show increased vitality. Bottom line: as the system goes, so go the subsystems.

⁓

Smart Sustainable Communities

When listing the characteristics of Community 4.0, I included the word *smart*. This is an important differentiator between Community 3.0 and Community 4.0. In Community 3.0 qualities, I listed the characteristic *pre-smart*. I'll define these terms from my perspective, and perhaps that will be helpful in noting the importance of community smart systems.

A smart community, in my opinion, is one that has a high degree of intellectual capital and such resources as highly-qualified educational institutions at all levels. It is even better if there are research universities functioning in the community. Additionally, the community ranks above the national average in the number of people holding bachelor's, master's, and doctor's degrees as well as professional designations. Supplementing the intellectual component to the smart systems definition is social capital, which (again, in my opinion) is the degree of people connectedness in the community while presuming that human rights are respected and all people are considered potentially valuable contributors to their community's sustainability.

In other words, intellect alone is not enough to build a smart community. Community Leaders 4.0 realize that for a community to be truly smart, it must be strong both intellectually and socially. Interaction of the social subsystems is as important as interaction of the intellectual subsystems. If both variables—intellectual and social—are considered to be part of the smart equation, then there are very few totally smart communities in existence today. However, it is possible, and very necessary, to be both intellectual and social in order to be sustainably smart. Community Leaders 4.0 will find this challenge to be one of their greatest in the next decade.

In product development and contemporary environmental literature, the term *smart city* is often used. In this context, the smart city is one that employs the sophisticated tools that will support a high-tech eco-friendly infrastructure. However, the definition I'm espousing for *smart* as a characteristic of Community 4.0 incorporates eco-friendliness plus socioeconomic capital—as I have been explaining in this chapter. And this broader definition of *smart* will be the definition used throughout this book.

Besides intellectual and social capital, a sustainable community is embarking on, or has already implemented, smart technology systems. These systems use sophisticated tools to maximize the efficiency of the community's infrastructure. Some examples of how these systems are being applied will be discussed later.

☙

Observations on Social Capital

Over the past several decades, social capital has been the subject of commentary and some degree of debate over its definition. This discussion was documented as far back as 1916 (Smith 2000-2009).

While growing up in the small town of McKinney, Texas (now much larger and one of the fastest-growing cities in the USA), I experienced social capital at its best. Therefore, my definition and perspective are favorable. We were a close-knit community wherein people were involved at all levels. Children's activities were centered around family, school, neighborhood, sports, and the faith-based community. Adults were involved in family, neighborhood organizations, civic groups, faith-based institutions, sports, volunteer work, associations, and numerous other venues. At a young age, I formed my definition of social capital as that of connectedness which produces a sense of security and trust. In other words, the positive connectedness made me feel a high degree of safety and a sense of belonging. Obviously, at the time, I did not possess the knowledge to call my perception *social capital*. Instead, as a child and young adult, I *felt* the process more than I verbalized it. It was only when I moved to a large city after college graduation, and felt a void created by a lesser degree of social capital than I had experienced growing up, that I recognized what a treasure my small-town life had offered.

As I matured in my profession, I expanded my definition of social capital. It is this: interpersonal connectedness supported by trustful interdependency, mutual responsibility to one another, and community participation. It seems to me that the quality of community life is positively correlated with social capital. When there is a high degree of social capital, the community's quality of life is good. And the opposite is also true: a low degree of social capital breeds a low quality of community life. As a result, the community suffers.

I have included social capital in the definition of a smart community in that relationships matter to the success of a community as much as intellectual capital. The two categories must coexist. However, I believe we must expand the definition of social capital to raise the degree of its existence in Community 4.0. The traditional ways a community connects are in decline. But other ways of connecting are coming into existence—for example, digital connectedness.

I feel that the degree of human rights experienced in a community is a very important part of human capital as is the degree of tolerance. Per my definition, tolerance is peaceful coexistence among people who are culturally, ethnically, socially, physically, economically, and/or philosophically different from one another.

Multiple digital social networking tools are tremendously popular and will serve as valuable techniques for social connectedness. I contend that the definition of social capital is generationally different in many respects. If communities are to be smart, and this will involve social connectedness, then Community Leaders 4.0 will necessarily find multiple ways to connect with different generations. Traditional connectional methods will eventually decrease even more while new methods of connectedness will increase. It is in successfully applying these new methods that Community Leaders 4.0 will be adding to the smart community equation.

༼ঔ

Examples of Smart Communities

The best way to explain smart communities is to present examples. No community is perfectly smart. Some communities may be highly intellectual but not rank as high in social capital and vice versa. Other cities may be implementing smart infrastructure but not rank as high intellectually or socially. However, the ideal sustainability strategy is that Community Leaders 4.0 should lay out community plans for implementation of all three elements: intellectual and social capital as well as smart technology infrastructure. With these three entities in place, a community's chances for sustainability will be substantially increased.

There are several global regions that can be classified as smart in one category or another. By combining social and intellectual capital plus smart technological infrastructure to define a smart community, many places are in the process of becoming smart. Discussed in the following paragraphs are three communities that are applying some degree of smart sustainability models.

Seattle. Nestled in the beautiful Pacific Northwest is a progressive region that is working hard to sustain itself. For 2009, Seattle was named by *Fast Company* magazine at its pick for "City of the Year" (Stein 2009).

This is one of the smartest of all regions in the United States. The state of Washington has a high social capital rating according to Dr. Robert Putnam's studies (2000). And in *The Social Capital Community Benchmark Survey* (The Saguaro Seminar 2000), Seattle had a high social capital rating among three dozen communities surveyed in America. There was a later survey conducted in 2006, but I found no record of Seattle's participation in that project.

In addition to ranking high in social capital, the Seattle area has the presence of a major public research university, the University of Washington. The people in the community have a high literacy level, read a great number of books per year per capita, and rank very high nationally in the percentage of higher level degrees. Such respected creative companies as Amazon.com, Starbuck's, Microsoft, and T-Mobile USA—to name a few—reside in the greater Seattle area. The community is also extremely eco-friendly.

Amsterdam. In this progressive-thinking capital and largest city of the Netherlands, a sustainability movement is underway. A number of projects are designed to make Amsterdam a leading European smart city in the sense that it will upgrade its infrastructure rather quickly by working renewable energy projects, reducing its carbon footprint, and using smart grid technology (Scott 2009). By the way, a smart grid uses information technology to measure energy usage and provide energy efficiency.

To create cooperative ventures leading to the goal of Amsterdam's becoming one of Europe's top five cities for businesses, Amsterdam has formed AIM (Amsterdam's Innovation Motor). According to the official website of Amsterdam's Innovation Motor (Amsterdam.nl, Amsterdam's Innovation Motor 2009), this program is designed to incorporate cooperation among businesses, local government, and educational institutions of the Northern Region. There are a number of organizations partnering in this effort including the two universities in Amsterdam—University of Amsterdam and The Free. More information can be obtained from their website as noted in the References and Notes section of this book.

I am additionally impressed with the degree of cooperation that is being beckoned for the purpose of moving Amsterdam forward (Amsterdam.nl,

Working Together 2009). Besides introducing green information technology, collaboration is a priority of Amsterdam's sustainability movement. From the official website information, it seems that Amsterdam's leaders are open to listening to ideas from those who would like to contribute to Amsterdam's becoming an innovative leader through cooperative efforts. It is building on social capital. The community is soliciting collective wisdom for becoming a leading 21st century vital place to live and work.

Raleigh-Durham. For over a half century, the Research Triangle region in North Carolina, anchored by Raleigh, Durham, and Chapel Hill, has prospered as one of the most intelligent regions in the United States. Based on intellectual capital, *The Daily Beast* named Raleigh-Durham as "America's Smartest City" for 2009. The criteria used to determine the cities rich with intellectual capital can be found on *The Daily Beast's* website as listed in the References and Notes section of this book. Also considered in this selection process was the degree of political involvement, which was measured by the percentage of eligible voters in the community who actually cast votes in the 2008 U.S. presidential election (*The Daily Beast* 2009). This is a form of social capital, and I applaud *The Daily Beast* for taking this item into consideration when choosing their winner. Actually, "Raleigh-Durham" is a combination of two cities—making up a dynamic community.

With the creation of The Research Triangle Park in the 1950s, the Research Triangle region has grown into a powerhouse of such high-tech companies as IBM Corporation, Cisco, Nortel, Sony, Ericsson, and many others according to The Research Triangle Park's official website (The Research Triangle Park 2009). The Research Triangle area has three renowned research universities, which have continually gained prominence. They are Duke University, University of North Carolina at Chapel Hill, and North Carolina State University. With this degree of intelligence gracing the community, the region is able to attract well-paying jobs and a highly qualified labor force.

According to Jodi Ann LaFreniere, former president of the Wake Forest, North Carolina, Chamber of Commerce (and current president of the McKinney, Texas, Chamber of Commerce), the Research Triangle region has a strong business community which is extremely well-organized. All the major entities in the region work together in a systems approach to making things happen. LaFreniere indicates that, in an effort to attract jobs to the area in the 1950s, community visionaries envisaged a hub of future activity in what was then a forest. The idea came forth with no paradigms from which to work. But, in spite of all the challenges, pioneering leaders created a sustainable community. Six decades later, the region continues to thrive.

LaFreniere further espouses that the idea of sustainability has been instilled in the Research Triangle region over multiple generations. The culture of respect, systems thinking, and community engagement continues to be embraced. The current generation wants to contribute to regional success as much as their predecessors. "The players in the region realize that they are responsible for doing something to further advance their geographical area. They know that nothing remains constant," comments LaFreniere. "With these thoughts in mind," LaFreniere further states, "participants in the Research Triangle community are always willing to develop new approaches and evaluate opportunities to respond to changing community dynamics and present day challenges" (LaFreniere 2010).

⌇

Community Leaders 4.0 Get It

Now that we've had a lengthy discussion about how systems thinking can promote sustainability, let's see how Community Leaders 4.0 can apply this concept to renewing the vitality of their communities. It is important that leaders wanting to advance their communities to 4.0 status "get it." This means that these leaders must understand how to successfully view a community as a complex system and learn to work the process in moving each of their communities forward.

To illustrate the application of systems thinking, I have developed a fictional case study, which is presented in the following section. Although this study is based on imaginary characters and events, it represents likely happenings in contemporary society. Any likenesses to real characters, communities, and events are purely coincidental.

❧

Emilio, the Grassroots Community Activist

As a former "Citizen of the Year" in his community, Emilio continues to lead efforts that will add vivacity to his city of 150,000 people located in a larger metropolitan area with 3.6 million people. For many years, Emilio has volunteered in community activities and served on numerous boards and committees. In fact, he has been president of several of the nonprofit boards. Emilio is generous with his time and money for worthy causes.

Because he has worked with many community agencies, businesses, and government entities, Emilio understands that his community is a system of many integrated subsystems. He also comprehends that if one subsystem is malfunctioning, the whole community system is affected. Therefore when he leads a campaign, he is careful to consider the subsystems' involvement in the project or problem solution. Owning his own engineering company, and having earned a degree in mechanical engineering followed by an MBA (Master of Business Administration), Emilio also understands systems thinking from a professional standpoint.

Since the 1980s, Emilio has been assessing global socioeconomic trends. He has studied communities and the manner in which they are either growing or declining. Having read literature on global competitiveness and the necessary characteristics for becoming an internationally competitive community, Emilio recognizes that his community is a Community 3.0 with great potential for moving to Community 4.0 status. He also realizes that it takes leaders who are functioning as Community Leaders 4.0 to drive a community to the 4.0 level. Emilio believes he can lead that charge in his community.

Emilio's reasons for categorizing his community as 3.0 are as follows:

- The community leaders do not reflect the diversity of the community.
- The perspective of the community as a whole tends to be locally minded without viewing itself as a regional player.
- Community leaders are uncomfortable with calculated risk and chaos.

- There is no long-term vision for the community's future and no consideration for global competitiveness.

The new rules for sustainability are not being applied in Emilio's community. The system is rather closed although as new populations enter the community, the numbers of new residents are forcing more openness and risk tolerance than in the past. Emilio senses an opportunity. That's why he is hopeful that his community can move to the 4.0 level that embraces creativity and innovation, global perspective, calculated risk, openness to change, smart technology, managed conflict, tolerance of some degree of chaos, and peaceful coexistence of very diverse populations. Emilio hopes to accomplish all this without having his community lose its family-friendly environment, positive values, respect for heritage and history, and esteem for community traditions. Largely a bedroom community, Emilio is awed by the city's beautiful rolling landscape and its ample well-planned green space. The community prides itself in being eco-friendly. It has a history of environmental conservation. So there is also potential for more use of green technology and recruiting of green companies to the region.

Emilio has been visiting with several other community leaders lately. He has good friends who lead the education system, local government, businesses, nonprofit organizations, and civic clubs. They all agree that the community must get a grip on its future. Otherwise, it will not experience sustainability by the year 2050. Because Emilio has the interest, time, money, and energy, his friends urge him to actively drive a campaign to convince leaders to move forward on a plan that would ensure a sustainable future for the community and the region of which it is a part. They must build a community that will attract high-level businesses and creative well-paid knowledge workers.

Emilio understands that he is not an elected or appointed leader. He feels, however, that he is someone who has considerable influence as a citizen-leader. He also recognizes that all subsystems must work together to produce a strong outcome. This issue is not merely one for local government or for the economic development commission to make in isolation. Taking that route could produce some unintended consequences which could damage the whole community. He accepts the challenge and goes to work to accomplish his goal of moving his community to 4.0 status. To do so, Emilio uses a systems approach.

He first conducts a great deal of research to build credibility for his cause. He reads and documents many studies concerning what successful global communities are doing to sustain their viability in a heavily competitive marketplace. He identifies key regions of the world that are projected to be strong in the years to come. Excitedly, he notes that his community is a part of one of the regions identified as a future "hot spot" in global socio-economic activity. This gives him more information to support his quest.

Next Emilio sets appointments to visit with leaders of as many of the subsystems in the community as possible including those who govern the infrastructure, the educational institutions, local government, community development, economic development, faith-based institutions, individual grassroots leaders, philanthropists, civic club leaders, business people, special interest groups, political activists, health care professionals, and many others. To reach these people, he either makes individual appointments or endeavors to be named as a speaker for the programs of various organizations to which these people belong. He also holds town hall meetings and solicits feedback. This is a long arduous task. It may take a year or more to reach all these people.

In addition to personally contacting people or speaking to groups, Emilio sets up a website and buys advertisements in local news and periodical publications asking people to access the website and express their opinions to his interactive blog. He also utilizes social networks and other digital methods to get his message out. He pulls out all the stops! He is on a campaign to enhance his community's future.

Emilio documents all his findings over this lengthy process and writes a report. This report is delivered in a special three-hour session to the key leaders in the community who have been invited. Emilio also tries to get as much publicity for the report as possible, including TV interviews, postings to websites, subjects of blogs, discussions on social networks, radio interviews, newspaper and periodical coverage, and yes... more speeches. He also, by now, has built a team of interested parties who will carry the torch for the cause, many of whom will spread the word through opinion editorial (op ed) pieces in the local and regional newspapers, blogs, and speeches to various organizations. There will be more town hall meetings with the citizens concerning the contents of the research paper that Emilio compiled.

Now that Emilio has built interest for moving his community forward, he calls for cooperation of all the subsystems in contributing funds for the hiring of a major consulting firm to come to the community, study all aspects of the system, and recommend steps for escalating the community (and the region) to a Community 4.0 status. He also gets a "buy-in" from the community leadership. They promise that once the results of the consulting study are provided, the subsystems of the community will cooperate to begin implementation of the recommendations.

From this brief case study, the process sounds easy. However, it was far from that. Emilio experienced rejection of his ideas, community chaos, polarization of various groups, political positioning, territorializing, citizen fear, and several other issues. Nevertheless, Emilio pushed forward and kept the challenge in front of the community leaders knowing that, in time, at least 20 to 30 percent of the population would buy into the idea. Eventually, perhaps 80 percent would approve of the idea if he kept repeating the concepts. He never expected 100 percent approval. In igniting change, that rarely, if ever, happens. Emilio persisted because he realized that one subsystem cannot act alone although it might have some authority to do so.

Emilio taught us some lessons. Homework must be done before implementing the change. People must be prepared to work together to implement outcomes of each subsystem. Interacting subsystems, toiling together toward a common community mission, work much more smoothly than various subsystems wanting to accomplish their own individual interests. When people selfishly vie for position and personal credit, the results will be community stagnation. That can kill sustainability. For sustainability efforts to be successful, teamwork must prevail.

⁓

Community Leadership 4.0 Strategies

One of the hottest topics concerning communities today is that of sustainability. To avoid decline, Community Leaders 4.0 must have a sustainability plan. In this chapter, I have defined sustainability in a broad sense and encouraged leaders to use systems thinking when working out a strategy to build and retain the community's vitality for many years hence.

1. Review the characteristics of a system.
2. Picture how a system's characteristics pertain to your community.
3. Lay out a diagram of your community's system while including the subsystems.
4. Review the definition of a smart sustainable community. Assess your community in light of that definition.
5. Review the case study on "Emilio, the Grassroots Activist." Describe how you would approach the same issue in your community.

Questions for Contemplation

1. Does your community have a sustainability plan?
2. If you answered "yes" to Question 1, express the plan in 50 or fewer words.
3. If you answered "yes" to Question 1, what is your community's definition of sustainability?
4. If you answered "no" to Question 1, why doesn't your community have a sustainability plan?
5. If you answered "no" to Question 1, what steps could you personally take to start the sustainability planning process in your community?
6. Choose a hot issue that has affected your community in the past two years. Discuss how your community acted as a system when trying to resolve the issue.
7. What green initiatives are being implemented in your community?
8. Is your community a smart system?
9. If you answered "yes" to Question 8, list the qualities that make your community smart.
10. If you answered "no" to Question 8, discuss why you believe your community is not smart.
11. What immediate contributions do you plan to make in helping your community become a better-functioning system?

CHAPTER FOUR

Balancing Paradoxes

IN A WORLD gone wiki, people wish to champion their ideas. They demand empowerment in an open-source environment. This situation often produces chaos, as I have mentioned earlier. When this chaotic atmosphere prevails, polarization often exists. As a result, paradoxes come into play. For discussion in this section, I will define paradoxes as contrasting qualities, ideas, values, philosophies, and viewpoints.

With the existence of paradoxes in mind, Community Leaders 4.0 must work to balance these contrasts so that the community will not be dominated by extremes. In this chapter, I will address the five sets of paradoxes listed below.

- Diversity Versus Homogeneity
- Individual Rights Versus Common Good
- Global Perspective Versus Local Emphasis
- Innovation Versus Tradition
- Quality of Life Versus Community As a Commodity

Diversity Versus Homogeneity

On one end of the community continuum is diversity (the presence of differences), and on the other end is homogeneity (sameness and consistency).

Historically, there has been debate over which type of community is better: homogeneous or diverse. I believe that there must be balance between the two. If a community is too diverse, it is difficult to find common ground. Polarization will happen. Gridlock will follow. If the community is too homogeneous, there is lack of creativity and excitement. It seems to me that eventual stagnation will take place. In the following paragraphs, I will discuss both homogeneity and diversity. Then I will argue that a blended balance will produce a healthier community.

Communities 3.0 (more than 4.0 communities) often enjoy the fact that there is uniformity in the citizens' values, ideas, philosophies, and cultures. Additionally, there is often similar race and/or ethnicity in the community. Everyone seems to be like everyone else. Not many differences exist. In a community of this type, a comfort zone is created. Citizens become quite content in their state of existence. Change is not desired nor is it welcomed. When this happens, normally there is mitigated ingenuity. Perhaps a sense of arrogance exists. Sometimes the citizens have bought into the idea that their current culture is better than the alternatives. Rather than accept differing views, which likely arise from diversity, it's easier to reduce conflict and be satiated by appeasement.

Recently I was participating in a focus group for the purpose of determining the sustainability of a small suburban community. One of the participants mentioned that he had gone out of state on vacation recently and visited a relatively small community that did not welcome change. He said that multiple generations live in the community and that most of the residents had lived there all their lives. Children were born there, educated in the school system, went away to college, then returned to the community to work, build their families, and live out the remainder of their days on earth. This continues from generation to generation. Social capital is so strong that not too many people leave permanently. The community is located in a prosperous, highly-educated metropolitan region offering well-paying jobs and all the amenities necessary for an economically secure lifestyle. The public school system in this community is superior. There are low crime rates and excellent closely located medical facilities.

The community is quite homogeneous and likes being that way. As a system, the community rejects the introduction of diversity, even in the architecture of new homes which are built on the lots of old homes as they are demolished. The focus group participant questioned how long this community could exist without introducing diversity. Actually, the person questioned the sustainability of such a system in the 21st century global society. The focus group's discussion led to the conclusion that this homogeneous community might eventually be forced to merge with a larger community if it didn't change its attitude toward diversity.

Consider the other end of the continuum. Can there be too much diversity? Can differences be so wide that adversarial notions prevail to the degree that no point of unity can be achieved? If a community cannot find common ground, then it's difficult, if not impossible, to move forward together. Disparity can be so severe that the community shatters. I have often brought up this question concerning too much diversity to discussion groups. Additionally, I have surveyed research data. Thus far, I have seen no definitive conclusion. So I turned to history to search for my answers.

I well remember as a high school student memorizing the lines from a speech that Abraham Lincoln delivered in 1858, two years before he was elected president of the United States. In that speech, he stated: "a house divided against itself cannot stand." He further mentioned in the speech that he did not feel that the U.S. government could endure with some states advocating slavery while others advocated freedom from slavery. Later, I found the same idea expressed by Jesus in Matthew 12:25. That verse in the King James Version of the *Holy Bible* says: "every kingdom divided against itself is brought to desolation; and every city or house divided against itself shall not stand." These two statements imply that differences can be so harsh that the whole will eventually break into parts. From a systems thinking viewpoint, the system will fracture. Thus, the interacting subsystems will then become dysfunctional. From historic information, I conclude that there can be too much diversity in some cases and that great harm can be done. In the case of the Civil War, the U.S. system was wrecked then was reassembled through a reconstruction process after the war.

This conclusion now begs other questions. How do I know when diversity is too extreme? When can the introduction of diversity shatter the whole system? Is the diversity being introduced worth the destruction of the entire system? Again, let's return to the Civil War days in America. My memories from the study of American history in school indicate that historians have drawn different conclusions concerning the cause of the Northern states and the Southern states going to war against one another. Some historians claim that the dispute was over slavery. Others espouse that the conflict involved states' rights. I don't think either answer fully explains the North-South dispute.

The situation was complex at best in the 1850s, the years leading up to the Civil War which lasted from 1861 to 1865. In assessing the intense feelings people had on both sides about states' rights and slavery, it seems that when deeply entrenched beliefs are challenged, people will defend those beliefs even to the point of war. There are philosophies about life that people feel are not negotiable. They are willing to die to defend those beliefs. These values can fall into several categories including religion, politics, family, and patriotism. Introducing diverse beliefs into deeply-held philosophies of religion, politics, family, historical values, and heritage can be enough to incite riots. Taking a lesson from history, Community Leaders 4.0 must count the cost of challenging long-held entrenched values.

We are witnessing this phenomenon today. In the United States, there are major conflicts over various social issues. Feelings are running deep. The nation is very divided. There is a great split over political ideologies. Definitions of *family* and *beginning of life* are being fiercely debated. Arguments over the separation of church and state are raging. Groups are arguing over the meaning of patriotism. There is conflict among religious groups. And many more discords are arising as this book is being written. Another question comes to mind. How far can we go without shattering our system?

Community 4.0 leaders realize that balance between homogeneity and diversity can be a helpful answer. They understand that a mosaic is being created in America. Each piece of the mosaic holds a group of people who have differences with people in other pieces of the mosaic. The best that might be expected is that the various groups housed in these very different pieces of the mosaic will agree to disagree. The hope is that groups will peacefully coexist in a very diverse community.

Either extreme—too diverse or too homogeneous— can endanger a community's sustainability. From my observations, having watched several major changes take place, it takes at least 30 years from the introduction of social change to the acceptance of it in society. Why a minimum of 30 years? That's the equivalent of at least a generation and a half. Introduction of strong change will be rejected by the current dominant generation, then the next generation will be more accepting if the change managers keep on pushing for the transformation. Many of the social changes that are in the process of being accepted today began as small campaigns in the 1960s and 1970s then expanded into national and international phenomena.

One example of the introduction of diversity is Earth Day. In 1970, the first Earth Day was held to bring attention to the preservation of the earth's resources. Until that time, people liked to think of themselves as concerned citizens who were stewards of the earth's resources, but the study of ecology did not dominate their attention. U.S. citizens weren't all that mindful of the finiteness of the earth's resources. The Earth Day movement was designed to begin planting the seeds of change in people's minds. It introduced diversity in that it initiated a different way of thinking about the environment.

I remember being in graduate school in 1970 and noting the handwritten signs being toted over the college campus announcing Earth Day. I didn't pay much attention and thought to myself that this movement would never go very far. However, the proponents persisted. The movement grew. Now, four decades later, there is great attention and money being devoted to the earth's environment. This introduction of diversity has created conflict between groups operating at opposite ends of the environmental spectrum. One extreme on the continuum is represented by groups advocating preservation of the earth's environment to the extent of blocking business development. On the other extreme, there are groups who do not believe the earth's environment is in any serious danger of depleting its resources; thus they advocate business progress in spite of environmental group protests. To move forward, these two extreme positions must find common ground. As Communities 4.0 participate in the environmental movement, it is important to maintain a healthy balance among their economic, social, and ecological systems. Too much investment of time, energy, and money in one of these areas can cause devastation of the other areas.

Think of the major social changes that have happened in your life-time. The acceptance of them happened through slow integration of the issues into mainstream society. At first they were rejected—perhaps boldly rejected. Then more people became accepting of them. Eventually the alterations became a part of society. It's all about the art of changing people's minds. Community Leaders 4.0 are aware of the techniques for introducing diversity into a homogeneous society. It must be done slowly while constantly communicating with the citizens to obtain their feed-back. Yes, there will be conflict and sometimes violent rejection of the new ideas, but Community Leaders 4.0 are prepared to stay the course if they feel the diversity being introduced is worth the struggle. It is important for Community Leaders 4.0 to analyze the probable long-term effects of the diversity introduced and ask themselves if the diversity is healthy for the future sustainability of the community.

It is very difficult to transform a close-minded community system to a more diverse system, but it can be done through perseverance. We men-tioned earlier that systems must have an immunosuppressive approach in order to be diverse. Communities 4.0 have mastered flexibility to the point that change is accepted. However, every community has a set of values. And in every community, some of the values are non-negotiable. When diversity comes up against these non-negotiable values, then the leaders have one of the greatest challenges of their careers in introduc-ing these changes. There is a risk that even the most flexible system can suffer damage if there is a threat to the community's value system. Wise Community 4.0 leaders assess the risk of introducing the diversity before they actually initiate the change process. In some cases, challenging the current system might not be worth destroying it. That's a tough call.

Individual Rights Versus Common Good

In many communities, the struggle for individual fulfillment often clashes with the desire to promote the common good. Picture a hori-zontal line. On one end of the line is the category of individual rights, and on the other end is the category of common good. Along the scale bridging these two extremes, society practices many applications of these ideas.

Since the ratification of the Bill of Rights to the U.S. Constitution in 1789, America has been known for its seemingly never-ending quest for individual rights. As a futurist, I have been tracking the empowerment of the individual for the past three decades as an indicator of social direction. The more individual rights are bestowed in a society, the freer the society becomes. When individuals are empowered, creativity rises, grassroots activities take root, entrepreneurism expands, and eventually, free people drive a healthy socioeconomic environment. This situation is workable up to a critical point. If people continue to demand their rights and begin to exclude the exercise of their individual responsibilities to their community, then the once healthy environment may bend toward harming the common good. Too much individual freedom, in extreme circumstances, can lead to anarchy, which is a state of lawlessness and mayhem without a strong-enough governing body to enforce the law. To have no governance and expect people to exercise their individual rights to their fullest extent while regarding the full rights of others in a pluralistic society is a pipedream.

The demand for individual rights without accompanying those liberties with some degree of responsibility to the community creates narcissism, which is a state of excessive self-absorption and self-centeredness. When an individual's full attention is on himself, then everything this person does is for the objective of self-promotion, self-satisfaction, and self-enhancement. When an individual exercises too much freedom for herself, then it might obstruct the freedom of others. For instance, if a person exercises her freedom of speech to the degree that she makes a slanderous statement about another person, she is impeding the other individual's freedom. Her freedom has crossed the other person's boundaries. The narcissistic individual has little consideration for how her actions will affect the whole community.

The narcissist has little empathy for others. For example, a few years ago there was a shortage of flu vaccines for the major portion of the flu season. Healthy people were asked to defer taking the vaccine to let others who had compromised health conditions have the available vaccines. This required using an honor system. In spite of the public appeal for personal sacrifice, many healthy people availed themselves of the flu vaccine without consideration for the well-being of others who might be more negatively affected if they contracted the flu. This narcissistic behavior showed an unwillingness of some people to make personal sacrifice for the common good.

I believe that there can also be group, or social, narcissism. Some groups feel that their demands are more important than those of other groups. They become so absorbed in the group's cause that they harm the ability of the community to move forward. Groups who try to dominate others at the expense of the common good become elitist and exclusive. Rather than work on issues with a compromising attitude, these groups endeavor to trump the actions of other groups and are constantly jockeying for a key position. This often happens in community political settings—from local politics all the way up to international policy-making entities. The groups become more concerned with dominating the political spectrum than compromising with other groups in order to help the community over the long term. Immediate power and control are more important to narcissistic groups than sustainable community prosperity.

However, the other extreme can also exist. There can be so much concern with the common good that individual rights are sacrificed. With diversity prevailing, there are many voices demanding to be heard. The world gone wiki necessitates the empowerment of multiple groups with equally important needs, philosophies, and mandates. With all this chaos, it is difficult to produce community ordinances that will satisfy the diverse needs of the population. To restore order and move forward in some direction, sometimes a ruling group obtains enough clout to overpower all other groups. The ruling majority determines that it will be better to equalize all collective interests for the common good. Thus, everything—including public safety, schools, parks, health care, transportation, utilities, many businesses, and a bulk of private capital—becomes part of the public domain. High taxes are levied on organizations and citizens to have services equally available to the total community. The common good trumps individual liberties.

This concept of common good surpassing individual freedom contradicts a capitalistic community philosophy and often follows the failure of the application of *pure* capitalism. The reason I emphasized *pure* is that the United States does not have pure capitalism. It has a quasi-capitalistic economy. In pure capitalism, only the strongest and most resilient people survive and prosper. There are no government safety nets. In a quasi-capitalistic society, there are such safety nets as unemployment compensation, social security, disability, and welfare payments available to the citizens who qualify for them.

In a purely capitalistic economy, eventually the gap between the rich and poor can become unmanageably wide. When this happens, the situation gives rise to the idea of collective equality. Anger breaks out between the *haves* and *have-nots*. At that point, implementation of the idea of "everything for the common good" arises. This extreme condition can choke the community's creativity and entrepreneurism. Often the opportunities for prosperity diminish when the interests of the common good are regarded as far more important than individual privileges.

By having many features of society commonly available, some people are not willing to do their share and thereby relinquish their responsibility to others. This often happens in group behavior. People will defer the major effort to others and will lag in their contributions. For example, potable water is a desired community commodity. It is to be made available to all. However, some people and companies may choose to pollute the water supply, i.e., they choose to renounce their responsibility for maintaining clean water. Thus, common good taken to the extreme can be harmful to the community's future.

There is a third option: balance between individual rights taken to the point of narcissism and common good taken to the point of the quest for total equality without regard for individual responsibility. Community Leaders 4.0 have grasped the idea that the world has gone wiki and that many people insist on being heard. A large number of interests exist in a diverse community. The job of Community 4.0 leaders is to find the lowest level common denominator on which all can agree. For example, not all citizens may agree on specific public ordinances. There may even be civil disobedience by some groups who consider some ordinances unjust. Thus, abiding by all laws may not be the point on which everyone agrees. Dr. Martin Luther King, Jr. in his "Letter from a Birmingham Jail" written on April 16, 1963, justified nonviolent demonstrations in the civil rights movement for what he called "unjust laws" (Ali-Dinar 2009). In the letter, Dr. King validated his reasons for interpreting the segregation laws as unjust.

Perhaps there can be community agreement on public safety issues or equal access to public parks. There may be many things on which all facets of society can agree. It is the responsibility of Community Leaders 4.0 to find these positions of agreement and build on them. Additionally, Community Leaders 4.0 are accountable for discovering points of disagreement and setting up dialogue sessions with the opposing parties in an effort to manage the conflict.

It is becoming increasingly difficult to find common ground on many issues as diverse cultures and philosophies permeate our communities. However, if we are all intending to do life together, it is imperative that we find common ground and work together for the common good without forsaking our individual rights. Community Leaders 4.0 have great responsibility in this area.

Quality of Life Versus Community As a Commodity

A community's quality of life (sometimes referred to as quality of place) embraces all aspects that make the community an inviting place in which to live. Among the features constituting quality of life are safety; availability of health care, arts, educational opportunities, good jobs, presence of nearby grocery stores, shopping choices, transportation, pleasing climate, and good air and water quality; degree of social capital, high quality infrastructure, choices of faith-based institutions, and community attractiveness. Additional features include caring, visionary leaders; a variety of sports and social activities; healthy government and business climates, low poverty level, acceptable cost of living, and a general feeling of well-being among citizens. Even this long list is not all-inclusive. I'm sure you have things you can add. Part of the mission of healthy communities is to maintain a high quality of life for all citizens.

On the other end of the spectrum is consideration of the community as a commodity. I view this as looking at the community from the perspective of a product to be marketed. With this in mind, community leaders concentrate heavily on selling the features of the community for competitive reasons. In the globalized society in which we live, there is intense competition among international communities and regions to attract talented workers and state-of-the-art profitable businesses. Many communities have economic development professionals working through local governments, the chambers of commerce, and other local entities to provide tax incentives, land, and other amenities in order to recruit profitable businesses and retain these organizations in the community.

Great Community 4.0 leaders recognize the importance of integrating these two extremes. If this doesn't happen, communities may have a good quality of life for residents (if that's what the leaders emphasize) but the tax base is so imbalanced that it's too expensive to live in that community. On the opposite end of the continuum, there may be too much concentration on recruiting and retaining businesses to the point of negatively affecting the quality of life of the citizens. Businesses may tend to dominate the community and dictate the direction it takes. There can be a real imbalance. Even the environment can suffer if the community is willing to compromise its ecological goals, and perhaps the safety of its citizens, to invite certain types of businesses into the community. Community 4.0 leaders know that economic development cannot be the sole mission. They understand that economic development must be integrated into quality of life issues.

A good example of the balance of quality of life and economic development is occurring in Seneca Falls, New York. This town of just over 9,000 people located in Seneca County approximately 45 miles west of Syracuse has managed to balance its quality of life with its community as a commodity through a relationship with IESI, a Fort Worth, Texas-based non-hazardous waste management company, which coexists with its sister company BFI Canada under the corporate name IESI-BFC Ltd. IESI has built the Seneca Meadows, Inc. Landfill in Seneca Falls. This is the largest active landfill in New York and serves the municipal, business, and industrial solid waste disposal needs of the Northeastern United States. Besides being a boon to economic development in the region surrounding Seneca Falls, Seneca Meadows, Inc. is a quality of life partner for the betterment of the region through its support of community activities, food drives, and such community green initiatives as helping citizens with household hazardous waste disposal and environmental education. Just under a fourth of the 2600-acre Seneca Meadows facility is a solid waste disposal program, which has a state-of-the-art eco-friendly design. It operates under very strict state and federal environmental standards.

Other programs are located on the 2600-acre site. The Tire Recycling Facility processes and chips an average of 1,500,000 tires per year. The chips are used in the landfill lining as well as in road construction and other civil engineering applications. Not only is the Tire Recycling Facility creating a useful product serving customers throughout the Northeastern United States, it is providing a way to rid the environment of huge stacks of old tires from cars and trucks.

Additionally, landfill gas is a byproduct of decomposition of organic materials. Seneca Meadows controls emissions from this organic waste by collecting it in a network of wells and burning it in the landfill gas-driven electric plants. Seneca Energy, Inc. owns two landfill gas-driven electric plants, which produce 18 MWh of electricity—enough to power over 18,000 homes. Thus, by working together, Seneca Meadows, Inc. and Seneca Energy, Inc. produce a marketable product which holds great potential in the emerging market of low-cost renewable energy (Seneca Meadows Landfill 2010).

To further capitalize on the electricity produced by the landfill, the IESI-Seneca Meadows Renewable Resource Park (RRP) is being developed. By locating in the RRP, organizations will experience significant savings in cost of electricity. Additionally, they will reap many environmental benefits as well as have access to waste management facilities and other such amenities as transportation and infrastructure. The RRP will add jobs and contribute to regional sustainability (Seneca Meadows Landfill 2005, 2009).

∾

While balancing quality of life and community as a commodity, Community 4.0 leaders must put systems thinking into action. Bringing an organization into a community will affect other community entities. For example, a corporate relocation might create hundreds of jobs that will bring scores of families to the community. So many families moving into the community simultaneously might overload the education system, create pressure on the infrastructure, and cause a housing shortage. This might drive both housing prices and labor costs up. The infrastructure may need to be updated while tapping into unplanned expenditures from the local government coffers. The lesson from this scenario is that before marketing the community as a commodity, plans should be made to check the implications for other quality of life issues that may be affected.

I have seen communities who aspire to balance quality of life and community as a commodity but lack the systems thinking to make it happen. Doing so takes time and visionary leadership. It may take a decade or more. Wishing doesn't make things happen. Strong Community Leaders 4.0 must work to implement the community vision by attaining committed alignment from leaders of the various community subsystems. After that alignment takes place, leaders must become responsible for the deliverables.

To really attain the balance that will sustain a community, it is imperative that communities cooperate on a regional basis. It takes adequate financial resources, foresight, creativity, time, and energy for a community to move forward as a commodity. Working in isolation doesn't allow a community to accumulate the adequate resources necessary for the high degree of competitiveness required for the global economy. Balancing community as a commodity with quality of life issues takes cooperation with other communities in the region. That equilibrium will be attained by working together.

Often communities fail to see beyond the competition with one another. "After all," they tell me, "we must consider our revenue stream. We don't see the logic in helping our neighboring community locate a business there rather than in our town." That might seem logical. However, there are instances when communities can work together. For example, it may seem obvious that the community next door is the best match for a company relocation. Maybe your community has a corporate airport. Working together to bring that corporation to the neighboring community will perhaps win the air transportation contract for your community.

I know what you are thinking. The above example is easy. But not all communities have an airport. If you are thinking this way, it's understandable. On the other hand, your community has its own value which translates into its own unique features. To identify that uniqueness, hold a focus group session and produce a list of your exceptional qualities or hire an outside consultant to observe, analyze, and list your community's strengths. When there is the possibility that a desirable business might relocate to your region, present your features as a unique benefit to the total transaction. By working in a cooperative mode, everybody wins.

Global Perspective Versus Local Emphasis

Community Leaders 4.0 recognize that becoming extremely global in scope or extremely locally minded can do harm to the community. If the system operates from only a global perspective, it will lose its local appeal. If leaders are caught up in the global movement, they may direct their communities in recruiting mostly global companies and work with citizens to convert the community to a multicultural environment while abandoning the community's local identity altogether. This extreme transformation may not be necessary.

On the other hand, some community leaders continue to maintain the community's local identity to the point that they isolate the community from global issues. The citizens advocate the avoidance of recruiting global organizations and stage a concerted campaign to "go local." It is important to retain the community's local identity, but it is also important to recognize that all communities are participants in a larger world. With the Internet, global trade agreements, emerging economies, and a global workforce, it is almost impossible to be so self-contained that these issues can be avoided. To ignore the socioeconomic globalization now taking place is dangerous to a community's sustainability.

As we have discussed in all the other paradoxes mentioned in this chapter, balance is the key to community sustainability. Participation in the global socioeconomic arena while maintaining a community's local flavor will be part of the 4.0 community's mission for protracted success in the ensuing decades.

Upstate, South Carolina

An important illustration to consider for this balance of paradoxes is the Upstate Region of South Carolina. This region is composed of ten counties with a population of approximately 1.3 million people in the northwest corner of the state and has more foreign investment per capita than any other region in the United States. To find out more about the Upstate, I talked with Ben Haskew, president and CEO of the Greater Greenville (South Carolina) Chamber of Commerce. He has been in that position since 2003. His background also includes service as president and CEO of the Spartanburg (South Carolina) Chamber of Commerce for ten years. Both of these cities are key communities in the business and commerce sphere, which stretches along the Interstate 85 (I-85) corridor of the Upstate. Thus, Haskew is literally a human encyclopedia on the topic (Haskew 2010). The Upstate works hard at balancing local culture with global flavor. Haskew indicated to me that the Upstate has over 220 companies from 24 countries. With that distribution of diversity and global significance, the actual local culture of the area has blended well with a global perspective. Haskew says that people in the region no longer think about two different extremes of the continuum. The area is so blended that a global outlook, coupled with the preservation of historical spots and the renewal of downtown areas, has become the common culture. Foreign nationals feel right at home in the Upstate. The local citizens consider it a part of their way of life to hear many different languages spoken in such places as grocery establishments and department stores.

Transition From Local to Global/Local

In the 1960s, South Carolina's governor, chambers of commerce, businesses, and local communities realized that something had to be done to create jobs to replace those lost in the declining textile industry, which had largely moved out of the United States. Visionary leaders recruited foreign manufacturers to the Upstate region. They worked together to accommodate the foreign nationals who would relocate to the Upstate for a specific period of time. Word of mouth caused more foreign companies to choose to locate in the Upstate. The largest early investment came when Michelin arrived. Now the North American headquarters, Michelin North America Inc., is located in Greenville.

In 1992, BMW announced the location of its first North American manufacturing operation in Spartanburg. First creating 450 jobs, the current employment has grown to 5,000 people and $4.2 billion in investment. Since locating to the Upstate, BMW has attracted 42 tier-one suppliers to the region. Other foreign companies in the Upstate include

Adidas, Alfmeier Corporation, BASF, Lab21 Inc. (biomedical company based in the United Kingdom)—and over 200 more.

The region also has many domestic companies and regional offices of U.S. companies. Milliken & Company, one of the largest privately held textile and chemical manufacturers in the world, is located in Spartanburg. Even though the textile industry to a great extent is located overseas, there continues to be many facets of the textile industry operating in the Upstate.

Balancing Local and Global

Upon my asking how the Upstate balances the local and global perspectives, Haskew answered: "We treat everyone the same. We are inclusive. We are all in this together." In order to help foreign nationals adapt to the Upstate, special Day Schools are available. They are set up for French, German, and Japanese families to help with language barriers. The Day Schools are also helpful in keeping the students on par with their schools back home. Foreign nationals usually stay in the Upstate an average of three years, then they return home. It is important that they not get behind educationally while in the United States. The foreign national workers who come to the Upstate usually speak English, but their families who accompany them may not. Upstate leaders feel that it is important to accommodate language barriers.

There are also various activities honoring the cultures of the many countries represented. The International Center of the Upstate (ICU), a nonprofit organization, was created to promote understanding between local and international cultures. ICU is available to help foreign nationals assimilate into the local culture by providing information for such things as getting a driver's license, meeting other people in the community, and availability of resources for making the transition easier. People from over 70 countries participate in ICU. Additionally, leaders in the Upstate also started an honorary consul program—where consuls were named to represent the interests of their home countries and to help the Upstate locals connect to travel and cultural interests in the honorary consul's homeland.

Upstate Economic Development

Everyone works on economic development, according to Haskew: "Cities, counties, chambers of commerce—all work together to make things happen. *Forbes* ranked Greenville County as fifth of all places that could best handle the recession in the United States (Coster 2008). BMW even expanded during the economic downturn. Our ten-county Upstate Alliance markets the Upstate to businesses around the world. Our vision is to be a premiere region on the global stage. We are already global. And we constantly seek to improve our position."

With education being an impressive partner in economic development, Haskew indicates that Clemson University and the University of South Carolina work closely with the Upstate through various programs and research institutes located in the area. The Upstate recognizes the importance of a close relationship between research university programs and the economic growth of the region.

Also playing a major role in economic development are the technical college and community college systems in the area. They work closely with businesses to provide state-of-the-art training to companies in the region. The community college system can also act as a feeder to four-year colleges in the area.

The major metric for measuring the Upstate's success is per capita income growth. Education, in partnership with businesses, can make this metric increase. The goal of the Upstate is that, by the year 2025, 40 percent of the adult population of the region over 25 years of age will hold a bachelor's degree or higher. The region wants to grow their own educated people in addition to recruiting creative, highly educated people from outside the region. Working with Dr. Michael Porter of Harvard University, the program to make the Upstate more globally competitive is called *New Carolina*.

When I asked Haskew why companies like to locate to the Upstate, he commented: "There are great transportation systems here—interstate highways, air, and a deep-water port at Charleston. We have had a very good business climate for over a century, and we continue to improve. And as the textile industry reduced its workforce, through global competition and automation of facilities, there was a very trainable workforce left. That provided a good cost factor."

Other exciting things on the horizon are the expansion of the University of South Carolina's medical school to a four-year program through Greenville's hospital system and the beginning of service of Southwest

Airlines in the spring of 2011 at the Greenville-Spartanburg airport. Haskew says that one of the best things that happened to the Upstate was the cooperation of Greenville and Spartanburg in the building of a regional airport in the 1960s. He firmly believes that communities must work together regionally in order to experience growth.

"It's a new age," comments Haskew. "It is important for communities to have a collaborative—rather than a competitive—spirit" (Haskew 2010).

Innovation Versus Tradition

As in the other four paradoxes discussed in this chapter, innovation and tradition exist on two opposite ends of a continuum. It is unhealthy to be too tradition-minded. Likewise, it is not beneficial to be extremely innovative without any consideration for community traditions.

Often communities that concentrate greatly on local identity lean heavily on tradition. Beliefs, stories, customs, culture, and heritage are strongly emphasized. Leaders try especially hard to preserve the way of life that has been handed down from generation to generation. There may be modern conveniences in the community, but the worldview is highly traditional. I have worked in many communities that strive to emphasize tradition over innovation. As I have proposed ideas for innovation, I have often heard: "I'm not sure that would work here. We have a specific way of doing things, and have successfully applied that philosophy for years. It seems to work well for us. So why change our approach if what we've always done continues to work?" More often than not, the above statements are made by Community Leaders 2.0 and 3.0. They don't even realize that they are on a journey of obsolescence. If they aren't operating in a defensive mode already, they soon will be doing so.

On the other end of the spectrum is innovation. I define an innovation as a new idea, product, or service; the combining of two or more products, ideas, or services now in use to produce something that is novel; or new applications for current ideas, products, or services. Innovation can happen in any area. Communities can become innovative in their marketing, building design, infrastructure, manner in which citizens connect, organizations they target for economic development, the education system, and in many other ways.

The question is: can a community become too innovative? That is possible although at this point, communities are being urged to become more innovative rather than less innovative. However, down the road, communities may become so innovative that they lose valuable traditions which they intended to keep. As in all cases of paradoxes, balance is the key to success.

As Community Leaders 4.0 work together to determine the balance necessary for community sustainability, they must first establish the traditions they wish to keep. In the future, communities will create a specific personality that will cause people of like minds to move to a particular place. Traditions will form the base of the community's personality. There is a big push for restoration in many communities. New Orleans, for example, is creating jobs for workers by having them restore historic homes in the community. Known for its proliferation of antique dwellings, city leaders are aware of the uniqueness these homes lend to New Orleans. There is great care taken to capture and retain the history of this distinctive Mississippi River city (Maloney 2009).

Other communities celebrate the stories of their past through plays and musicals. History is depicted in museums of all kinds. The distinctiveness of each community can be found in its history and heritage. Communities must be careful not to lose their stories in their quest for new development and innovation. Preservation of the past is not always easy. It takes hard work, passion, and perseverance—as in the case of Big Spring, Texas.

Big Spring Preserves Its Past

As America quests for alternative energy sources, West Texas is capitalizing on wind energy. This effort will bring innovation to the region. Yet such West Texas cities as Big Spring, Texas, which has a population of just under 25,000 people, don't want to lose the stories of their past. Rich with military history, Big Spring is proud of its traditions. It was the home of the Big Spring Army Air Field from 1942 to 1945, where approximately 5000 aviation cadets were trained as bombardiers. In 1951, the airfield was reactivated as Big Spring Air Force Base and was later renamed Webb Air Force Base in 1952. During its life, Web Air Force Base trained approximately 10,000 pilots.

In 1977, the base was closed, and a major portion of the installation was turned over to the city of Big Spring, which converted the facility into an air park. Later an Air Park Development Board was formed. One of the board members, Bobby McDonald, noted the deteriorating hangars on the property and was inspired in 1995 to organize an effort to preserve one of the hangars for use as a museum. Since these hangars were scheduled for demolition, McDonald hastened to present his idea to community leaders. He met opposition. But undeterred, McDonald persisted (Hangar 25 Air Museum 2010).

Because of his passion for Big Spring's contribution to America's freedom, McDonald continued his quest. He presented his idea to the Air Park Development Board at least 12 times. He took the idea to the Big Spring City Council, and that governing body voted "no" to the idea but granted permission for money to be raised to save one of the hangars. Over time and by marching through numerous obstacles, grants were received and community fundraisers were held. Finally, there were enough funds to renovate one of the hangers by combining distinctive features of both deteriorating and damaged hangars.

By 1999, the project was complete. Today, the Hangar 25 Air Museum is an impressive tribute to Big Spring's role in American history. It has hosted more than 35,000 visitors from all 50 states and 31 foreign countries. For his work on this project and many others, McDonald was named Big Spring's "Man of the Year" in 2004. Currently, his wife, Gloria McDonald, who also enthusiastically worked in the Hangar 25 restoration efforts, is serving her third term on the Big Spring City Council. She has also served in the capacity of mayor pro tem of Big Spring as well as on numerous boards and committees throughout the city.

Saving portions of a community's history sometimes takes the enthusiasm of just one person. That zeal becomes contagious. Then great things happen. The website for the Hangar 25 Air Museum can be accessed at www.hangar25airmuseum.com (McDonald 2010).

Personality Created By Community Values

Community values—which are principles and ideals the community deems to be important—help create its personality. Some communities emphasize family life or high achievement. Others support the values of a specific political orientation woven throughout the population. Many communities carry the values dictated by an explicit population strata. In the future, people will more likely choose to live in a place based on its fit to their personality. In other words, the community's personality will match the citizen's personality. Dr. Richard Florida in his book *Who's Your City?* indicates that where we live ranks very high in our happiness quotient (Florida 2008). As I mentioned earlier, globalization is causing people to want to establish a sense of place. The traditions that a community preserves—and the values it emphasizes—will help to determine that feeling of a physical anchor.

Advantage of Innovation

On the other hand, spending the majority of leadership time on preservation of traditions without implementation of innovation can impede economic viability. As communities globalize, and moreover, as America continues to be globally competitive, The Council on Competitiveness in a published report entitled *Compete*, states that "ideas, imagination, and creativity are the most important factors of production" (Council on Competitiveness 2008). *The 9/11 Report* indicates that one of the failures resulting in America's inability to anticipate the terrorist attacks on New York City and the Pentagon on September 11, 2001, was the lack of imagination (The National Commission on Terrorist Attacks Upon the United States 2004). Without the ability to imagine, i.e., to create a mental image, it is impossible to be innovative. Our communities must produce people who have the thinking skills that will result in their ability to envision the possibilities and provide new ways of dealing with prevailing issues. New problems demand new solutions. Too often, communities are trying to solve today's problems with yesterday's solutions. These attempts for resolution are not working, and the community is falling behind in its quest for global competitiveness.

It is heartening to read the *2009 Legatum Prosperity Index*™ and find that the United States ranks first among 104 nations assessed in the category of Entrepreneurship and Innovation. This index is produced by The Legatum Institute, a privately-funded think tank located in London (Legatum Institute 2009). This report additionally reflects that the U.S. does not rank first in its other eight categories.

Further examination indicates that although America outranks other nations in innovation at this time, there is intense competition for this coveted global position looming on the near horizon. There is urgency for the labor force of the United States to become better prepared to compete in the international marketplace. And it becomes the responsibility of communities to prepare their citizens for this global challenge. America will compete with its ideas and innovation. I feel that Community Leaders 4.0 must create a sense of urgency for innovation much like the urgency created in the 1960s when the United States set a goal to land a person on the moon before 1970.

Analysis points to the fact that America's greatest need for innovation lies in how we provide education and training for everyone in our society—from very young students to the seasoned workforce. We must first tool our people for the future then continue to retool our citizens as changes demand. Coupled with continuing education is the need for continued high quality research and development residing in both public and private institutions and public-private partnerships. It is going to be very difficult for a community to be highly competitive unless they have at least a regional relationship with a major research university.

The power of innovation lies with regional cooperation. Much like the Greek city-states of ancient times, strong regions (a form of region-states) of the world will dominate the global arena within the next decade. It is imperative that those communities who wish to be global players identify themselves with a major region and work cooperatively to cluster their industries so that these organizations are interactive both horizontally (with suppliers) and vertically (as a participant in the supply chain) with one another and with the regional education system.

Balancing Tradition and Innovation

Of course there are myriad ways to balance tradition and innovation. Even the marketing of a community's traditions through its museums, restored downtowns, historic districts, dramas, and other methods can be innovative. The personality—for example, connected, caring, and compassionate—of the community that has prevailed over the years can be preserved as new people immigrate to the community from other areas of the same country or from entirely different countries. While contributing to new ideas and innovations, the blending of cultures can still adhere to overarching values. Innovations can happen in several areas:

the community's ecology, in the education system, in how people connect in novel ways, and how the infrastructure becomes smarter and therefore more productive—just to name a few.

Our communities are at the intersection of two crossroads. One leads to stagnation. The other leads to new life. On the journey to 4.0 status, communities must learn to balance the way they were with the way they can potentially be.

⁓

Community Leadership 4.0 Strategies

With many opinions being expressed in a world gone wiki, communities are experiencing polarization. Extreme polarization eventually produces gridlock unless some degree of balance between the two extremes can be established. This chapter deals with five sets of paradoxes: diversity versus homogeneity, individual rights versus common good, global versus local perspective, innovation versus tradition, and quality of life versus community as a commodity. A community's sustainability depends on how well Community Leaders 4.0 address the balancing of the issues involved in these paradoxes.

1. Review each of the paradoxes we have discussed.
2. Draw five horizontal lines and label each with the words from the paradoxes depicting the extremes of each continuum. For example, draw a horizontal line with the word *Diversity* on the left and the word *Homogeneity* on the right. Then do the same using the words from the other four paradoxes mentioned in this chapter.
3. Now that you have drawn each set of paradoxes on a separate continuum, put a mark along each line indicating where your community falls between the two extremes.
4. Analyze all five paradoxes and how your community is plotted along the lines.
5. If you did not plot your community's position near the midpoint of the line on any continuum, think about how your community can become more balanced.

Questions for Contemplation

1. Do you feel that a community can become too diverse?
2. If your answer to Question 1 is "yes," how would you handle the situation?
3. If you live in a community that is too homogeneous, how would you introduce diversity?
4. Do you have a community to use as a model of good balance between diversity and homogeneity?
5. How do you feel your community ranks on the spectrum of individual rights versus common good?
6. Choose three nations to discuss. Through group dialogue, decide whether these nations have too much emphasis on either individual rights or common good. Then discuss the outcomes of having too much emphasis on one or the other extreme.
7. Name a community which has too much emphasis on quality of life as opposed to achieving balance with community as a commodity. How does too much emphasis on quality of life affect the lives of the citizens? How is the tax base affected?
8. Do you know of a community that emphasizes marketing itself as a commodity at the expense of achieving quality of life for its citizens? What are the outcomes of this community perspective?
9. Does your community have an organization which lends to its quality of life as does IESI in Seneca Falls, New York? If so, who is that organization? There may be multiple organizations that add to your community's quality of life. If so, who are they? Are there additional ways in which your community can work with these organizations to enhance both quality of life and community as a commodity?
10. How does having businesses in the community (community as a commodity) help your community enhance its quality of life?
11. How is your community balancing its local perspective with its need to compete in the global marketplace?
12. If, by answering Question 11, you feel that your community needs to implement steps to attain a more global perspective, list some ideas for achieving this status.

13. Is it possible for your community to organize an initiative, perhaps in a whole different business category, to achieve similar success in globalization to that experienced by the Greenville-Spartanburg corridor in South Carolina?

14. If your answer is "yes" to Question 13, how would you go about starting a grassroots effort to ultimately achieve such globalization success? In what business category would you concentrate?

15. What are some ideas for sustaining your community by balancing tradition and innovation?

16. What measures are your community leaders taking to join a regional movement for innovation?

17. Does your community have a relationship with a major research university or other research entity? How can your community make that happen if there is no present relationship?

18. In viewing your community's position in these five paradoxes, what do you feel are your community's vulnerabilities? What steps can you personally take to address these vulnerabilities?

Critical Community Leadership 4.0 Initiatives

CHAPTER FIVE

Begin Within

Thee are many actions that Community Leaders 4.0 can take to experience success. However, there are five vital initiatives. I will deal with those actions in this and the following four chapters. The first critical initiative is to begin within yourself. This chapter will help you in acquiring that essential knowledge.

Self-Knowledge

Going inside herself to procure self-knowledge is often the last thing a leader does rather than the first action taken. To lead a 4.0 community, it is imperative that leaders have accurate intrapersonal insight. Experts indicate that self-knowledge is rarely taught and is difficult to attain. The information gained about the inner self can be inaccurate, especially if the individual is doing her own analysis (Wilson 2009). Even with that caveat in mind, I continue to recommend that a leader go through the process of introspection.

Before we proceed, please consider the questions in the exercise below entitled "Self-Assessment Questions." These questions are intentionally open-ended and are designed to cause you to think deeply about your answers. Please respond to the questions as you perceive them. I have not provided definitions or explanations. I want you to freely explore your *self* through these inquiries. It will be helpful if you take the time to write your answers.

ᥱᴑ

Self-Assessment Questions

1. What is your major life purpose?
2. How do you handle uncertainty?
3. What are your strengths?
4. What are your weaknesses?
5. What are your greatest fears?
6. When do you feel most courageous?
7. What motivates you to have courage?
8. What three things do you value most in life?
9. What motivates you to reach your goals?
10. What are your greatest sources of self-esteem and personal value?
11. What would you do if you had unlimited money?
12. How can you make your greatest difference in life?
13. What brings you peace?
14. Does your career bring you a sense of satisfaction and happiness?
15. How do you determine the difference between right and wrong?
16. What is your belief about God?
17. Does your answer to Question 16 relate in any way to your answer to Question 15?
18. What triggers your anger?
19. What triggers your fears?
20. What makes you sad?
21. What triggers your happiness?
22. How are your emotions affecting your physical health?
23. When faced with new problems, what steps do you take?
24. In interactions with others, how do you read their reactions to you?
25. How do you exercise empathy with others?

ᥱᴑ

Now that you have thoroughly thought about your answers to these questions, let's discuss some ideas concerning how your responses will contribute to your leadership philosophy and style. I will discuss a few subjects in the following sections. In other places throughout this book, I will focus on the additional topics addressed in the preceding exercise.

Life Purpose

If you are a person who believes that each individual has a purpose for his life, then I'm sure you will want to spend time searching for your mission. It takes a lot of thought coupled with trial-and-error experimentation to define what your life purpose is. It is helpful if you can state your life purpose in ten or fewer words or, even better, if you can state it in three or four words. If a person doesn't have a life purpose, it might be difficult to stay on course because life purpose can be the anchor for one's leadership philosophy. When making important decisions, life purpose is one of the standards by which a leader measures her judgment calls.

For example, if you believe your life purpose on earth is to be an encourager to others, your leadership philosophy will cause you to measure your decisions based on whether they will ultimately encourage or discourage others. You will, therefore, lean toward encouraging resolutions. Another example might be this: you feel that your purpose on earth is to make your community the most economically competitive entity in its region. Your decisions and aspirations will all be measured by whether they contribute to your community's positive economic growth and whether they will place your community in a high-level financial position in the region. In other words, you measure your personal and leadership success by the degree to which you estimate that you are attaining your life purpose.

Handling Uncertainty

Uncertainty is the norm in today's community environment. The rapidity of change causes unexpected results to happen frequently. Community Leaders 4.0 will continually be asked to solve problems which they have never before confronted. Because of prevailing insecurity for the last several decades, we have been immersed in what has been called the "age of anxiety." Today, a renewed sense of disquiet has emerged. In fact, we have entered the "age of neo-anxiety." Leaders who allow uncertainty to elicit apprehension will find their jobs to be difficult.

Community Leaders 4.0 must approach uncertainty with a sense of calm assurance that problems will be solved in due time. Operating in a constant state of anxiety will eventually take its mental and physical toll. In this age of neo-anxiety, Community Leaders 4.0 must be aware that people are searching for a sense of security and peace. Although they cannot guarantee this state of existence in any community, leaders must do everything possible to create the perception of stability.

Awareness of Strengths and Weaknesses

When you recognize your strengths and weaknesses, you are going a long way toward understanding yourself. It is important to identify those areas in which you are a strong performer and those areas in which you do not perform well. Community Leaders 4.0 will be called on to play to their strengths. Be aware of your expertise and use that know-how to excel. Success in a 4.0 community will demand focus. There will be so much to know about such a narrow spectrum that the Community Leader 4.0 must be able to gather information for decision-making from experts in various areas. It is helpful if one of the major strengths of the Community Leader 4.0 is that of synthesis—i.e., fusion of information from diverse sources.

Weaknesses must also be considered. Many people go too far and allow themselves to be controlled by their vulnerabilities. Recognition of weaknesses is not for the purpose of destroying self-esteem, but for building strengths and avoiding situations wherein your weaknesses would cause potential harm. An example of this state of affairs might be when a person understands that her weakness is in her definition of leadership itself. She might think that leadership and management require the same functions. Therefore, she perceives that skills of leadership should be applied just like she would practice management. She leads people by directing, controlling, planning, and organizing—i.e., as a leader, she tries to micromanage other people's assigned tasks. I have often heard that some boards try to micromanage the executive director. A leader who micromanages situations when he should be leading people is playing from weakness, not strength. By recognizing this weakness, the micromanaging member of the board can lighten up on the executive director and trust her to do her job.

Often people's personality strengths can become weaknesses when those strengths are taken to extremes. For example, a very nurturing person (a strength) might take nurturing to the extreme and become an enabler (a weakness). A competitive individual (strength) might become so competitive that she tries to set every situation up to be a win-lose contest while she is always vying to be the winner at all costs (weakness). Great Community 4.0 leaders are aware of their personality strengths and are careful not to take them to extremes that become weaknesses which do harm to themselves, their communities, and to others.

Personal Satisfaction

By analyzing what brings you peace, you will gain insight into how to achieve personal satisfaction. I have met many young people who yearn to make a difference. However, by the time individuals reach ages 50 to 70 or older, countless numbers of them seem to have an even deeper desire to make a difference. Perhaps it's because they have spent time in a career and have experienced success, and now they have more free time. Or perhaps they realize that approximately half or more of their life has already been lived. Or, there is a third option: they have had enough experiences and consequences (both positive and negative) from their life-journey that they are ready to name those things that truly matter and make a long-term difference in the world around them. Whatever their reasons, there seems to be a quest to make a real impact. The search for the methods that would make a difference often gains momentum in middle age or later. You may be one of these people.

If you think about what you would do if you had unlimited financial resources, you may get a hint about how you would contribute your time, energy, and money to worthy causes. When pursuing a task or being with special people, you may experience an extremely peaceful feeling. That's an indication that you need to spend more time with those people and activities. It is important to search for the things that bring you happiness and deep satisfaction. Then pursue them as soon as it is practical to do so.

Motivations

What motivates you? Something causes you to move in the direction of your goals and dreams, and it is important to be able to identify that "something." Some motives for achievement are healthy while others are not. Generally, there are three motivational categories in which you operate. These categories are based on Dr. Abraham Maslow's hierarchy of needs (Maslow 1943).

Most people who have had college courses in leadership, management, education, and other related areas have been exposed to the work of Maslow. Through my career, I have applied his theory and have simplified it in a personal theory that is easy to practice. My own theory indicates that, basically, humans have three overarching motives that drive their behavior. When one motive is satisfied, then humans are ready to move up the ladder to a more advanced motive. The third motive is the most sophisticated and expresses itself in various ways. These three motives are safety, community, and validity. First, humans seek to be psychologically and physically safe. They will be driven to achieve these ends. For example, you are in an important deal-breaking meeting that you have been anticipating for several weeks. Someone yells that a tornado is headed directly for the building in which you are assembled. You will immediately forget how important that meeting is and will be motivated to seek shelter from the violent storm. Your safety needs have surfaced.

If the tornado lifts back into the air just before it hits the building and does little damage to your community, you will take a moment to recover, and then you will probably return to your meeting agenda. Safety needs have been met, and you are ready for the next rung on the ladder. In fact, you are probably up two rungs on the ladder if you are in a deal-maker meeting.

The second motivational category is community. This gives you interaction and a sense of belonging to something greater than yourself. If you are part of a family, business organization, volunteer group, or city/town with good social capital, then you probably have this need met. The deal-breaker meeting meets the third motive—validity. This motive helps you feel valued. It indicates to you that your life counts and that you are truly making a difference.

When you exercise these motives in a healthy manner, they work for you. Pursuit of them in unhealthy ways can eventually cause your behaviors to work against you. For instance, some people want to belong to someone or some group to the extent that they become addicted to affection. On the third level, validity, some individuals might pursue public service careers for the wrong reasons. Instead of helping the community thrive for the community's sake, they do good works for attention, which validates their self-worth. One use of the validity motive is selfless; the other use is selfish—and can be addictive and unhealthy.

Community Leaders 4.0 must be mentally healthy enough to know the reasons for their actions. By assessing their motives, they can determine whether they are pursuing their community work for healthy or unhealthy reasons.

Understanding Your Emotions

Feelings are indicators. They help you in the decision-making process, provide guidelines for monitoring satisfaction and dissatisfaction, give you hints concerning paths to follow, and can be motivators for your behaviors. Community 4.0 leaders will find it to be a great boon if they are tuned in to their emotions and can gauge what they are feeling, why they are feeling that way, and how to change their emotions if necessary.

However, making decisions totally based on emotions is dangerous. It is helpful to validate your emotions with rational thinking. Feelings are temporary. They can change quickly. What you would do when you are happy may be completely different from a decision you would make if you are angry. Community 4.0 leaders will be called on to demonstrate consistency and stability. Since emotions fluctuate, making decisions solely based on feelings will cause a leader to be inconsistent and unstable. When that happens, it will be easy for a leader to lose credibility.

To acquire emotional self-knowledge, it is important to learn the triggers for your dominant emotions. When you have that knowledge, supposing that you are insightful enough to accurately assess your feelings, then you can learn to control those behaviors that result from your varying emotions. A valuable leadership skill is the ability to understand the triggers for a range of emotions.

To connect your emotional patterns, one suggestion is to keep a journal of your feelings and the triggers for these feelings each hour during your waking time for 30 days. At the end of each day, review your feelings and their triggers. After analyzing your feelings for the 30-day period, look for common themes. Typical journal entries might resemble the fictional example that follows. It is viewed from the first-person perspective.

$\backsim$

Journal Entry

7:00 A.M. Have started my day with optimism. Looks like a great day ahead.

8:00 A.M. Telephone call from client who needs to call a meeting within the next three hours. I am having a small amount of anxiety since my day is already full, and now I must try to change my schedule to accommodate this important client.

9:00 A.M. Schedule has been shifted. I feel relieved.

10:00 A.M. My mother telephoned to tell me that my dad is ill and that they are on the way to the hospital. I feel tense (in fact, my stomach hurts) because my schedule has been interrupted. I'm worried about my dad and am anxious because I'm wondering how I can again shift my schedule so that I can meet my parents at the emergency room.

11:00 A.M. After a couple of phone calls, my brother said that he could meet Dad and Mom at the emergency room. I can now carry out my morning schedule.

12:00 noon. Attended the client meeting. All went smoothly. I feel at peace about my contract with them. In fact, I feel excited about all the possibilities that lie ahead with this new client relationship.

1:00 P.M. Stopped at the local fast food restaurant and had a grilled chicken salad. Ate rapidly in order to hurry back to the office to work on a project.

2:00 P.M. My brother telephoned to see if I could come to the hospital to relieve him. My dad is still in the emergency room waiting for a diagnosis. Again, I feel stressed. My schedule is packed. The clock is ticking on my project deadline. And now off to the hospital. I will take my laptop to get work done while I'm waiting with my parents for a diagnosis. Excitement about the new client blends with anxiety about a jampacked schedule compounded by worry about Dad.

3:00 P.M. Working on my laptop. Still no diagnosis for Dad.

4:00 P.M. Physician has read some of the preliminary reports and decided to keep Dad in the hospital for more tests. Could be heart problems. Doctor isn't certain.

5:00 P.M. Dad has been assigned to a hospital room. He is resting comfortably. Mom tells me to go to my daughter's school play since my daughter is counting on my being there. Mom says that she and Dad will be fine. She will telephone me if she needs me later tonight. I feel at peace.

6:00 P.M. Home for a quick dinner then off to the school play. I feel myself relaxing.

7:00-9:00 P.M. My spirits are lightened. It's always fun to be with my wife and daughter. Being at the school play significantly reduces my stress. The kids are so funny. And they are having so much fun getting into character. I feel my stress level dropping.

9:00 P.M. Mom calls. Dad is having chest pains. I am going back to the hospital. Again, I feel stressed. I am worried about Dad plus I had intended to work on my client project for a couple of hours after the school play. My brother and sister will be at the hospital, and with the talking and meeting with physicians, there is no way to work on my project.

10:00-11:30 P.M. At the hospital. The doctor will run more tests tomorrow and does not believe Dad is in danger. Mom wants to spend the night at the hospital and sends my brother, my sister, and me home since we all must go to work tomorrow morning.

Midnight. I'm now at home. My neck muscles are tense. I feel a sense of anger and angst concerning all the expectations people seem to have of me. Then I feel guilty because I love my Dad, and know I shouldn't feel angry because of my schedule. He has been so good to me all my life. I want to be there for him. The anxiety and stress are building. I am going to try to get some sleep. Hope I don't toss and turn too much tonight because I have a busy day tomorrow. And tomorrow night is the city council meeting. I need to prepare for it. Since I've been elected to the city council, I feel a responsibility to the citizens of my community to serve them to the best of my ability. After all, they showed confidence in me by casting their votes in my direction. My jam-packed schedule begins all over again. There seems to be no end to all my activities.

Daily Analysis of Journal Entry

There is a common thread running through my emotional themes. Stress, anger, and anxiety are being experienced with intermittent feelings of optimism, peace, and joy. The stress tends to dominate my day. When viewed in hour-by-hour perspective, it appears that I have lots of responsibilities in the areas of work, family, and community. My schedule seems to control my emotions. When my schedule is smooth and things are paced well, I am at peace. When my schedule is interrupted or it has too many activities packed into it, then stress and anxiety prevail.

If this persists, then I have two choices: (1) work to reduce the pressure induced by my schedule or (2) make some changes within myself so that I can handle the chaotic life I'm living at work, with the family, and in my community activities. I will first analyze my schedule over the remaining 29 days of this month to see if the stress continues to be triggered by schedule interruptions—most of which I don't control—like Dad's illness or the key client calling for an immediate appointment. If this hectic pace continues, then I will analyze what I can reorganize or activities from which I can take a leave of absence to find some downtime during the day and evening.

In combination with reorganizing my schedule, I will intentionally engage in activities that reduce stress—meditation, daily exercise, healthy diet, self-talk when stress rises, and perhaps counseling with a specialist in anger and anxiety management. I will find pathways to peace. Cognitively, I will learn to exercise self-talk when things are closing in on me and I'm beginning to panic about my tight schedule and inability to get everything done that is expected of me. I will deliberately pursue activities that produce peace through humor—like reading entertaining books, watching funny movies, purposely socializing with positive, upbeat friends, and delegating tasks as much as possible.

I will continue to monitor the triggers to my negative and positive emotions. From looking only at this one day, I'm already realizing that I may take life too seriously. Even though some heavy things are happening, I need to lighten up and realize that life has its ups and downs and that there is only a limited amount of happenings that I can control. My expectations of myself might be too exacting. I have always been a perfectionist. I need to lighten up and not try to do everything perfectly. I need to understand that there is a difference between perfectionism and excellence. With a balanced schedule and proper stress-relieving activities, I can still produce with excellence.

Stress and anger can eventually lead to physical problems and in some severe cases can lead to an early death. Anxiety can also lead to panic attacks. Anger, I've always heard, can turn inward and exhibit itself as depression—which would be another negative emotion I would then have to deal with.

After monitoring my behaviors and feelings for the remainder of the month, if I'm continuing to draw the same conclusions, then I will set goals to reduce my stress. In fact, setting goals now would be beneficial. I will begin to walk for 30 minutes per day starting tomorrow morning. And tomorrow is not too early to begin a healthy diet. I will then work on the other goals over the next month.

˜

From this very lengthy example in the fictional but realistic journaling and emotional analysis exercise, it is important to note that you can find patterns in both your feelings and behaviors. You may not be as tuned in to your emotions and actions as the person in the example, but you can learn to conduct an effective analysis. You don't have to write out a lengthy report as this person did. You can instead jot short notes to yourself so that you can establish patterns over a defined period of time. If you are at a loss concerning how you really feel, you can consult a professional counselor to help you sort out all your emotions. The counselor can then help you with your journal entries and show you ways to continue your introspection. Eventually, you can learn to conduct this exercise independently.

Without knowing yourself, it is difficult to become a Community Leader 4.0—especially in this world gone wiki.

Courage

For many years, I have been searching for an appropriate definition of the word *courage*. Not much can be accomplished without its presence. My own definition of courage is this: getting up when you'd rather stay down, keeping on when it would be easier to quit, and looking ahead with hope when others are turning back in despair.

Most courageous people are not necessarily fearless. Instead, it is their ability to act in spite of their fears that causes them to accomplish great feats. Community Leaders 4.0 have the ability to muster the strength to do that which is right regardless of the consequences.

As a Community Leader 4.0, one of the most difficult things that you must face is criticism. When you dare to stand up and speak out, you immediately subject yourself to unfavorable opinions. You will not get through your leadership career without feeling the sting resulting from harsh remarks made about your decisions, choices, or philosophies. In fact, you (and perhaps your family members) will likely be personally attacked by discordant words or misleading statements from your critics. Thus, you must be emotionally prepared to handle the negativity and blistering comments that are hurled your way.

When you are faced with critical comments, it is helpful to use rational self-talk. Tell yourself that it's easy for your critics to sit on the sidelines and fire cutting remarks in your direction. But it's difficult to be the one immersed in the battle for a mighty goal—one that you believe to be the right thing for your community. Review the stories of past heroes who have suffered mightily for a worthy cause. Remember America's president, Franklin D. Roosevelt, and the United Kingdom's prime minister, Sir Winston Churchill: both of them refused to quit in the dark days of World War II. Review the labors of Thomas Edison who tried repeatedly to find just the right formula for the incandescent light bulb. When his naysayers suggested that he quit, he doubled his efforts and kept on trying. Recall the Jewish-American patriot, Haym Salomon who although in grave danger, furnished money to finance a huge portion of America's Revolutionary War.

You will experience failures now and then—but you will also give victory a chance. However, your detractors who are warming the benches on the sidelines will never know the pain of the scars or the exhilaration of the stars resulting from an energetic quest for a worthy cause.

What is the Right Thing?

I mentioned earlier that courage empowers leaders to do the right thing in spite of the consequences. In facilitating Community 4.0 leadership classes, I often open discussion with participants on how a leader will recognize that which is the right thing. People have different perspectives on the definition of *right thing*. The participants often mention several determinants—among them are power, good feelings, majority rule, culture, situation, and one's religion or faith. Let's apply these concepts to how people might be thinking about ethical community leadership. As you read the information on each definition, consider the pros and cons—and whether it would be advantageous in the long term.

The strongest people, groups, or nations will determine what is right.

If a community group demonstrates the most power, then the philosophy that it espouses will be considered the correct one. In war, the strongest side often wins. If this theory applies, then the right side won in the opinion of those who adhere to the theory that strength determines the right thing.

This belief system, however, might not always be true. Throughout history, strong nations have dominated weak nations. If they are really aggressive, they seize those nations and control the people. Strong nations sometimes even enslaved the citizens of weaker nations. If the strength theory for determining the right thing holds true, then slavery would have been the right thing in ancient empires. Personally, I don't believe that slavery has ever been the right thing. So this theory is not always true. Just because a person, group, or nation is strong enough to be dominant does not indicate that this theory is true all the time.

An action or belief is right if a person feels good about it.

If leaders let their feelings guide their determination for doing the right thing, then those feelings won't always guide them onto the most effective path. As I have mentioned before in this book, feelings are temporary and can change quickly. A particular behavioral choice might feel appealing and exciting. Thus, you determine that this option might be the appropriate one.

However, future consequences may indicate otherwise. Before taking action, it is important to back up your choices with rational thinking. If your mind tells you that you are getting ready to make a dangerous choice, and your feelings tell you that you are making a wise choice, the contrast between emotions and intellect tells you that you need to do more homework. The governor in your brain is indicating to you that you are not taking the rational path and that the consequences down the road may be unpleasant.

The majority rule determines the right thing.

When leaders believe that the majority is always right, it leaves little room for the opinions and desires of the minority to be expressed. If only the majority is empowered to determine what is right, then the minority, by exclusion, is always wrong. It seems to me that this precept will cause oppression of the minority and arrogance of the majority. It is possible that the majority can be wrong about an issue or action. Listening to the minority can be wise. Community Leaders 4.0 understand the value of considering all sides of an issue before making a judgment call and taking action.

The culture dictates that which is right.

In a nation, state, or local community, there is always an abiding culture. This embraces current values, beliefs, behaviors, preferences, and even people's habits. Culture can shift due to the arrival of a strong leader who possesses the ability to influence people toward making cultural changes. Additionally, different cultures blend in a community due to the influx of new people. As a result, the culture eventually shifts. If culture dictates what is right, then those people who do not adhere to the community's cultural preferences are considered to be wrong. Leaders must view the fairness of such reasoning. When community culture alters, then those who do not shift their beliefs and actions as the culture changes are considered to be wrong. Leaders should contemplate the rationality of such expectations.

The situation determines the right thing.

People who subscribe to this definition of *right thing* do not believe in moral absolutes. Instead, they believe that morals are relative to the situation at hand. For example, some people believe that stealing is always wrong while others would justify stealing if they were stranded in a snowstorm and were hungry. Their car might have broken down and they were walking to find help. Perhaps they came to a house and discovered that the inhabitants weren't at home. Yet there was a probability that food would be inside. People who subscribe to this belief system would break into the house and steal food to survive. They believe that survival is of higher order than stealing from someone. Individuals themselves determine the rightness or wrongness of an action depending on the situation and their own system of ethical priorities.

The above scenario often makes a good point of discussion and debate. Most people say that they would steal for survival if that was their only option. This may be an easy, desperate decision. There are other decisions that are more complex. Another example is when two people are together and decide that they are both reasonable adults. They decide on a debatable action, but both of them agree that it feels right. They are accessing the "if it feels right" theory in combination with this situational theory. They decide that if both of them feel good about the action, and the situation seems to call for that particular action, then it must be right.

Rational thinking must prevail in this context, and leaders must look beyond feelings and situations to determine the right thing. People often suffer negative long-term consequences when they combine "feels right" with a "situational" definition of *right thing*.

A person's religion or faith determines what is right.

Often people use the beliefs of their faith or religion to provide the guiding principles of what determines right from wrong. Different faiths provide different edicts of rightness and wrongness. Even people of the same faith often interpret their religious teachings differently. In the "Self-Assessment Questions" exercise that you considered earlier in this chapter, one of the questions addressed your perception of right and wrong while other questions asked you about your perception of God and whether these two views were connected.

In communities where faith groups are homogeneous, it is often easier to agree on a common definition of the right thing. In communities where there is diversity among faith groups, there can be different beliefs about what constitutes the right thing. Therefore, it is sometimes difficult to find common ground on this subject. Through the ages, there have been harsh disagreements and even hostile wars waged over faith-based determination of the right thing. People often have clashed over whose faith advocates the real truth. In a religiously diverse community, leaders should be aware that social polarization can happen when seeking to do the right thing by reflecting the beliefs of a particular faith. This is a sensitive matter because many people's religious beliefs are non-negotiable. Thus, the issue invokes the question: if a majority of people living in a community practice a specific faith-based belief system, does that guarantee that their concepts of right and wrong are correct? This query usually ignites deep debate; and rarely is there a definite conclusion reached in the think tanks, focus groups, or classes where I have addressed this topic.

What Now?

There are probably several other points of view on what determines that which is right. It's a complex subject. As you mentally assess the various definitions of *right thing*, it is important to determine those constructs which form your model for defining the difference between right and wrong. Community Leaders 4.0 will be called on to have a solid value system and to be sure about what they believe. My suggestion is that you spend an ample amount of time delving into the ideas listed here and even explore literature on the subject to become certain about the roots of your thinking. Your core values will determine what you believe about *truth*. What you believe to be true then determines what you believe to be the right thing.

In summary, it is difficult to be courageous without a firm definition of *right thing*.

⁓

A Study of Courage: Greensburg, Kansas

Tragedy has turned to triumph in Greensburg, Kansas. On May 4, 2007, the most severe category (EF5) tornado devastated this small rural town. Winds were clocked at greater than 200 miles per hour. After the tornado damage was assessed, it was determined that 95 percent of the town was totally destroyed, and 11 people had been killed. In the months following the devastation, approximately 700 people moved from Greensburg, leaving the population numbers hovering around 800.

Rather than feeling victimized by such tragedy, the leaders and citizens of Greensburg sought opportunity. Operating from a tent where people gathered for town planning meetings, church services, and sharing meals, the community leaders carved out a vision for Greensburg's future. The town meetings were intense. People were hurting but determined to rebuild—and to rebuild bigger and more sustainable than before the tornado struck.

The vision was to go "green." Because many of the citizens were involved in agriculture, there was already a love of the land expressed by an appreciation for preserving the environment. Also the word *green* was in the name of the town. Additionally, the leaders and citizens felt that a green city theme would be a fantastic economic development tool for attracting new businesses to the community. The city council passed a resolution declaring that the town would build its structures to Leadership in Energy and Environmental Design (LEED) platinum standards. With that declaration, Greensburg would be the first town in the nation to build all structures according to these strict environmental standards. Short-term, the cost would be higher than restoring the town to the former building designs. But the leaders and citizens determined that the green plan would reap profits in many ways for Greensburg in the long-term.

This vision and plan execution takes a generous dose of courage. New home construction is costing the people much more than the replacement value of their former homes, therefore their mortgages are a great deal higher. Some of them are working two jobs to afford the luxury of building to green standards. They, however, feel that it's worth the investment. A majority of the townspeople have a firm faith in God and feel that there is a Providential hand guiding Greensburg's future. Citizens are willing to work hard to execute the community's vision.

Greensburg GreenTown is a nonprofit organization whose mission is to help make green building principles easy to understand and aid in the reconstruction of Greensburg. People and businesses from a broad spectrum are donating through GreenTown to help Greensburg in its green building efforts. For more information on GreenTown, please access its website at http://www.greensburggreentown.org.

Greensburg is indeed moving toward many qualities of a Community Leadership 4.0 model. The leaders and townspeople have a unique spirit that drives them to live out the definition of courage that I mentioned earlier: getting up when you had rather stay down, keeping on when it would be easier to quit, and looking ahead with hope when others are turning back in despair.

~

What Is Your Ethical Foundation?

If courage demands that you do the right thing in spite of the consequences, then you will need to have a firm concept of your ethics. My personal definition of the word *ethics* is the art and science of doing the right thing. Thus, between demonstrating courage and making ethical decisions, you can easily go in circles. By the way, in this book, you will find that I use the words *morals* and *ethics* interchangeably. For this application, I consider them synonymous.

Often ethics is listed in such categories as professional ethics, public service ethics, and personal ethics. I pose this question: can ethics be categorized or do you operate with a master set of ethics that covers all categories? It is my opinion that your core values drive your ethical choices in the decision-making process. Each person has a code of ethics—whatever that might be. This code has been derived from education, training, and personal experiences along with religious and other influences throughout one's life. Therefore, your sum total of life exposures, and how you have processed them, will help define your ethics and the resulting actions you take.

As I commented earlier, it is important for Community Leaders 4.0 to delve into their belief system and truly be in touch with how they determine right from wrong and good from bad—then act accordingly. I mentioned that ethics is both an art and a science. It is an art in that often the answers to hard questions are not exact, and you must intuitively find the answers. It is a science because there are some clear-cut, absolute formulas that work every time. For example, the murder of humans is considered to be universally wrong (Kidder 1995). That's the science part. However, killing humans under some conditions (self-defense or war, for example) is accepted in most cultures. Those conditions are not always clear-cut. That's the art part of ethics, in my opinion.

Several years ago, my hometown was building a new high school. Our alumni group was asked to name a few ethical values that we wanted to pass forward to the students in that school. Because our group had raised money for the new library, a plaque listing those ethics was to be posted in the library entrance. Coming up with just a few high-level ethics was a challenging exercise. It demanded that we think deeply about right and wrong, be clear on definitions, and prioritize our values. Obviously, the plaque had limited space, thus we couldn't list all the ethics we wanted to convey.

Such a task might be helpful to you in determining your ethics. Please take some time to do the following exercise.

ᥱᦓ

Exercise: Passing Your Ethics Forward

Let's suppose that you have been asked to list your five core ethics on a plaque that is to be displayed in the entry hallway of your local high school. You feel that there are really more than five ethical values that are important to you. List all of them. Think about their definitions. Then prioritize those morals so that you can choose the top five ethics to be placed on the plaque. Take some time to go through this process.

ᥱᦓ

Often, in class sessions, I ask participants to do this exercise. Over the years, the answers are remarkably similar. Participants usually mention honesty, integrity, love, responsibility, tolerance, fairness, loyalty, teamwork, respect, peace, and hard work—to name a few. We then go into their personal definitions of each of these words. Often participants' points of view differ concerning the definition of each word. Our discussion then leads to understanding diversity and different cultures. The word *respect* may mean different things to different people. In fact, all these words are open to diverse interpretations. In a world gone global and wiki, it is important to understand that differences do exist. People don't always define things similarly. The word *love* in the context of love for family differs among cultures and has changed down through history. In some cultures, love is prioritized in the immediate family structure depending on a family member's role in the family and the gender of the family member. That differs greatly from my definition of love for family.

Ethical Decision-Making

Decisions involve making choices. Often ethical choices are hard. In this section, we will consider three categories of options. To better understand these decision categories, I have developed fictional examples. Unless otherwise stated, they are based on imaginary characters, companies, communities, circumstances, and events. However, they represent possible happenings in contemporary society. Any likenesses to real characters, communities, organizations, circumstances, and events are purely coincidental.

One situation: Internal Dilemma Concerning Appropriate Actions

In this case, there is one situation. Yet there is internal conflict: to do or not to do. For example, you are serving on your community's city council. And you have a good friend who is also serving on the council. The friendship has existed for several years, and you have learned to trust your friend. However, with the recent economic downturn, you have suspected that your friend is having financial problems.

A company has approached the city council with some ideas for bringing a unique project to your city. The city council members are in conflict due to the company's past reputation in other communities. The corporation needs two more council votes to move the project forward. You suspect that the company is courting your friend. You even suspect that your friend has accepted a bribe from this organization—a sum of money in exchange for your friend's voting "yes" for the proposed project.

The ethical decision you are having to make is hard. You have maintained a friendship with this person for several years, and you know that if she is indeed involved in this bribe, she's not thinking straight. You suspect that she must be in dire financial straits. However, you also know that this activity is illegal. You see that the choice is obvious. You must report your suspicions concerning your friend's dishonesty. The proper authorities can then take it from there to secure proof of various transactions that are probably taking place.

This decision is very emotional for you. It boils down to this: report your suspicions or not. After all, you could justify the fact that you don't know the situation for certain. You do not have first-hand information. You have not seen anything. You, however, are fairly sure of her guilt based on subtle cues she has given you. You truly suspect that she is doing something illegal. However, after much emotional turmoil, you determine that there is only one choice. It boils down to reporting the suspected illegal activity for further investigation in order to do the right thing.

Two or More Situations: Good Outcomes, Choose One

Often people don't see much of a problem with having two or more pleasant situations from which to choose. However, the pressure comes with having to choose just one, especially when choosing one will eliminate the other. A case I often present in the community leadership classes to illustrate this point involves two positive situations, but the person must choose between the two. Here is this case.

You are a guru in your profession and are founder and president of a prominent consulting company. You have just been informed that your company is a candidate for an enormous contract. The prospect's company is located in London. To consummate the deal, the prospective client insists that you come to London and meet with certain "powers that be" in his company. The only day available for this meeting that will make or break the deal is May 18. You need this contract to keep your business competitive. In fact, if you don't get this contract, your company may even have to declare bankruptcy due to some cash flow problems that have surfaced during the sagging economy.

However, your only child, a daughter, is getting married on that same day. You and your wife have planned a huge costly wedding and dinner following the ceremony with 500 expected guests. Of course, you, as the father, have been planning on "giving your daughter away" in the wedding ceremony. In fact, you have been envisioning this sacred moment since she was a little girl. If you don't attend, she will be severely disappointed, and there will be tremendous pressure on your wife in this social situation. But if you don't go to London to meet with the prospective client, your company may be in big trouble. You want to do both. But you must choose.

Which choice would you make?

I'm sure you can see the great dilemma here. Leadership class participants argue this situation from every angle. There is no right or wrong answer. In most sessions, the participants first try to find a way to do both. They endeavor to negotiate with one or both parties, try to change dates, and truly want both good things for their lives. However, in the end, they must choose. And that choice is hard. Being forced to choose either good thing causes disappointment for the option not chosen. What a dilemma! Often, leaders must make these hard choices. And leaders must be prepared for their own emotional turmoil that happens as a result of the choices they have made.

Two or More Situations: Painful Outcomes, Choose One

This scenario is probably toughest of all. A choice must be made. The outcome will be painful. As a case in point during the past century, Americans have watched as Congress has had to deliver these types of decisions. Going to war against a country that has attacked the United States is one example. If soldiers are committed to war, then they will, for certain, be put in danger and many will lose their lives. Choosing an alternative like economic sanctions and not choosing to go to war might endanger the citizens of the United States in the future, and potentially millions of lives could be lost. Not going to war against a threatening country could destroy the United States in the long term. Congress must decide. The decision seems clear, especially when the U.S. has been attacked. But the outcomes of the decision are painful. It takes great courage and emotional stability to lead a country during wartime. And it takes great courage to declare a just war.

On the local community level, such decisions might not mean life and death. However, they can be painful. Several years ago, I heard a story on a national newscast about a dilemma that a community was facing concerning the sale of alcoholic beverages in that city. The community's leaders had decided that the city was going to promote wholesome family values and would not sell alcoholic beverages within its boundaries. That value system was advertised and had become the city's norm over several decades. From that story, I have developed the following fictional example of what happened in that city for your ethical consideration. Any likenesses to specific people or events are purely coincidental.

The city then began to suffer economic hard times. Discussion came up about putting the sale of alcoholic beverages on the ballot to improve sales tax revenues. The community's churches argued that a vote in favor of alcoholic beverage sales would reverse the wholesome image that the city wanted to portray. Other community leaders countered with arguments that more revenue was needed to give property tax relief to the residents, many of whom were deeply hurt by the recession. Eventually, the sale of alcoholic beverages went on the ballot.

Many leaders of the community's churches had to make a choice between two situations. Should they stage a campaign to defeat the sale of alcohol? Or should they remain quiet and perhaps bring tax relief to their members, who were also citizens of the community? A successful public church anti-alcoholic beverage campaign could perhaps defeat the vote but could cause some members to suffer financial difficulties. If the churches held no campaign, perhaps their silence would mean tacit approval. If the final vote count resulted in favor of alcohol sales, then city revenues would be much higher; and the city could prosper during the economic downturn. For church leaders, either outcome was painful in some way. The decision was hard.

The dilemma mentioned above can also be considered much like the first dilemma previously discussed; i.e., to do or not to do. You can view it as one situation or as two emotionally negative situations. Much of your perception depends on your belief system. Two people may view this concept differently. Either perception still generates much discussion and potentially negative feelings.

In elevating this situation to a higher level, we can consider the two sides that are representing the alcohol sales. One side is carrying out an economic development campaign for the approval of alcohol sales to attract more businesses to the community and lower citizens' property taxes. Several churches whose belief systems do not advocate the consumption of alcoholic beverages are staging a campaign against voting for alcohol sales.

The community's mayor is a volunteer leader in one of those churches that are against the issue. The mayor himself is personally backing the church side of the conflict but has not stated his position publicly. The citizens of the community are now demanding that the mayor let them know how he views this controversy. He must go public with his viewpoint. He is conflicted over how to make his statement. No matter which side he would have chosen, there would have been many citizens voicing their disapproval of his choice.

How to Employ the Decision-Making Process

When making an ethical decision, no matter what kind it is, it is helpful to consider some questions. There is no substitute for doing your homework and for considering every angle of a situation before drawing a conclusion and taking action. If quick decisions are demanded and you don't have time to do research, then you will need to call on all the intelligence available from trusted sources and all the knowledge that you have accumulated from past experiences. That's why it's important to constantly study situations and rehearse what you would do when confronted with specific decisions. Although some decisions must be quick in emergency situations, most decisions can be deliberated. Here are some questions to mull over. After answering these questions in each situation, you will be in a better position to make a sound decision.

1. What are the legal implications involved in this decision?
2. If I play out all possible scenarios involved in this decision, what are the long-term implications to all people affected in each scenario?

3. Have others been in a similar situation? What did they do? What were the outcomes?
4. Is research available on my various choices?
5. What are the probabilities of success for each scenario of my decision?
6. If I am a person subscribing to a particular faith, what do the tenets of my faith suggest that I do?
7. Will anyone be adversely affected by my decision that I'm contemplating? If so, to what degree?
8. Is the decision I'm leaning toward a wise one?
9. Can I live with the consequences of my decision in the years to come?
10. If someone else were in my place making this decision and I was the one being affected by the outcome, what would I want done to me?
11. Gut level, what is the right decision?
12. How will my decision affect the common good?

Community Leadership 4.0 Strategies

It is important to build a foundation for Community Leadership 4.0 by beginning with your *self* through deep introspection. This chapter emphasizes the need to acquire self-knowledge by taking ample time to study your *self*. Your motives for the actions you take and the decisions you make, your emotional triggers, your strengths and weaknesses, and what you consider as truth are critical to your success as a leader.

Courage is a necessary ingredient for Community Leadership 4.0. How you demonstrate courage and why you allow yourself to speak up and step out in spite of your fears projects a picture of your character. In the chaos of a world gone wiki, courage is important to the ultimate competitiveness of your community.

You will be called on to make critical judgment calls in your position as a community leader. Making ethical choices concerning the *right thing* is often difficult but necessary. Many factors are involved in the development and execution of moral options.

1. Have you ever had an ethical dilemma? If so, how did you solve it?
2. In ten or fewer words, describe your *self* as you know it.
3. Have you ever had to demonstrate courage? If so, what actions did you take?
4. What are your goals for developing a greater understanding of your *self*?
5. How can you acquire more courage?
6. What is your standard for measuring whether your decisions are ethical?

Questions for Contemplation

Since there have been numerous exercises with questions for your consideration and analysis in this chapter, there will be only one summary question in this section. Here it is:

Based on all you have learned about your *self* by applying principles discussed in this chapter, what is your leadership philosophy?

It would be a great idea to write your leadership philosophy to keep handy for constant review and editing as you continue to have leadership experiences.

When writing your leadership philosophy, please include your leadership mission, your ideas on how to treat people, how to determine right from wrong, your ethical priorities, how you see yourself leading your community, and ways you can demonstrate courage in moving your community forward. And please go beyond these suggestions to develop a philosophy that is original to you. This philosophy will be your operational foundation for your Community Leadership 4.0 status.

CHAPTER SIX

Imagine the Future

WHEN DISCUSSING THE topic "Innovation versus Tradition" in Chapter Four, I mentioned that *The 9/11 Report* credits lack of imagination as a factor in America's failure to anticipate the acts of terrorism on September 11, 2001. Judging by the number of lives lost in New York City, at the Pentagon, and on United Airlines Flight 93, which crashed in Pennsylvania, the inability to imagine these horrific events ahead of time was very costly.

Community Leaders 4.0 recognize that imagination is a critical skill and that imagining the future is an essential initiative for surviving and thriving in the remaining decades of the 21st century. Several years ago I wrote a book on lifeskills necessary for success in the 21st century. One of those necessary skills was what I called *futuring* (Corbin 1993). Now the term *futuring* is used frequently in the profession of futurism. From my point of view, futuring is the art and science of anticipating tomorrow. Therefore, when you imagine the future, you are actually practicing the skill of futuring. Without this skill, it will be difficult to make accurate judgment calls. A good textbook on the futuring process is *Futuring: The Exploration of the Future* by Edward Cornish (2004). I highly recommend this very thorough work.

Futuring Basics

Four terms are necessary for understanding the basics of futuring—trends, conditions, issues, and window of opportunity. Please consult Figure 6.1 as you read the explanation of these terms.

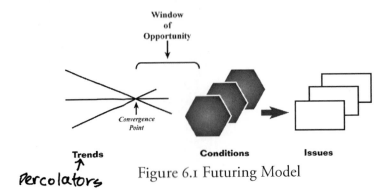

Percolators

Figure 6.1 Futuring Model

Trends are general directions. *Conditions* happen when multiple trends converge. *Issues* are outcomes. They are all things with which you must deal. The *window of opportunity* is the timeframe that exists between the convergence of trends and the actual occurrence of ensuing conditions. By understanding these four terms, you can be well on your way to successful futuring.

Let's take an example. The states of Nebraska, Kansas, Oklahoma, and Texas are included in an area labeled "Tornado Alley." Inhabitants of these states are well aware of the likelihood of a tornado in the springtime and are constantly on the alert for such an occurrence. Violent weather is expected especially in April and May of each year.

Citizens who live in Tornado Alley instinctively watch for weather trends. Since I live in Texas, I often become uneasy when I notice the sky becoming dark, the barometer dropping, the humidity rising, and the wind becoming eerily still. Either of these trends might not be dangerous alone, but the peril happens when these trends converge. The resulting condition is likely to be a powerful storm or tornado. After a strong storm or tornado, there would normally be issues with which I would need to deal. There might be damage to my house, insurance claims to negotiate, yard to clean up, and electricity to be restored. If my house were severely damaged, I would need to make other living arrangements.

Normally, between the time when the trends collide and the result-ing tornado or storm, there is a window of opportunity. By watching the trends develop on their collision course, there will often be an indication of approaching violent weather an hour or two before the storm strikes. Even after a tornado hits the ground, there is often enough time to issue a warning and blow a siren so that people can take cover. Sometimes there are as many as 20 minutes in the window of opportunity after a tornado is on the ground. Many lives have been saved by people taking advantage of the warning signals and seeking shelter from the storm.

Knowing that I live in Tornado Alley, I have futured the possibility of a tornado—i.e., I have envisioned how I would exercise my window of opportunity and deal with various issues should this catastrophic event occur. In other words, I have imagined the future using the model in Figure 6.1. The Homeland Security departments of the federal, state, and local governments have requested that organizations and families for-mulate a plan for all sorts of catastrophes ranging from adverse weather conditions to terrorist attacks. What these governmental agencies have asked us to do is to imagine the future.

The model in Figure 6.1 can be applied in communities anywhere in the world. Community Leaders 4.0 are always on the lookout for emerg-ing trends and trying to project ensuing conditions and issues. They are formulating ways to exercise the window of opportunity. One significant caveat for futuring is to always imagine the improbable. Often leaders fail to spend time on improbabilities for four reasons: (1) the risk of the condition happening is small and not considered to be worth the leader's time to deliberate; (2) the condition is unpleasant or too horrible to think about; (3) bringing up the condition to an advisory group might make members of the group uncomfortable for various reasons; and (4) since the risk of the event is so low, it's not worth spending money on preven-tion when economic resources are tight. Thus, things that might happen are mentally and emotionally avoided. If and when they do happen, lead-ers are then unprepared to handle them. For instance, you may live in a small rural community that has a low degree of risk for terrorism. Thus, you decide to avoid futuring in that area. Doing so might be a dangerous precedent in that an incident which might happen—perhaps perpetrated by a disgruntled citizen—has all the qualities of a terrorist attack. Then your community would be ill-prepared. The risk of such an incident is slight, but communities must be ready just the same.

Great Community 4.0 leaders spend many hours creating scenarios relating to every aspect of the future by anticipating both the possibilities and the probabilities. Leaders also picture the window of opportunity and take appropriate actions. By creating pictorial images of the future, community 4.0 leaders are often able to know what seems unknowable and pre-empt an unfavorable condition.

More About the Window of Opportunity

Between every set of converging trends and the resulting condition is a window of opportunity. Community Leaders 4.0 should be prepared to take advantage of this window of opportunity. Wise leaders anticipate the future and intervene. While it is often in our human nature to wait and react, the exercise of wisdom dictates that Community Leaders 4.0 should be proactive.

Let's look at an example from local government. There may be early signs of racial unrest in a community over disagreement about specific issues. Different ethnic groups, for example, may disagree over city governmental policies. Leaders of various groups may become very vocal, and street wars could break out from time to time. For the past several years, certain groups may have been asserting that local governmental officials are ignoring them. While these conditions continue, one of the scenarios that city officials might imagine would be a riot—a condition based on overt trends.

In the early stages of this scenario, there is time to take advantage of the window of opportunity. Either elected leaders, salaried public servants, and/or perhaps grassroots leaders could step up to the plate. Problem-solving groups could be formed throughout the community to detect any hot spots of ethic unrest. The goal is to pinpoint the roots of the agitation. Valid complaints should be taken seriously, and fixes should be initiated. Negotiations for policy improvements involving dissenting groups could take place. Leaders might hold diversity training events. I'm sure that conflict areas could be uncovered, and open discussions would be possible.

Wise leaders will see the trends developing. They will then create scenarios about various conditions and issues that might arise. After composing the scenarios, leaders will try to pre-empt any chaos that might occur. By taking advantage of the window of opportunity, serious problems can possibly be averted. Wise leaders never operate in ignorance but face potential problems head-on and seek solutions.

Principles for Applying the Futuring Model

Keeping the model in Figure 6.1 in mind, it is important to begin with assessment of trends, then envision possible conditions, and finally, project likely issues that might arise. After working with these three phases of futuring, then you should evaluate your window of opportunity and choose an action. More detail on the principles of futuring is contained in the subsequent material.

Determine important trends.

People often ask me: "How in the world do I discover a trend? And if I find a trend, what should I do about it?" As a first step in determining trends, it is helpful to answer these two preceding questions. Discovering trends will eventually become instinctive if you practice the habit of constantly being on the lookout for them. And I will later give you some hints concerning what you can do if you identify an authentic trend.

To discover trends, read everything possible—newspapers, magazines, websites, blogs, recent polls, professional journals, and research studies. View all sorts of TV programs and movies. Listen to speakers on a variety of topics. Scan YouTube and various social media. Ask questions of everyone you meet. Gather data in rare places—for instance, converse with taxi and other transportation drivers about all sorts of interesting subjects in every city you visit. In other words, continually be searching for common themes and patterns. This process is termed *environmental scanning.* For example, over 40 years ago, I noticed that there was an increasing amount of oil imported by the United States. In the 1970s, Honda was competing with U.S. automobile manufacturers on American soil. Imports into the United States were increasing from other parts of the world. People in America in the 1980s were increasingly doing business with Japanese banks. Business experts were beginning to declare the importance of China for future trade. On January 1, 1994, the United States entered into the North American Free Trade Agreement (NAFTA). As the years passed, the United States began to do a great volume of business with other countries. Companies from other countries were physically locating manufacturing facilities in the United States. By the early to mid-1990s, it was very obvious that the United States had gone global. In my book, *Strategies 2000*, published in 1986, I had already gathered enough data to determine that the United States was in a process of globalization—which would, as a result, thrust the United States into strong worldwide rivalry (Corbin 1986). In that book, I cited some collateral effects of that international competition.

When I began noticing these trends back in the 1970s, I developed a distinctive mental radar that seemed to find more happenings that indicated globalization. As I found these separate—but connected—streams of happenings, I kept notes on them. I watched to see if the trends were increasing or decreasing, speeding up or slowing down, tending to go away or having more of a presence. I also analyzed whether these trends might constitute a fad or were truly developing into forces to be reckoned with. Obviously, these trends were huge forces eventually intersecting to produce the condition of globalization, which has generated impacting structural changes in the socioeconomics and politics of the world.

It is important to differentiate between a fad and a trend. A fad is not a trend. It is a temporary event, happening, or movement whereas a trend has staying power. When I was in elementary school, the hula hoop was introduced into American society. Sales skyrocketed, and it appeared to me at the time that almost everybody bought one—at least most preteens in my small community seemed to have one. People were seen "hooping" on television shows. Hula hooping contests were held all over America. Popular songs of the late 1950s and early 1960s referred to the hula hoop. However, the popularity eventually waned. Sales of hula hoops dropped. Recently there has been a resurgence in hula hoop sales, but it has never again reached the high percentage of sales of all toys sold as it did in the late 1950s and early 1960s. The sales of the hula hoop followed a parabolic curve—i.e., they went up rapidly, leveled for a very short while, and came down almost as rapidly as they went up. This describes a fad.

Generate an organized system for following the trends.

You will want to keep records on how the trends are moving. Over time, you can discern patterns. Because I am a socioeconomic futurist, I have identified trends in five broad areas that I find of interest: (1) the relative socioeconomic position of the United States compared to the remainder of the world; (2) changing demographics in the Unites States weighed against those changes in other world powers; (3) technological movement and innovations; (4) the impact of business on society; and (5) the power of the individual in society.

By following trends in these five broad areas over the past 25 years, I have been able to determine some general socioeconomic directions of the world. Often, trends seem to be moving in a forward direction; then they begin to move in the opposite direction. It is important to observe the timeframe of a backward movement to determine if there is truly counter trending taking place or if there is only a brief reversal in a bigger forward thrust. For example, in the year 2000, it seemed obvious that for the United States to be globally competitive, it would need to rein in its spending. With looming entitlement programs ballooning in the next two decades and beyond, it seemed logical that the United States would need to cut programs and balance the budget to the best of its ability. Now that we are down the road a decade later, it seems that spending is at an all-time high and that the economy of the United States is being questioned by U.S. citizens and even other nations. Hopefully, this economic insecurity is a short-lived phenomenon on the forward trendline—which is to continue to cut expenses and be watchful of the looming budget requirements. America has always been conscious of its competitiveness with the rest of the world. As a result, I believe that America, in the long term, will become more economically conservative.

Additionally, you will want to review structural changes that occurred during the past 30 to 40 years. Often the aftershocks and vibrations of structural changes are felt more intensely three to four decades after the initial event. For example, as we discussed in Chapter Two, Japanese competition in the U.S. automobile market, first identified in the 1970s, had a giant aftershock. That impact eventually became a factor in the competitively compromised position in 2008-2009 of two major automobile manufacturers—General Motors and Chrysler. As another example, various bills and laws passed in the 1960s and 1970s are now having a social and economic impact.

With these examples in mind, not only should Community Leaders 4.0 look back to structural changes in past decades, but they should also analyze current bills, laws, and political decisions for possible future impacts. Additionally, such events as wars in the Middle East and the 2008 U.S. economic meltdown will affect America 30 to 40 years hence as a result of continuing socioeconomic vibrations. It will be interesting to determine the ways in which communities will be affected in the future based on the structural changes of today.

Create paradigms of possible intersecting trends to identify probable conditions.

When trends intersect, that convergence produces conditions which will impact your world both locally and globally. Here's a case in point: as the U.S. and other countries continue to globalize, and as the Internet continues to become even more sophisticated and useful than it is today, the convergence of these two trends will produce several conditions.

One condition is that of being able to do complex intellectual work any time and anywhere. Another condition will be the ability to commit digital espionage and to sabotage local and national infrastructures. Yet another condition that will occur is the capability of building relationships worldwide, thereby producing better understanding among various cultures. There are many other conditions that the intersection of these two forces can cause. Great leaders will create models for various intersections and will determine the positive and negative conditions likely to affect their communities.

Devise a plan for dealing with the issues arising from the conditions.

When conditions occur, there will always be issues with which you must deal. To increase your chances for success in dealing with the issues, you should engage in mental rehearsal. In the previous discussion, I mentioned the trend of increasing technological sophistication and innovation intersecting with the trend of increasing connectedness and trade throughout the world.

One outcome of this intersection was the condition of any time, any place work. We are already seeing indications that this is happening today.

This condition will generate such issues as job shifts offshore, decreased community revenues in some locales as well as increased revenues in other places, increased job opportunities overseas, relocations of workers to communities with preferred quality of life, and many other possibilities.

As a Community Leader 4.0, you must make certain that the leaders and community stakeholders have developed plans for handling these conditions should they arise. If, for instance, a company in your community shifts most of its jobs overseas to cut costs and physically moves its operations offshore, your community will feel the impact. Although the company may allow many of its knowledge workers to live in your community while working in its overseas operation, loss of this organization will cause a revenue drop. How will your community handle loss of revenue? By looking ahead at this issue, it will be easier to have plans to replace the revenue from losses incurred when companies located in your community move away while taking most of their employees with them.

At the Center for the 21st Century, we have always recommended reviewing projected future issues at least once every six months. By doing so, you can better defend against happenings that otherwise would have been devastating surprises.

Calculate your actions resulting from the window of opportunity.

There are five possibilities to consider when addressing the window of opportunity (WOO). First, as accurately as possible, determine the amount of time created by the WOO. Often, there can be five or more years' lead time for action. We have found in our research at the Center for the 21st Century that there can be as many as 14 or more years before a condition occurs—even after you have spotted the trends. For example, decision makers in the federal government of the United States have known for several decades that the trend of the increasingly aging population would intersect with the trend of depleting funds for Social Security and Medicare. It has been recognized that this intersection would create a crisis condition of the Social Security and Medicare systems well before the middle of the 21st century. There have been at least two decades (and really more) in the WOO when specific actions could have been taken. The whole idea is to be on constant lookout for trends and their possible intersections. Once the resulting probable conditions have been identified, then you will estimate the WOO timetable for taking action.

The next four possibilities are actions that you can choose to take once you have calculated your WOO.

Denial. Some leaders suffer from the ostrich syndrome. They bury their heads in the sand, deny the existence of the circumstances they observe, and ignore the danger signals. Although you might think that denial nullifies action, it is really premeditated behavior (in my opinion). In fact, taking no action is actually an act of avoidance.

Refusing to consider that your community might someday need to file for bankruptcy, therefore making no plans for dealing with the condition, is a form of denial. Not planning for a disaster, racial unrest, or terrorist attack because your town is too small is a type of denial. Yes, avoidance of possible conditions and the ensuing issues is an action.

Often in 3.0 communities, there are citizens who would like to see the city move to 4.0 status. At a grassroots level, some of the citizens are visionaries. As we have mentioned earlier in this book, no community has achieved full Community 4.0 status at this point. However, the citizens would perhaps like to see their community enter the beginning phase of 4.0 status within the next five years. However, the leadership of the community may not be able to grasp the vision of moving from 3.0 to 4.0 status. They have no idea how to proceed. The leaders live in denial that the more advanced community status could ever be achieved. They are holding up progress. Because there might be a threat to their power, the leaders choose to avoid moving the community forward. Instead, they choose the status quo. In effect, this choice is truly a move backward. Thus, denial is an action—and can be a very destructive choice.

Ignorance. Often trends present themselves, but leaders don't see them even though they may be in plain sight. If they are ignorant of the trends, then they won't see the intersections producing the conditions. In other words, their judgment calls will be greatly affected by their inability to detect key happenings. Throughout my career as a futurist, I have observed that a major reason that leaders miss forthcoming happenings is because of "success arrogance." I have noticed this phenomenon happening across organizational spectrums. Once thriving cities have concentrated too heavily on specific industries that are either candidates for off-shoring or that are not competitive in the global marketplace. Because these industries have always been successful, the community leaders fail to recognize the coming disaster. Success arrogance can produce igno-rance. What we know (or think we know) determines what we see. What we see determines our destination.

Arrogance isn't the only reason we don't see trends. Not knowing how to look for them, or simply missing them, is also a factor. Many communities are not realizing the importance of producing a high qual-ity of life/place that attracts an educated workforce. Additionally, they aren't making the effort to incorporate the whole community in a drive to see that all children get a quality education. Thirdly, the leaders don't realize the need for a connection with a research university, without which they won't be able to attract world-class businesses. Ignorance is an action because it is a deliberate choice. And a choice is definitely an action. When leaders choose not to pursue futuring techniques and thus remain blind to the future, they have acted in a way that can damage the community's competitive edge.

Acceptance. When things are going well for a community, the lead-ers often choose to accept the favorable climate. When times are good, it is often difficult to plan for times when things will not be good. It is easier to accept the current situation. Several years ago, I worked with a nonprofit organization which was prospering well in the late 1990s. They were surmising that their future would be a continuation of the present—that things would get better every year. They accepted the good times as a permanent condition and didn't have plans in place for an economic downturn. Then came the economic slump of the early 2000s. That caught them by surprise. Today they are again experiencing a criti-cal situation resulting from the worst economic recession since the Great Depression. It will take that agency several years to work through the collateral damage from the severe economic slump. Because they were in a state of acceptance over the last decade, no plans were in place to secure their revenue flow in bad times. The staff and board are working very long hours to meet their financial obligations. Cuts in staff and other operational reductions have taken place. Refusing to make plans for bad times in the midst of good times can spell catastrophe down the road.

Often the opposite happens. A community might find itself in a seemingly hopeless situation and can't find the strength and foresight to envision itself prospering again. Thus, the leaders accept the current sad set of circumstances and fail to plan for a flourishing future. Many rural towns across the U.S. were experiencing economic woes even before the Great Recession of 2008 and beyond. Rather than looking for ways to make a comeback, they are choosing to let their towns die. Under some circumstances, that may be the reality these towns must accept. However, leaders should try to create alternative positive futures for their communities before accepting the option of demise. Often, good ideas help towns overcome adversity. Remember the awesome story of Greensburg, Kansas, that we discussed earlier.

Purposeful intervention. This action is the most targeted of all. It results from vigilant futuring and careful planning. For example, if the school district's leaders observe test scores continually declining in a particular group and simultaneously notice that this specific demographic population's numbers are increasing in the district, the leaders will surmise that test scores will continue to drop. Wise school leaders will plan targeted interventions with that group in question to increase their test scores. Perhaps mentors could be appointed to each individual in that group. Schools could be adopted by various civic groups and churches to help with requested family needs as well as coaching in student studies.

The U.S. Department of Homeland Security practices purposeful intervention frequently. They set up surveillance of suspected terrorists and often intervene in their activities before they have a chance to strike a community. That's evident from national news reports. To keep America safe, that governmental agency must constantly employ investigative and futuring techniques. Once they have identified probable conditions, then they must implement resolute intercession.

I could continue indefinitely with examples of purposeful intervention, but I'm sure you understand the importance of such action by now. Eternal vigilance and strategic action are requisites of Community Leadership 4.0.

Tools for Imagining the Future

I personally like to anticipate the future by using the model in Figure 6.1. Everything else I do builds on that paradigm. As you imagine the future, you too will eventually develop your own favorite methods and tools that work best for you. Discussed in the following paragraphs are some instruments I use to support my futuring activities. One of my favorites, environmental scanning, has already been discussed in the explanation of trend analysis earlier in this chapter.

Scenario. This tool is old. Stories have been handed down throughout history since humans learned to communicate with one another. A scenario is a story. Using this instrument effectively can create a picture of various alternatives that might happen in the future. It is helpful to use this tool when you are creating a vision of the future. In community work, I like to create group activities. I often ask the participants in planning sessions to develop a story of life as they see it in their community 30 years into the future. It is always interesting to review the results of the assignment, which calls for individual free-flow of ideas. I then ask the group to look for key words used by most of the participants. By identifying commonalities, the group will discover potential trends.

However, there is more to scenario development than asking each person to use her imagination to compose a story about the future. That's the easy part. The difficulty arises in applying pattern analysis since there is no assigned structure to the project except for the subject on which the participants are writing.

When you have a specific problem to solve, there are two important scenario ingredients to consider: (1) the knowledge level of the participants and (2) the way you have structured the plan for developing the scenario. In this case, I suggest that a group develop a collective scenario or set of scenarios rather than have each person write an individual story. Community Leaders 4.0 realize that their ability to choose the right people for the scenario composition will help determine the success of the project. I always like to choose experts from various professions and walks of life. It is often dangerous when the leader builds the group from one distinct area. Also, Community Leaders 4.0 will recognize the importance of soliciting recommendations for group composition from knowledgeable people throughout the community. Often, when community problem-solving groups are selected, participants are chosen for political reasons. This does not necessarily guarantee that the best people have been chosen to create a scenario about the community's future.

Community Leaders 4.0 should be careful to identify the appropriate people for participation in the group activities. However, it is advisable to include some political appointments in the group composition to have well-connected stakeholders who can influence the implementation of the project findings.

Once the scenario group has formed, the specifications for the scenario must be developed. First, identify the elements in the scenario. For example, I normally have the group name the characters they will be writing about and their involvement in the social, technological, economic, environmental, and political areas of the community. Such a case might involve the school superintendent and the school district's board of trustees as the major characters. The scenario might depict a day in the life of each character 30 years hence. During that day, the characters would come in contact with various social situations involving education, religion, the media, and maybe sports and entertainment venues. Imagination will dictate the areas defined in the social category. For the technical area, the characters would be interacting with computers, perhaps artificial intelligence, converged technology, telecommunication systems, a future version of the Internet, various biotech devices, and a number of other technological inventions that the group envisions down the road.

The group would also include in the story some of the environmental issues for 30 years hence, the infrastructure that would be in place, information about the food and water supply, and any other environmental conditions worthy of note. The economy is always a concern. Jobs, income levels, how business is conducted, the community's position in the world economy, the labor force—all these and more would be included in the scenario. And we wouldn't want to exclude the political system that the group envisions for three decades into the future. Some topics to include would be as follows: specific laws that are likely to be enacted, regulations, taxes, wars likely being waged in 30 years, the status of Social Security, Medicare, and Medicaid three decades from now, and the general philosophy of government which will be in force.

After identifying the elements of the scenario, the group will produce an outline and create a storyboard housing the flow of the story—just like producers use in movies or TV commercials. This storyboard can be hand crafted and very simple. It is used to picture the flow of events and interaction of all the elements. Once the flow of the scenario has been designed, then the third step, the actual writing, is ready to begin.

Someone from the group will write the scenario. Others in the group will edit and proof the document. It becomes a wiki instrument in that all the group members produce this scenario in an open-source environment.

The final step is to present the finished product for analysis. From there, the group and community leaders can create a strategic plan to make the scenario come to life.

Scenarios are limited only by leadership creativity. I often suggest that the group take a variable and vary it at least three different ways. For each state of the variable, a separate scenario can be devised. For instance, the identified variable might be the economy. Three scenarios could be created using the elements listed earlier. One scenario could depict the community 30 years hence as the economy grows at two percent per annum. A second scenario could be devised to reflect fast growth over the next 30 years—maybe eight percent per annum. Then a third scenario could be written assuming a sharp drop of 15 percent five years hence then a rebound at a sluggish rate of one percent for five years, and then leveling out at a two percent rate of growth to reach the 30 year planning goal. The same idea might involve other such variables as population growth, a change in political philosophy, or a variation in environmental conditions. Scenarios are a great way to capture group imagination.

History. A valuable tool for assessing the impact of events, innovations, financial changes, ideas, and actions is the study of history. Beneficial lessons can be extracted by analyzing outcomes of earlier happenings. When you are confronted with important decisions, it is advantageous to think back over history and review situations similar to the one you are now facing. By noting instruction from historical occurrences, you can more easily address the current problem. You are also more likely to avoid potential pitfalls.

During the 1990s, the Internet brought irrational enthusiasm to the marketplace. People were investing in stocks without even giving rational thought to the wisdom of the investment. Companies were forming around Internet applications. Many people were building companies and then selling them for huge sums of money. There was an Internet obsession. Many investors thought that the bubble would never burst. But it did!

Had people analyzed history, they would have realized that such exuberance often follows the introduction of a popular innovation. Many automobile manufacturers emerged after the invention of the automobile. Most of those companies failed. When television became popular in the late 1940s and early 1950s, there were many production companies competing for business. Many of them failed. In the cases of the automobile and the television, only a handful of large manufacturers and producers eventually dominated the market. The lesson from history concerning an innovation is that the pioneering product or service becomes a magnet for business competition. However, after several years of competition, only a few companies are left standing to service the innovation.

History also provides instructions on human nature. For example, when given unfettered freedom, many people will be disrespectful of the boundaries of others. Lawlessness never works. There must be rules, and these regulations must be enforced. Anarchy can cause a nation or community to implode. Therefore, there is always a role for government in any society. However, there are also lessons in history concerning outcomes of oppressive regimes, heavy-handed governmental regulation, small deregulated governments, and many other combinations. When governments seek to change their structures, it is wise to consult history. When seeking the degree of balance between government and individual citizen empowerment, sound examples can be found somewhere in history.

There is definitely a place for historical scrutiny in planning the future. Although history doesn't repeat itself detail by detail, there are valuable big-picture lessons available to all who are willing to spend their time mining for historical patterns.

Metaphor. This tool is one of my favorites for envisioning the future. A metaphor, as applied to my futuring experiences, is something from a completely different area that helps me envision what might happen in the category that I'm studying. In other words, I create my model for the problem that I'm solving by using an example from a completely different class or discipline. I am always on the lookout for paradigms that pose similarity to the situation at hand. Several years ago, I was volunteering on a church committee. We were discussing the plans for church expansion and growth. The first inclination was to study benchmarks from other churches, which had gone through similar growing pains. Thus, we did that.

However, there were alternative options that would expand our thinking and perhaps show us other unique and more productive methods. In addition to exploring growth strategies of other churches throughout the United States, we decided to study the growth strategies of banks. In so doing, we discovered one overarching theme in bank expansion: banks were going to the people rather than expecting people to come to them. For decades, banks had one central site, and people were expected to drive to that site to do business. Then, as communities grew, banks located satellite offices more convenient to neighborhoods so that customers wouldn't have to drive so far to do business. Then, with the advent of the Internet, online banking became available so that customers could conduct their banking transactions from a location of their choice.

Resulting from our church committee research, we decided to follow the path of the banks in church expansion. We decided to create satellite sites in the suburbs as extensions of the main church, which was located in the downtown area. We would also offer online services to accommodate those who preferred to virtually connect with the church. Since this committee assembled several years ago, churches weren't developing satellite sites like they are today. This was a new phenomenon at the time. Our committee's idea wasn't derived from best practices of churches but from best practices of banks. The future vision was borrowed from a metaphor.

Closely related to the metaphor is the bellwether, which is a leading indicator. For example, by observing California, a leading socioeconomic indicator for the United States, other states can envision what might happen socioeconomically in their locales several years hence. It is helpful to identify the roots of the problems and the constructive solutions applied in California in order to intervene in various social problems that might occur later in your community. In finding a bellwether, look for a state, city, or country that has similar issues now that you anticipate might happen later in your local community, state, or country. Record the various advantages and disadvantages of actions taken in the bellwether so that you will know what works and doesn't work for problem solution should a similar situation arise in your area.

As you gather data on various indicators, you will be able to watch certain gauges for your community's performance. You can, therefore, identify potential problems before they occur.

Discrete source. By far, this tool holds the greatest mystique in the futuring process. Community Leaders 4.0 should spot resources that are helpful in their identification of trends and ensuing conditions. Normally, the compilation of these sources is proprietary to the specific leader who locates them—i.e., the compilation is under the ownership of the leader, but the sources themselves are most likely not owned by the leader. Professional futurists use this technique to brand themselves and protect their intellectual property. However, community leaders can also use this means for making judgment calls about the future. The research for such sources demands hard work and testing the sources for accuracy. Leaders must be careful to use only sources that have a track record and time-proven credibility. Over the past 30 years, I have compiled a long list of sources that have proven themselves to be credible time and again.

To start your list of discrete sources, scan the Internet for research studies, contact universities for critical information, tag experts from various professional fields, connect with dependable professional associations, read scores of periodicals, newspapers, polls, books, and journals, watch varied TV shows and movies, and review the work of numerous think tanks. Check the accuracy of their work over time and compile your findings. After a number of years, you will have a quantity of sources uniquely designed to help you solve problems and envision the future. Constantly connect with these entities to stay abreast of global happenings. Discrete sourcing is both an art and a science. It is in large part detective work.

The Introduction of Surprise

With careful analysis using a number of methods, many future conditions can be projected. However, there is always the possibility of a surprise occurrence. Futurists refer to highly impacting, improbable happenings as wild cards—which can be classified as either positive or negative. Examples of positive wild cards are winning the lottery, inclement weather stopping a planned terrorist attack, and a multi-million dollar inheritance from a long-lost relative you didn't even know. Many wild cards can be classified as random events.

It seems that most of the focus is on negative wild cards, and that's the type of wild card I will concentrate on in this section. Examples of negative wild cards might be the sudden death of a key world leader during important peace talks, a nuclear attack on an American city, a rapidly-spreading plague, the landing of a space ship from another planet, the sudden strike of a meteoroid on Planet Earth, an earthquake, an oil spill, a volcanic eruption, or a mass shooting in a shopping mall. Some of these events are more probable than others. However, they hold something in common: they are difficult to predict.

One of the most puzzling elements in the prediction of wild cards is identifying the specific date and time of an occurrence. The United States government, for example, had considered the likelihood of a terrorist attack on the World Trade Center in its scenario planning. But the problem was that those involved in the planning had not identified the method, date, and time of the attack. Earthquakes are expected in California. It is difficult to place the exact date, time, and severity of the earthquake's occurrence. Scientists already suspect that an asteroid may strike somewhere on Planet Earth within the next four decades, but little is known yet about when and where. Thus, even if we suspect the character of the surprise, it is still virtually unpredictable.

Wild cards can change our existence. An earthquake or nuclear attack can destroy a city and bring death and untold misery to the inhabitants. Sudden attacks by a nation's enemy can forever shift the world's power structure. Abrupt financial collapses can wipe out trillions of dollars of global wealth. Thus, prospecting for wild cards is an important part of the futuring process.

Leaders should identify and plan for as many wild cards as they can imagine. Using the futuring techniques cited in this chapter, leaders can imagine the unimaginable and think the unthinkable. Many wild cards can be pinpointed, and catastrophes can be avoided. For example, earthquakes can be detected with sensitive equipment. With sophisticated technology—which will be available in the future—the place, magnitude, date, and time of the earthquake can possibly be named within a window of opportunity wide enough to save many lives and avert heavy property damage. Approaching meteoroids and asteroids can be detected and perhaps burst into smaller pieces by spacecraft or lasers in the future. With proper intelligence gathering, international cooperation, and smart technology, "surprise" attacks by enemy nations can be averted. The key to identifying and preventing negative wild cards lies in becoming proficient at the futuring process and then devising exact methods (including the invention of new technology) for the prevention of these happenings and/or alleviation of their impact.

Even with all the expertise in the world, there will still be negative wild cards. Not all of them can be prevented. However, many wild cards can be either foiled or mitigated through careful futuring, accurate planning, the invention and application of sophisticated technology, and decisive leadership action.

☙

Community Leadership 4.0 Strategies

Imagination is critical to the success of fashioning a competitive community. The process of futuring must take place to construct a strategy for growth and development in a global playing field. Anticipating tomorrow is a skill that is necessary but rare. However, it will be a necessity for Community Leaders 4.0.

1. Review Figure 6.1 and make certain that you understand trends, conditions, issues, and the window of opportunity.

2. There are a number of tools for imagining the future. Becoming proficient in the application of these tools will enhance your futuring skills.

3. The element of surprise can throw your strategic plan off its path. Try to identify as many improbabilities as you can. Consider the possibility of outrageous happenings and devise plans for handling them should they occur.

Questions for Contemplation

1. What are some significant trends that are now happening that might affect the future of your community?

2. Are there points of intersection of various trends that could produce one or more conditions that might impact your community? If so, what are they?

3. Can you identify certain conditions that could generate specific issues which would need to be addressed? If so, what are they?

4. In the above question, you may have identified some conditions that generate issues. What issues were generated? How would you handle these issues should they arise?

5. Have you ever had to calculate a window of opportunity and then apply specific actions? If so, what did you do?

6. After reviewing various tools for imagining the future mentioned in this chapter, which ones will you feel most comfortable using? Are there other tools that you have researched which you like better than the ones mentioned in this chapter? If so, name them.

7. Have you ever experienced a wild card? If so, how did you handle it?

8. Identify the top three wild cards that might upset your community's strategic plan. How do you plan to handle them?

CHAPTER SEVEN
_____

Think!

YOU HAVE PROBABLY noticed that this is the only chapter title ending in an exclamation point. I purposefully included this punctuation mark to indicate the intensity of this initiative. Community Leaders 4.0 will be required to think in order to lead their communities to world-class status.

Without possessing the ability to think, it's impossible to make good decisions. Thinking skills are necessary for imagining the future. In fact, most everything required for success in life involves some type of thinking skill. High-level skills in recalling, generalizing, comparing, analyzing, synthesizing, calculating, deducing, empathizing, creating, assessing, connecting, and criticizing—among many other cognitive skills—are involved in thinking.

The definition that I use for _thinking_ is this: self-talk using the brain's ability to analyze, reason, synthesize, form patterns, create, and visualize. You may have your own definition of the phenomena. It doesn't matter what the technical definition is as long as you have the ability to understand the importance of thinking skills and are able to apply these skills in life and work.

The good news is this: thinking skills can be learned. It's never too late to improve the thinking process as long as an individual is mentally healthy.

Principles of Thinking

There are some general principles of thinking that I've discovered throughout my many years of researching and speaking on the subject. I was fortunate to have been exposed to these skills early in my career as a futurist. My initial corporate assignments in this field required multidisciplinary training. I implemented many of my futurism projects through use of systems analysis and design. I also wrote software programs which required in-depth logic and abstract thinking. My training was directed by the corporation for which I worked—through extensive class work and applications—in the areas of reasoning and systems thinking.

As I pursued my career, first in the corporate world, then as an entrepreneurial futurist, I continued to hone these skills. I will be forever grateful for the intensive training provided by my excellent corporate educators and mentors during the initial years of my career. They set the stage for all phases of my life's work. As a result, here are some principles that I've developed and tested throughout my career that hopefully will be helpful to you as you lead your community forward. You may individually apply these standards or create a team to pursue them.

Define your thinking goal.

If you are solving a problem, you must envision the problem as exactly as you can. For example, let's say that you are trying to recruit new businesses to your community. Before you can devise a plan, you must define the industries you are targeting for recruitment by size, revenue, environmental friendliness, community engagement, and several other factors. The problem, in the form of a question, can then be stated something like this example: how do we go about recruiting businesses with specific characteristics [name the characteristics] that will grow our community's tax revenue base by twenty percent over the next five years?

Make a plan and initiate it.

After setting your ultimate goal, make a plan for achieving your desired results. Among numerous possibilities open to you, list promising research resources; people you wish to interview; Internet sites from which to glean data; places to visit; benchmarks for excellence; software simulation programs, if available; think tanks to access; consultants to hire; and any other sources that you and your team deem necessary. After drawing up your plan, assign responsibilities to various people, and then activate the plan.

Set deadlines.

I don't personally have a neurological explanation concerning what happens cognitively when you set thinking deadlines, but I know that this principle works a great percentage of the time. To explore the subject more thoroughly, you will need to consult experts in the field of brain science.

I do know, however, that something happens subconsciously when you set a deadline for a thinking project. It has been proven over and again to me as I have authored several books. When I wrote my first book in 1985, I outlined the book by chapters and created a schedule for the book's completion. I decided to finish a chapter every two weeks. Some chapters took more research than others. But, to a great extent, the work to be performed for each chapter balanced out by the end of the book.

I wrote the first chapter rather easily. The second chapter was a slight bit more difficult, but not too hard. Then I started the third chapter. I was affected by writer's block. Then I panicked. I began to think catastrophically about all the things that were going to happen if I never finished the book. The anxiety grew—and for certain, the writer's block intensified. I would sit for hours at a time staring at a blank page. No ideas would flow. Then, through self-talk, I realized that I simply needed to calm down and continue to research and work my plan. About three days before my two-week deadline arrived, ideas began to flow. I was making connections among all the disparate data I had gathered! Aha! Insight had occurred. In three days, I wrote the entire third chapter and met the deadline to my editor.

Several times during the course of writing that first book, a similar occurrence happened. Yet I always met my deadlines. Then I wrote more books. Similar things took place while authoring each book. I began to realize that there was a pattern. My subconscious mind knew the deadline and was working toward it. My conscious mind didn't see how I could reach the mark, but the subconscious mind had my project under control. I've also noticed that same principle often works in solving other types of problems. I can't explain how my mind works, but solutions do happen in a great percentage of my life and work cases—and just in time for the deadline to be met.

Think slowly and deliberately.

In today's fast-paced society, the emphasis is on quick decision-making capacity. However, rapid-fire decisions are required in relatively few cases. Most of the time, leaders can negotiate for time to think slowly and deliberately—even when others are demanding an immediate decision.

Obviously, there are times when quick decisions must be made. Emergencies arise. Leaders are expected to respond wisely and quickly. However, even in emergency situations, there has often been time in the past to simulate future crises which might occur. In such cases, necessary rapid responses will be much easier.

However, in most cases, thinking slowly and deliberately will provide the best results. Take adequate time to explore all necessary avenues required to draw accurate conclusions. Review data, make connections, consider consequences, analyze, deduce, and call on as many cognitive skills as you can muster. Often, when you are pursuing a path, you will be linked to other sources of interesting information. Follow those paths to see where they will take you. Solving problems and making decisions take a lot of detective work.

Impulsive people are often tempted to make a decision based on limited data. They are not willing to take the necessary time to explore all options that can be pursued within a sensible timeframe. Often bad judgment calls are made due to restricted information. The opposite can also happen. Some people are fearful of making decisions to the point that they continuously search for more information. They never seem to have enough data from which to draw a conclusion. They are so risk-averse that decisions are difficult. They are afraid to be wrong.

Thus, when thinking slowly and deliberately, common sense must prevail. Taking too much or too little time can be equally ineffective. However, you may find it helpful to employ a backup confirmation system. Since I was in graduate school in the early 1970s—when I wrote my master's thesis on the subject of intuition—I have been using my gut-level response as a secondary indicator. Sometimes a leader's thought processes on all the available data will provide a clear indication of a problem solution. But the leader just doesn't feel right about his conclusion. Intuitively, he feels that there is more to be explored. He concludes that his answer isn't correct. By basing his analysis on intuition—not on data—he is alert to an alarm signal being sent by his backup system. He chooses to pay attention to the secondary indicator. He then seeks more information.

This phenomenon, which has been explored for many years, was revisited in Malcolm Gladwell's book *Blink* (2005). Gladwell thoroughly examines cases and presents the idea that quick decisions can be as accurate as slow, careful, deliberate decisions. He examines modern research in brain science to add credibility to his conclusions. Many years ago, we knew that hunches and intuition existed. Today's added research explains why, in many instances, those gut-level reactions can be credible.

On the other hand, Michael Mauboussin (2010) insightfully concludes that poor decisions come from people who have overconfidence, which leads to three illusions: feelings of superiority, too much personal optimism, and the erroneous belief that they can influence chance events. Adding to Mauboussin's ideas, I believe that—from a community perspective—overconfidence can also arise from limited thinking—which, in turn, provides limited knowledge. Often normal community leaders can become delusional because their thinking isn't high-level enough, and their world is too small. They are ill-equipped to handle complex situations. All decisions involving communities introduce some level of complex systems thinking—as I have discussed earlier in this book.

I have often heard people say: "That guy is so hard-headed. You can't tell him anything. He refuses to listen. He is so impulsive." Chances are that this guy has a record of poor decisions. He doesn't think slowly and deliberately. He uses limited data and depends heavily on gut-level impulses for making complex decisions.

How can leaders reconcile the diverse ideas on how to think? Of course, the first answer is to ask them to think through all the ideas themselves. My personal conclusion is to think slowly and deliberately while using my common sense to know when I've gathered enough data to formulate a decision. Then I'll use my gut-level indicator to check my decision.

Immerse yourself into a state of flow.

Community 4.0 leaders should set aside lengthy blocks of uninterrupted time for thinking. This works for individuals thinking alone and will also work for groups in a brainstorming activity or retreat setting. In a warp-speed world, it is difficult to find a segment of time to devote entirely to contemplation. However, to be an effective thinker, it is important to carve out several uninterrupted hours for environmental scanning, processing information, gathering data from various sources, creating possible scenarios, and developing strategies. This process requires both anticipatory planning and discipline.

When you are solving a problem, simply write your thinking time into your schedule. I periodically block off a whole 24-hour period or even three contiguous 24-hour timeframes for the thinking process. Do not allow other appointments to eat away at your timetable. It is tempting to set appointments for lunch or in the middle of the block of time that you have set aside. Discipline yourself in a way that disallows interruptions. When someone asks for an appointment within that timeframe you have reserved, tell them you have a schedule conflict and that you can't meet with them. Propose an alternative time to meet. Of course, there are crises which cannot be anticipated. These will interrupt your timeframe. But they won't happen often with proper planning and scheduling regulation.

When you are thinking during that time segment, it is important to put yourself into a state of flow and think around a central theme. It is possible to compartmentalize your thinking so that you can block out other distracting thoughts. The flow-state happens only when you have controlled all distractions and are concentrating on your thinking goal. While feeling relaxed, focused, and unhurried, you can then access your higher consciousness—from which ideas and possible solutions seem to flow easily.

To create an ideal environment for achieving a state of flow, you will want to have either soft, relaxing background music or silence. In a place where there are colorful plants (and/or green plants) and lots of sunlight, you can sense a higher degree of energy. In an unhurried state with no interruptions, you are free to have ideas, take informational paths for experimentation, eliminate the ideas which eventually don't seem workable, and pursue those thoughts that lead to problem solutions.

It is also helpful to engage all your senses in the thinking and deliberating process. Call on your visual skills for envisioning possible outcomes and/or various paths for resolutions. Engage your sense of taste, touch, and smell if necessary. Try to hear sounds that will be involved in scenarios you create during the thinking journey. In your mind, imagine the actions that will be taken as you apply various alternatives. Rehearse them mentally step by step. It is amazing how the mind works out details and how your imagination can replicate actions so realistically. In fact, there may be actual simulation software programs available which can help you determine the best path to take. They will also support your thinking skills in complex problem situations.

Open up.

To achieve effective thinking, you must employ an open mind. You may have tried something before, and the outcome wasn't favorable. That doesn't necessarily mean that the idea was bad. It may mean that you need to try again using different methods. I have had personal experience with a nonprofit organization which decided to do the same thing over again but pursue it differently. The board of trustees and staff experienced great success on the second try. Their story is in the following section.

๛

Open-Mindedness Pays Off:
The McKinney Education Foundation Advisor Story

As a member of the board of trustees of the McKinney Education Foundation (MEF), I was engaged in a strategic planning session in the year 2000 for expanding MEF's endowment fund to meet the needs of the burgeoning population of McKinney's high schools during the next several decades. The number of students in the public school system was exploding. In anticipation of even more student growth, the board was gearing up to pursue innovative solutions to challenges they perceived to be lurking on the horizon.

MEF is a nonprofit organization which offers several programs to enrich education in McKinney. In one of its programs, MEF awards scholarships to McKinney Independent School District graduates. That was what the board was concentrating on in the 2000 strategic planning session. It was quickly discovered that the amount of money needed in the endowment fund for future student scholarships was not easily attainable in a city the size of McKinney. By 2010, student population growth was going to outstrip MEF's ability to award the percentage of scholarships per the student population in the dollar amount that they were achieving in 2000. The board felt the need to find a way to supplement the current method of acquiring scholarship capital.

After deliberating on the challenge, the MEF board decided to emulate programs used in private institutions: i.e., hire an advisor solely dedicated to helping students apply for scholarships and find other funds for college. This would leverage both money and energy and could possibly bring a fantastic return on investment for MEF. The advisor would be a gift from MEF to the public school system.

As the advisor idea was deliberated, various board members brought up objections. Some thought it wouldn't work because very few public schools offered a special person to help only with college fund-finding. This advisor position was mostly a function of private schools. Some board members felt that the counselors already in place in the school system should handle that responsibility along with their many other duties. Others cited the fact that for a short while in the past, MEF had tried that idea with a person spending part of her time on the job helping find money for student college financing and scholarships. That person was quite successful considering the time spent on the program, but she had retired, and the idea was dropped. So some board members didn't want to try the idea again. Very few of the board members, on the other hand, were familiar with the situation as it had prevailed earlier.

However, after much consideration, wisdom prevailed. The MEF board decided to hire an advisor for the sole purpose of helping students find money for college. They spent a few years gathering data and planning the program. Local businesses were asked to fund the program, and they enthusiastically supported the function financially. Immediately after inception, the program was a great success. McKinney Independent School District continued to grow. Now there are three MEF advisors—one in each high school. Beginning with that one advisor, the program has now been progressing for six years. In that period of time, the advisors have helped McKinney graduates find and receive funds totaling over $35,000,000 (figures as of 2010). The program has been, and continues to be, a phenomenal success. There will be more high school capacity built as McKinney grows. The student population will continue to multiply. And MEF will be challenged to keep this very successful program in force to help students attend institutions of higher education.

Wisely, MEF didn't let the idea that they had tried something before interfere with the challenge of trying the same thing again—but pursuing it in a different manner. Doubts were overcome by optimism. Calculated risk was balanced by the possibility of great reward. Because of the open-mindedness demonstrated by the MEF board of trustees, many students—many of whom would otherwise have not been able to pursue their dreams—have been able to attend college (McKinney Education Foundation 2010).

☙

Other forms of open-mindedness should also prevail. Often people's opinions are not based on fact. They are merely suppositions. I've even seen some cases wherein opinion is based on delusion. People operate under the false assumption that "thinking makes it so." That's not necessarily true—especially when an individual draws false conclusions.

Prejudice also contradicts open-mindedness. This prejudgment of a situation or person happens when someone forms an opinion without knowing the real facts. For example, you may prejudge a person's capability for handling a job assignment by basing your opinion solely on the college he attended. Prejudice usually indicates negativity, but it can also be a sign of positive bias. Prejudgment can cause you to erroneously make good or bad decisions.

Another threat to open-mindedness is too much concentration on tradition. I've heard it said so many times: "we've always done it this way, so why should we change anything now?" Heavy concentration on tradition can blind leaders to innovation. As I discussed earlier in the book, there must be a balance between tradition and innovation. By the same token, too much attention to innovation can cause tradition to be abandoned. In either case, close-mindedness happens. Thus, erroneous thinking can take place.

Evaluation of all incoming information through a specific frame of reference (the philosophical prism through which you view the world) can also prevent open-mindedness. When you have a strongly dominant philosophical frame of reference, everything you think about is explained by the information held in that frame of reference. For example, if you hold a dominant frame of reference concerning a particular religious orientation, most all the things that happen to you in life will be judged as good or bad based on their fit into your religious frame of reference. In this case, you may have religious issues which are non-negotiable and consciously choose not to open your mind to other religions. That is certainly your personal prerogative. However, it is important to be aware that others may not share your particular philosophical frame of reference.

Another less obvious example is the frame of reference created by TV shows in the 1950s. Many early Baby Boomers (those born from 1946-1953 of all Baby Boomers born from 1946-1964) have no idea that they are measuring their behaviors and attitudes toward life based on the TV-show philosophical frame of reference. Many of the fictional children's shows in the 1950s had a similar plot: good fought against evil for most of the show; then, in the end, good always prevailed; and valuable lessons were learned. Everything always turned out all right. The shows were normally optimistic and uplifting while containing lessons in character building, patriotism, and civility.

However, depending on the viewer's perspective, there could have been a subtle message in those shows which produced unintended consequences. Early Baby Boomers generally adopted a rosy everything-will-be-okay-in-the-end attitude throughout their lives. Many Baby Boomers today are suffering from the close-mindedness that came from operating by the TV-show frame of reference without questioning their magical thinking and without understanding that they have responsibilities for their life outcomes. They have not invested their funds adequately for retirement because they actually believed that everything would magically turn out all right without any planning on their part. They felt that they would be rescued by an anonymous hero—just like the 1950s shows portrayed. This example illustrates that dependence on a frame of reference, which you may unknowingly approach through faulty thinking, can injure your reasoning ability. Please let me emphasize, however, that not all frames of reference are faulty. In fact, most are not. However, you are responsible for doing the homework necessary for discerning the flawed from the credible frames of reference that will potentially shape your life.

Although there are several threats to open-mindedness we have not discussed, I'll just mention one more: jumping to conclusions based on first impressions alone. It is almost common knowledge in the sales profession that a salesperson has only a few seconds to make a favorable first impression. And I feel that most leaders are aware of the importance of first impressions. But there is a caveat in all this. Community 4.0 leaders should be cautious about forming judgments based solely on first impressions. I know that I've jumped to conclusions about people, situations, and ideas based on my first impression. After thinking about it, I realized that my first impression was wrong. Had I have acted on my first impression—which may have been good or bad—I may have made a dangerously wrong decision. Therefore, it is important to register your first impression, but allow time and events to test that first impression before drawing ultimate conclusions.

It is important to be aware of the need for open-mindedness in the thinking process to avoid erroneous judgment calls. By being on the lookout for potential causes of close-mindedness, Community Leaders 4.0 can think more lucidly and achieve more accurate results.

Employ the art of free-thought.

Making connections among seemingly unrelated issues, events, and people utilizes the free-thought process. Sometimes thinking freely makes no sense at first, then the ideas start to flow; and linkages begin to happen. Use of the free-thought process is especially beneficial for creative thinking, which will be discussed in the next section of this chapter.

For example, you may be trying to decide whether to serve on a board of a local charity. Your schedule is jam-packed, but you feel motivated to assume the responsibility. You are in internal conflict over what to do. In this case, it is best to quit concentrating on finding an immediate answer. Let your subconscious mind work on the problem. You will probably notice that answers will appear from unusual places to help you with your decision. You may get an idea that you can relate to your situation from a novel you are reading. If you proactively practice a particular religion, you might get an indicator from the teachings of one of your religious leaders. Or, while driving down the road, you may see a billboard that causes you to get a sudden "aha" about the right decision for you. I've even gotten ideas from reading stories to children. The moral of the children's story seemed to pertain to a problem I was trying to solve.

I have also found that the subconscious mind keeps on working while I sleep. I make it a habit to keep a recorder or a notepad beside my bed so that if I suddenly awake after achieving insight while I'm asleep, I can immediately record the idea. If I wait until later, I may forget the inspiration. Often, my dreams will offer solutions to a problem I have been deliberately thinking about all day. In that case, I also record the ideas as soon as I wake up.

Through many years of applying the free-thought process, I've found that putting the problem aside allows your subconscious mind to freely think about the dilemma. You will be both surprised and gratified when you find a solution. Plus the process is normally quite enjoyable.

Five Essential Thinking Skills

To envision the effects of leadership decisions on the multitude of factors in a complex system, Community Leaders 4.0 need to access their higher-level cognitive proficiencies. There are at least five important types of thinking skills which will enhance prudent judgment calls when leaders are faced with critical decisions. These types of thinking skills are consequential, contrarian, critical, creative, and connectional. By working as a futurist for many years, I have developed my own definitions and approaches for using these skills. I will share those ideas with you in the paragraphs that follow.

Consequential Thinking

I call this type of thinking "if . . . then thinking." It requires a person to think about the consequences of her decisions and actions. Following the word *if* is a condition, and following the word *then* is a possible consequence. For example, in applying this thinking skill to an investment I'm about to make in the stock market, I would say to myself, "If I buy 100 shares of XYZ Corporation, then its stock price is likely to rise 20 percent over the next year, and I can make a good profit." Or, as another example of an action I'm about to take, I might say to myself, "If I decide to run in the school board election this year and win, then the amount of time I will need to commit to school board work in such a growing community will displace time I normally spend with my family." In both of these "if . . . then thinking" statements, I would have to make a decision concerning whether I desire the projected consequences. If I want the consequences, then I'd choose to take the action.

Also, there is another consideration for consequential thinking. Remember that in our discussion on the topic of courage, I mentioned that courage can be defined as a decision to do the right thing in spite of the consequences. Thus, you might consider the action you are about to take or a decision you are about to make, then decide whether you believe that it's the right action or decision. If it is the right decision, in your opinion, then you must assess the probable and potential consequences. If you can live with the ultimate consequences that you might have to face, then your internal voice of courage would motivate you to make the decision or take the particular action.

The consequential thinking skill requires the ability to exercise foresight and decide between right and wrong and good and bad. This involves the brain's prefrontal cortex (Anissimov 2003-2010). Brain scientists indicate that this part of the brain is not fully developed until approximately age 25 (Cornish 2010). As a result, children, teenagers, and adults under the age of 25 may have difficulty making an accurate assessment of the projected consequences of their actions or decisions.

In assessing the consequences of their actions and decisions on a complex system, leaders must watch for effects on all the subsystems. There may be unintended effects. For instance, major legislation might be passed to help specific groups. Yet that same legislation might negatively affect other groups. The negative outcome on one particular systemic node was not intended, but it happened due to the lack of effective consequential thinking.

Consequential thinking is very important in making ethical decisions. This topic has already been discussed in Chapter Five. You may wish to refer to that chapter before moving on to the next topic, contrarian thinking.

Contrarian Thinking

This cognitive skill goes against the general flow of ideas. As a hypothetical example, let's consider the following application. There is a common assumption that Social Security benefits will continue to be paid to beneficiaries far into the future. A thought contrary to that idea is that Social Security will be eliminated. Often contrarian thinking uses "what if" statements. Thus, if the common assumption is that Social Security will continue forever, then a contrarian thinker might pose the question: what if Social Security is eliminated?

To answer the "what if" questions, leaders must use all other thinking skills mentioned in this chapter. Certainly, consequential thinking will be employed. Assessment must be made concerning all the nodes of the national community that would be affected should Social Security no longer exist.

Contrarian thinking is often used to prevent groupthink, which is a situation in which all or most members of a group enter into a similar thinking pattern. Contrarian thinkers interrupt the conforming patterns and can even throw the group into chaos. Assumptions are questioned. Beliefs are challenged. And the group might even polarize over the choices of future directions. This polarization could end in gridlock. Thus, contrarian thinking can be very powerful and is to be used very carefully, thoughtfully, and strategically.

If you choose to enter into contrarian thinking and verbalize your thoughts about an issue, it is important to stick to that issue and approach the situation diplomatically. The verbalization of your contrarian thoughts should happen only if you feel that is it necessary to challenge the current flow of ideas or as a confrontation of the status quo. Some people express contrarian thoughts just because they want to be difficult or to draw attention to themselves. However, contrarian thinking, and the expression of those thoughts, is a serious matter. This can be a very productive tool when used conscientiously.

True contrarian thinking takes a great deal of skill. When forming think tanks, I specifically ask for people to join the group who are adept at seeing the other side of most issues. This skill reduces groupthink thereby mitigating mistakes in judgment.

Critical Thinking

The process of standing back from a situation and establishing its positives and negatives without assigning value judgments is known as critical thinking. In the section on principles of thinking that was developed earlier in this chapter, the ideas of open-mindedness and objectivity were discussed. In the critical thinking process, it is imperative to apply these principles if you wish to see things as they are rather than slanted toward how you imagine them to be based on your prejudices, personal values, and even your delusions. To clarify your thinking, it is beneficial to research the issue thoroughly. Ask questions of wise counselors. Pour through research data. Make certain that your positives and negatives concerning the issue are credible.

❧

An exercise I often use in my community leadership classes involves thinking clearly about the future of work. I pose the following situation and ask the class to divide into groups and discuss it:

> What if artificially intelligent machines could do any work that people could do, thus rendering work as we know it obsolete as a way of making money?

After each group has posed the positives and negatives of artificially intelligent machines replacing people as workers, the discussion becomes very interesting. Over the past several years, groups have never failed to derive valid positives and negatives about the situation. Of course, they are asked to keep their preconceived notions out of the thinking procedure because that would influence their thoughts and perhaps prevent a valid conclusion.

If preconceptions were involved, the first obvious prejudice that would arise would produce panic over the elimination of a way to make a living from work. Because most people think of work as a way to make money to be exchanged for their needs and wants in life, they fall into the habit of believing that's the only way to make money—or that money is the only valuable exchange factor for their wants and needs. Thus, that one prejudice shuts down the process, and the groups stack the negatives one on top of the other. Once the group members begin to think about the situation minus the traditional way of making a living, then the process can proceed.

❧

In the highly diverse, and often polarized, community environment in which leaders must function, it is difficult but necessary to think critically about many issues. By viewing issues objectively, leaders can evaluate the positives and negatives which will be helpful in the decision-making process. It is also important to apply all the principles of thinking previously discussed. Without the ability to be a critical thinker, it is difficult to be an effective Community Leader 4.0.

Creative Thinking

Innovation is the trump card that many communities play in the game of global competitiveness. And creativity is the process that produces innovation.

There are at least three ways to innovate. You can search for new combinations of things that presently exist; create something entirely new; and/or find new uses for something that is now available. For example, technology is converging. The convergence of the telephone, camera, and television into one instrument is a way of taking things that already exist and combining them. Another example of an innovation is to invent something entirely new, like the automobile, television, airplane, microchip, or the personal computer. You might argue that these items are extensions of things that already existed in some form. That may be true, but even if the process involves a progression of steps, the outcome is still a new invention that is useful for a specific purpose. A third example comes from finding new uses for existing entities. Ibuprofen was originally used for relief of arthritis symptoms. Its applications have broadened throughout the years as new uses were found.

These three avenues to innovation can be used in numerous applications. In every instance, creative thinking is involved. Usually a problem prompts the creative thinking process. Sometimes creative thinking yields immediate results. It is more common, however, for the process to require time-consuming trial and error. I'm sure you have read the stories of inventors who try many things and eliminate what won't work before they find something that does work to solve a problem.

Often leaders form brainstorming groups or work in think tanks or committees to produce an innovation. Creative thinking can be very strong when ideas are shared among several resourceful people. One person's idea can be expanded or amended by the group members to produce an entirely different approach to problem solution. Ideas that any one person could have never thought of alone are often generated from vigorous group exchange.

When thinking creatively, make certain that you look at the problem from every angle. Use ideas from metaphors, make connections from things you see in nature and everyday life, and try to get ideas from reading various articles and trying to transfer those ideas to the problem you are trying to solve. In group activities, play off one another's thoughts and opinions.

Again, please review the principles of thinking discussed earlier in this chapter. Learn to follow these principles when you are thinking creatively. Make certain that you have crafted a physical environment in which to work that is conducive to energetic and lively idea generation.

Connectional Thinking

This type of thinking is like a connect-the-dots exercise. Leaders endeavor to connect seemingly unrelated events, people, activities, and data to form patterns for analysis. Once the models are formulated, possible conditions can be identified and issues addressed. Connectional thinking involves all other kinds of thinking. The best way to illustrate this type of thinking is by an example, which is detailed in the next paragraphs.

‿

Consider the following trends:
- The population of the United States is aging.
- Social Security projections are troubling.
- Many jobs are being relocated overseas.
- There are large numbers of retirements in the future due to Baby Boomer aging.
- Internet capabilities are expanding.
- There is increasing concern over global economics.

Some of the above trends might seem connected in some way, and some may seem to not relate at all. However, through the connectional thinking process, these trends can be linked. An aging population considered with Baby Boomer retirements while Social Security is projected to have future financial problems can intersect to form several conditions.

With people presently drawing Social Security projected to live longer healthier lives, and the ranks being expanded daily by Baby Boomers taking early retirement or even waiting until the full retirement age of 66 to start drawing benefits, it is obvious that one condition is quite predictable: Social Security insolvency. The issues surrounding this condition will involve how to fix Social Security so that it does not go broke and leave those who have depended on it in dire straits. There are several options for fixing the system. Some of them are as follows: raise taxes, extend the age at which Social Security benefits start paying beneficiaries, or stop paying Social Security benefits to those who are younger—hopefully giving them fair warning so that they can plan adequately for their retirement. It is wise for community leaders, especially federal community leaders, to deal with these issues now to deflect problems that might arise later on.

There are still other connections to be made in this list. With jobs being offshored and the Internet expanding in sophistication and applications, many people who live overseas can now compete in the global marketplace. They can do jobs offshored from the United States to their countries, or they can work from their homes in other countries via the Internet and do jobs located in the United States. This opens up the labor market to global competition for jobs. People in the United States must keep their skills sharp to compete in the globally competitive job market. Whereas 25 years ago, many jobs in America were domestic in nature, now these jobs can be performed by a trained labor force located anywhere in the world.

With the latest global economic downturn, many countries are suffering financially. Unemployment rates are high. In other countries, for example China, the economy is doing better than in many other Western countries. This downturn in the West will give China a chance to move forward more rapidly in global competition. This economic situation provides the opportunity for China to buy real estate, debt obligations, and businesses in other countries—which will give China a foothold in various markets. Some other Asian countries are also doing better than Western countries during the Great Recession and will be strategically placed to be highly competitive when the Great Recession recedes. Thus, one condition from connecting these points becomes: heavy Asian global competition. As a result, the issues with which America and the

West must deal will center around interest rates on debt obligations, high unemployment rates, job creation, and competition for position in the global marketplace of products and ideas.

With ever-growing obligations to the elderly, jobs being sent overseas, and a compromised financial situation, Community Leaders 4.0 in America can connect the dots to discover that their communities will need to be innovative in order to sustain themselves throughout the first half of the 21st century. They must deal with the ensuing issues today to assure for themselves a better tomorrow. Such issues as attracting talent and jobs to their communities, keeping the tax base balanced, developing a healthy quality of life, and offering hope and prosperity to their citizens are just some of the challenges that are shaped by the trends listed above.

❦

The case just described is only one example of connectional thinking. This type of thinking must be employed on a regular basis. When trends intersect and conditions prevail, the ensuing issues can be very challenging. It is much more profitable to be ahead of the curve and prepare for the projected issues in advance rather than to be surprised—and perhaps overwhelmed—as a result of having no plan in place. Community Leaders 4.0 realize the immense value of connectional thinking.

❦

Community Leadership 4.0 Strategies

At least five types of thinking skills are important to the art and science of leadership. These skills can be learned in any stage of leadership development. Community Leaders 4.0 will find them helpful in making good judgment calls.

1. Employing consequential, contrarian, critical, creative, and connectional thinking skills will sharpen your decision-making prowess.
2. Review the principles of thinking. Make certain you understand each principle as it applies to all the five thinking types.

Questions for Contemplation

1. Think of a problem that you have solved in the past. How did you go about it? Did you employ any of the principles of thinking? If so, which ones?

2. Have you ever gone through the creative thinking process to produce an innovation? If so, what principles of thinking did you use? Were they helpful?

3. If you could gather five people to form a think tank for problem solving, who would you ask to be in that think tank? What criteria would you use for selecting each individual to participate?

4. Have you ever entered into a state of flow when thinking deeply? What did you accomplish as a result?

5. Have you ever made a decision solely on intuition or gut-level feeling? What was the outcome?

6. Have you ever thought through a problem slowly and deliberately? What was the ultimate result?

7. Are you open-minded while thinking? If not, in what areas do you need to improve?

8. Have you ever employed the art of free-thought? How did it turn out?

9. Do you apply consequential thinking skills often? List two examples of consequential thinking you have employed in the past year.

10. Cite an instance where you have used contrarian thinking. Did you then stand up and challenge the group to approach the issue differently?

11. Are you good at critical thinking? What is a situation in which you have applied critical thinking skills in the last year?

12. Do you make a habit of connectional thinking? If so, how successful have you been at identifying conditions and issues that have been likely to occur?

CHAPTER EIGHT

Harness Chaos

A S CHANGES CONTINUE to occur more frequently, chaos will increase. This systemic imbalance can cause a community to suffer greatly if the disorder is not handled properly. Leaders have a significant role in guiding their communities through the inevitable chaos which will happen as our world is experiencing global transformation.

It is interesting to study the mathematical concepts of chaos. These laws can be highly simplified and used as a metaphor for creating an organizational nonmathematical paradigm that will work for businesses, nonprofit organizations, governmental agencies, and communities. When I detected the common patterns, I determined that a model could be drawn. It is that model that I'm using in this chapter to enhance discussion of Community Leadership 4.0's role in harnessing chaos.

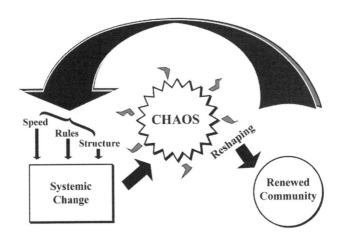

Figure 8.1 Chaos Model

In my earlier book, *Great Leaders See the Future First* (Corbin 2000), I included a chapter on the pre-emption of chaos as a necessity of 21st century leadership. During the decade that followed, I worked constantly with this model, which has continued to evolve as global conditions have become more complex.

As you will note in Figure 8.1, I have indicated that three changes will alter a system: change in speed, change in rules, and change in structure. Any one of these changes will cause the system to be different. Two of these changes happening simultaneously will cause even more alteration. And all three changes operating together will cause a great deal of systemic modification.

Please let me emphasize that as long as life exists, there will be chaos. Some degree of chaos is helpful. Otherwise there would be no vivacity in the system. However, it is the ability to pre-empt and control severe chaos and to lead systems through this hectic stage that will determine the degree of a community's sustainability.

Speed

The world is changing at warp speed. As countries with emerging economies enter the marketplace, competition becomes stiffer in all communities. Jobs, in many cases, can be executed any time and anywhere. Therefore, many jobs that were held domestically are now offshored.

Unemployment is unusually high in the United States due to a deep recession as well as a change in the labor system.

When economic conditions are good, and markets are growing, the speed of growth causes change. Likewise, when economies are shrinking, the speed of the downward spiral causes communities to alter. As speed increases in either direction—up or down—the occurrence of chaos is stimulated.

Rules

The April 2010 eruption of the volcano in Iceland changed the rules in the lives of many travelers. Airspace was shut down over at least 24 European nations causing travelers to be stranded for several days. Some grounded passengers ran out of money for food and lodging. Thousands of flights were cancelled. Appointments were missed. The airlines lost a great deal of money. People's budgets were blown. A change in the rules of travel caused many communities to suffer and chaos to prevail.

Natural disasters cause rules to change in communities. In just an hour, hurricanes can wipe out whole cities. Tsunamis can wreck entire villages. Earthquakes can devastate civilizations. In a matter of hours, communities can move from normalcy to total bedlam. Economies can be wrecked, and lives can be lost.

Structure

The systemic shape of communities can change. If several businesses go bankrupt and move from the community, the community structure is altered. Likewise, if several new institutions, such as hospitals, are built in the community, the systemic structure of health care and of the community as a whole changes. By the introduction of competition, the subsystem of health care may be thrown into chaos until a new state of normalcy can be established.

Any time that subsystems of the total community system change, then the whole system alters. This situation will always introduce some degree of chaos into the system. For example, in 2005, Hurricane Katrina hit New Orleans, Louisiana. That was a definite structural change, as well as a rules change, for that city especially after the levee systems failed and flooded the city. However, there were also repercussions among Louisiana's neighboring states. Victims of the hurricane took refuge in other communities, even in other states. The structure of many communities changed as a result. Many students were suddenly added to the school systems. New residents were living in shelters provided by various communities. In fact, Hurricane Katrina caused changes in speed, rules, and structure of many communities—not to mention the degree of chaos it caused in New Orleans.

Chaos Stage

When changes in speed, rules, or structure stimulate change in the community system, some degree of chaos will always prevail. During this stage, there is turmoil—both physically and emotionally. The degree of chaos that is instigated depends on the severity of the changes that have taken place. Often, there is only a mild degree of chaos. Sometimes, chaos is severe to the point of devastation of property and loss of lives. The timeframe for chaos varies from short to lengthy.

Often the expertise of leadership determines the degree of chaos and the timeframe of involvement. Visionary leaders will imagine various scenarios that can produce chaos and will then put plans in place to forestall much of the disruption that might occur. Frequently, the degree of chaos that happens in a community can be controlled through use of forward-thinking and pre-emptive actions. The Department of Homeland Security has disaster plans in place to mitigate the chaos that would normally occur if a disaster were a complete surprise. Communities have rehearsed disaster plans to offset pandemonium. Of course, not all disasters have been foreseen or rehearsed. The terrorist attack on New York City on September 11, 2001, was a surprise. However, the first responders had prepared for fires and other disasters and quickly translated that training to this surprise attack. New York City did a very good job of calming the chaos in a wild-card situation.

When chaos occurs, conflict will result. In the emotional and physical confusion that prevails, eventual conflict will take place among parties who disagree over various issues that will arise. Community Leaders 4.0 are aware that chaos and conflict management skills are necessary to keep serious clashes from happening. Of course, the ultimate exhibition of conflict is war. In extreme community (which includes national and international) conflict, there is the possibility that war can break out. Leaders want to prevent hostilities if at all possible.

In my studies of chaos in organizations and communities, I have discovered that if failure is going to happen, it normally happens during the chaos stage. Often leaders who guide the organization cannot lead it through chaos. However, I've seen exceptions—especially when leaders are brought into communities to induce change in speed, rules, and structure. When they purposefully stimulate change, thereby producing chaos, often those leaders are successful. They are experts at such activities. However, they too can fail if opposition is so great that people refuse to change. Also, conflict can become so intense that gridlock occurs in the governing bodies. Or, in severe cases, the community splits, and each side goes its separate way. In those cases, there will be failure to guide the whole system to the other side of chaos. Conflict can be produced by chaos. Polarization often results. It takes immense skill in leadership to guide a community past the polarization stage back to unity. This will be discussed further in the next chapter on conflict management.

Reshaping

I define the process of changing from "what was" to "what will be" as *reshaping*. During reshaping, the community environment is highly frenzied and volatile. It can be both confusing and threatening. High stress levels exist in those who are journeying through this progression.

Renewed Community

After reshaping takes place, there will be a renewed community system. The structure that comes out of the chaos stage is not the same as the one that enters the chaos stage. Often it is hard to adjust to the new system. Many participants will be able to alter their perspectives and behaviors, but there will also be others who will never be able to adapt to the new organization. It will be completely out of their comfort zone.

☙

In Figure 8.1, please note that there is a large arrow pointing from the renewed community back to speed, rules, and structure that cause systemic change. That arrow indicates that there is a constant loop of change and chaos happening in the system. Just about the time everything seems to smooth out from the period of turmoil, more change happens that hurls the system back into chaos thereby producing another changed system. In the 21st century, Community Leaders 4.0 can expect to experience constant chaos. There will be little time for peace and rest between changes that occur.

☙

The Cost of Chaos

Chaos can be very costly to the community. It is imperative that Community Leaders 4.0 realize the importance of understanding the principles of leadership that are required for guiding their communities through the threatening turmoil to the other side. These principles will be discussed later in this chapter and in the following chapter.

The ultimate cost of chaos is system failure. Often conflict and the resulting polarization can become so severe that the system shuts down and cannot move forward. Gridlock and stagnation stop progress. At this point, leaders are often asked to relinquish their responsibilities, and a new leader is appointed or elected.

Lesser costs also accompany inappropriately handled chaos. Communication problems can prevail for many years hence, thus affecting the harmony of the community. Financial difficulties can compromise the community's ability to compete with other communities in the region—and, in turn, certainly prevent the community's capability of competing globally. People tend to lose hope during the chaos stage, thus lack the faith to move the community forward. Often people abandon the community completely if leaders do not demonstrate acumen in chaos management.

During the chaos stage, you will often notice the following behaviors—many of which will affect the peak performance of the community.

Urge to Return

When the systemic turmoil becomes uncomfortable, many people will join a movement to return to the way things were before the change took place. Going back is impossible, but people's comfort zone has been disturbed. New attitudes and behaviors are being required. They are feeling pain. In this discomfort, they have a strong motivation to return to their comfort zone.

Polarization

People with strong feelings will band together and form an active group that will vocalize their strong beliefs concerning the community's future direction. Others who feel the opposite way will also join up to oppose the other side's ideas for moving forward. The two sides will often clash verbally. In extreme cases, they will physically clash. Polarization is often a direct occurrence of conflict—which arises from chaos. In this process, heroes of the movement arise. People will choose whom to follow—deciding which side to take in the hotly debated issues.

Often, when war is declared by a nation or a controversial bill is passed in Congress, polarization is immediate. On the local level, ordinances passed by the city council can cause polarization. For example, a nonsmoking ordinance can cause people to take sides and express their opinions in the media and, in some cases, actually march in the streets. There are several ways to observe the city's ability to control where people smoke. Issues of curbing of citizen freedom, financial effects on businesses, public health matters, individual choices, and other topics are open for debate concerning the nonsmoking ordinance.

Isolation

When people feel vulnerable, they often withdraw from community activities. I have seen this happen after tough election campaigns. When the contest is especially brutal, the candidate who was not chosen sometimes isolates himself from the community for a timeframe ranging from several months to permanently. I have had candidates tell me that, after such a rough campaign, they will not involve themselves in community issues again. It is a shame that elections, especially on the local level, can become so brutal that the candidates deviate from debating the issues and resort to personal attacks on their opponents and their families. This verbal brutality is costing the community the involvement of very capable citizens in moving the community into a productive future.

Stress

During chaos, many people suffer the effects of stress. Everything from tense muscles to serious diseases might occur. When stress happens, it is often difficult to perform to maximum productivity levels. Often, when stress proliferates, communication problems take place. When miscommunication abounds, turmoil is often created—thus increasing the chaos that is causing the stress in the first place. An abundance of both physical and emotional stress can negatively affect a community and impede its progress.

Markers of Chaos

I have spent many years studying organizational chaos. As I continue to learn the effects of this phenomenon on communities, it is obvious that Community Leaders 4.0 must get ahead of the chaos and try to control it as much as they can. When chaos first began to proliferate in the 1980s, it was noted that leaders needed to react in the most effective way possible. However, as time marches forward, it is obvious that leaders must do more than just wait for chaos to prevail and then react. They must instead anticipate the chaos as much as possible and do their best to pre-empt the turbulence in order to mitigate its effects on the community.

Throughout the past 25 years, I have noticed that there are six predictable effects of chaos. There may be more, or they may be stated in different ways, but I have noticed that these six outcomes are present in every chaotic situation I've witnessed—whether the chaos resulted from growth, shrinkage, sudden change, or an unanticipated disaster. In the paragraphs that follow, I will cite these markers and offer discussion of each of them.

Uncaring Leaders

In the confusion of the volatile environment, leaders often get busy with the priorities that demand their attention. They are operating under much stress and are forced to multi-task to keep up with their rigorous schedules. They sometimes forget that people are waiting for them to communicate messages of hope and assurance. They get so wrapped up in their own busy worlds that they disregard the fact that people are depending on their leadership.

When leaders fail to communicate, people interpret this oversight as lack of caring about the future of the community and the people in it. This causes all sorts of fallout. The perception of ambiguous leadership expectations is one result. This can lay the groundwork for anarchy. People start making up their own rules and following various emergent grassroots leaders. There may be no unified direction for marching through the chaos to a better tomorrow.

People also feel isolated from leadership when leaders fail to communicate and/or meet the people face to face. They feel disempowered and confused, which can lead to conflict and disorderly behavior.

Mistrust

When people believe that the leaders don't care about them or their community, they begin to mistrust the leaders themselves. Any information that the leaders disseminate is suspect. People conclude that important information is being withheld. They even go so far as to disbelieve, and often say publicly, that the information conveyed by the leaders is untrue. Then fear arises. The people believe that mistakes will be punished. They imagine the worst motives from their leaders.

Lack of Focus

During chaos, keeping proper focus is difficult. Thoughts race through people's minds. There is no clear direction. They jump from one thing to another, thus they start majoring in minors. Priorities are difficult to set unless leaders are strong. There is never enough time to get everything done. Because of the related stress conditions, thoughts dance in people's minds while going off in many directions. Everything seems vague—including the rewards for staying the course.

Inadequate Resources

When chaos is present, there are rarely enough resources to do adequate work. People sense shortness of time, money, and people to get the job done. In an economic downturn, for example, there will be some degree of chaos. Leaders will be doing their best to handle priorities. Yet there is a shortage of money. That might cause layoffs and force those who are left on the job to work harder and faster due to the heavier workload. This increases productivity while, at the same time, it augments fatigue. There is a greater chance that mistakes will be made. There just seems to be more expected of people than there are resources available.

Lack of Preparation

When time is compressed and resources are diminished, there may be performance requirements for which the people are not adequately trained. This environment is highly stressful and begs an increase in errors. There is an overarching feeling that failure is imminent. People begin to lose hope and feel ill at ease.

Burnout

With the other five markers of chaos in place, people often suffer the sixth marker—burnout. When there is a burden of work and not enough resources to get adequate results, people begin to experience exhaustion and feel used up. As a result, they begin to think about abandoning the cause. They may even plan to leave the community. People eventually tire of enduring the constant pressure.

Countering the Markers of Chaos

By knowing the six indicators that happen during chaos, it then becomes possible to lessen the degree of chaos that takes place. As a leader, you may not be able to control all the chaos, but you can manage reasonably under the circumstances in which you find yourself. Obviously, there are times when conditions are beyond your control. However, in most cases, you can minimize the chaos by having prepared for the issues beforehand.

By establishing counter markers for chaos, Community Leaders 4.0 can go a long way in maintaining order during tumult. In the discussion below are some suggestions for calming the torrents of pandemonium and change.

Caring Leadership

It is critical for Community Leaders 4.0 to let people know that they care about them. Authenticity, i.e., being real, is demanded of leaders today. As we discussed previously, when leaders isolate themselves from the people, that action is interpreted as a lack of interest. Thus, the opposite action will indicate attention and concern, which are best demonstrated by proficient communication. This involves actively listening to the people as much as it involves talking with the people. Community participants like to be asked a very significant question: what do you think? They want to be heard.

During chaos, Community Leaders 4.0 should contribute a portion of their valuable time to providing periodic status reports. They must continually tell the people what is happening and how things are progressing. Leaders should leave nothing—that is within their power to explain—to the people's imagination. Caring leaders will approach subject matter with a sense of openness. This includes offering open access to information not considered confidential or that will not breach community security.

Leaders will appear before the people often. They will make speeches. Additionally, they will visit with organizations and individuals throughout the community. In other words, they will be constantly visible. A good example of openness and visibility is that of Mayor Rudy Guiliani after the attack on the World Trade Center in New York City on September 11, 2001. The mayor was constantly walking among the people, dialoguing with them, and providing status reports. This was probably the greatest chaos to ever hit New York City in modern times.

There is no substitute for genuinely caring for people. Citizens can sense the sincerity of their leaders by the degree of kindness, compassion, and sensitivity they demonstrate.

Trust

To secure the trust of others, leaders must be trustworthy. Reputations take a lifetime to build. People are aware of your actions. And your actions are more influential than your words. It is important to constantly be aware of how your behavior will resonate with others' impressions of you. The people with whom you associate, and your record of honesty and integrity, constitute historical files accessible to anyone wishing to check your past performance. If you are known for inaccurate judgment calls, or if you are known for lack of openness and forthrightness, then that reputation can build into a lack of trustworthiness. When people don't trust leaders, it is difficult for leaders to persuade them to buy into their ideas.

To build trust, Community 4.0 leaders should be open about their actions as long as they are not risking community security or the privacy of others. Common sense should prevail in determining how open you should be. If decisions involve others, and most often they do in a community environment, leaders should ask for input from those who are affected. When people have a chance to make a contribution to the decision-making process, they are much more trusting of the leader's judgment calls.

Communication also builds trust. As has been mentioned earlier, leaders should circulate and interact with the community members on a regular basis. Not only does communication cause the members to feel important, but it also creates a bond of faith in the leaders' skills.

Focus

To prevent people from majoring in minors during chaos, Community Leaders 4.0 must help people focus on their priorities. In an age when people are accustomed to multi-tasking, it may seem reasonable to let the wiki community take off in multiple directions without some sense of cohesiveness. In a chaotic wiki environment, sharp contemporary leadership skills are necessary to keep things moving forward in a productive fashion.

It is also important for leaders to keep the people focused on the new community that is being shaped by the chaos. They should continually paint a clear vision of the situation that lies on the other side of this chaos. Additionally, leaders should repetitively explain the rewards for treading through the chaos to the other side. This vision will provide the courage to keep going when the road gets tough during the chaos stage.

Community Leaders 4.0 should be aware that lack of focus can eventually produce anarchy—and ultimately systemic failure. Whether you are an emergent grassroots leader for a project or an elected community leader, focus will be necessary for moving a community through chaos. You must possess the skill to determine how much freedom is allowable and how much guidance to impress on the people.

It is an incorrect impression that a wiki community totally manages itself. One person or a group of people must always assume a role of gentle guidance to find some degree of unity. Without unity, a community cannot progress. There must always be guidelines in order for a community to thrive. And there must be enforced consequences for failure to follow the guidelines.

During chaos, leaders will work with people to set priorities and execute mutually acceptable tasks. When each person is responsible for her task in a subsystem, then all the subsystems will begin to interact in an acceptable manner. In times of tremendous chaos, such as war, then leaders must make more direct decisions—and the focus must be very exact. A wiki community does not eliminate the need for leaders. In fact, it increases the need for leaders. Instead of the traditional form of top-down leadership, many people residing in the community will likely be called on to lead from time to time.

Resource Priorities

When there is a shortage of resources as is often the case in chaos, then leaders must work with the community members to increase productivity while using the resources that are available. This is an excellent time for innovation. When a need exists, human nature can employ the process of creativity and come up with one or more solutions. During the deep recession that affected many businesses in the latter part of the 21st century's first decade, organizations found ways to become more productive by using technology and reducing the number of people on the payroll. Additionally, instead of making trips to global meetings, the companies employed more telepresence capabilities and saved a great deal of both time and money. Many communities facing bankruptcy during the recession were forced to prioritize resources and apply them for the greater common good. In a time of growing entitlement programs in the United States, the nation's leaders will be forced to prioritize programs and alter them in ways that will serve the nation better in the long term. The solutions presented for resource allocation during chaos may not always be popular among affected groups, but those solutions may be necessary for the survival of the nation as a whole.

During chaos, leaders knowledgeable in crisis resource allocation are in great demand. Often, productivity increases wrought by chaos can engender lasting advantages well into the period after the recession has passed.

Work/Task Preparedness

Training and education services are likely to be some of the first things to be cut when resources are compromised. In the pressure-cooker environment of chaos, people are often called on to deliver outcomes for tasks they are not prepared to handle. However, the period in the course of chaos is the time to allocate adequate resources for training and education. During this phase, it is important for leaders to provide adequate preparation for required performance.

In a time of resource crunch, leaders can employ creativity in training people for the necessary tasks. Innovative methods can save both time and money. In times of growth, there may be enough money, but not enough time or people. Thus, training time will need to be compressed without losing critical skills training. And innovative techniques can be employed to draw vital talent to the community.

Burnout Prevention

Often discussed in the context of organizations, burnout is alive and well during chaos. However, burnout can also exist in communities undergoing tumult and confusion. Although this factor is seldom if ever addressed, it is certainly real. During community growth cycles, there is so much to be done, and too few people to do it. During downturns, resources are scarce. Conflict, polarization, blaming, anger, and even personal attacks can happen in chaos. In both scenarios, elected and salaried leaders, as well as volunteers, can easily suffer burnout. Especially vulnerable are elected officials and those volunteers who chair commissions, boards, and committees.

By virtue of the fact that many community positions are propelled by volunteers, not all of them have an equal degree of commitment to an assigned task. And, since the task is a volunteer activity, some volunteers encounter other priorities and cannot deliver the needed results. The chairperson is left with work overload. Individuals who volunteer for many activities throughout the community will experience burnout at one time or another.

Community Leaders 4.0 must be astute in recognizing burnout and in pre-empting it in key community influencers. Sensitive leaders can hold workshops encouraging life balance for people who are engaged heavily in volunteer activities. Stress management techniques such as meditation, exercise, use of humor, social support, and mental compartmentalization can be reviewed.

Additionally, leaders in charge of volunteer assignments can question those being assigned leadership responsibilities and determine whether they are under additional duress before assuming another responsibility. Community Leaders 4.0 realize that some people just can't say "no." Being unable to draw boundaries is not a favor to the individual or the community. In the end, everyone is penalized.

Also, Community Leaders 4.0 themselves can suffer burnout. It is helpful if they can become aware of the life/work balance techniques applicable to burnout prevention. Stress can easily affect leadership effectiveness. And burnout of key people can impede community progress. Often, during burnout, important leaders misdiagnose the root of their problem and quit their responsibilities. The community can then suffer significant setbacks. Burnout prevention and management are important lifeskills for Community Leaders 4.0.

Interpersonal Insight

Without interpersonal insight, leaders cannot harness chaos. During the confusion that the stimulation of systemic change in speed, rules, and/or structure brings, Community Leaders 4.0 must constantly demonstrate mastery of relational skills. In showing that you care for the people and exhibiting trustworthiness, interpersonal skills are vital. Leaders should become adept in empathy, sensitivity to personality and mood variances, teamwork, and verbal and nonverbal communication. These skills are also essential to conflict management, which will be discussed in the next chapter. Obviously, it would take volumes to thoroughly discuss each of the topics in this section. College courses and commercial programs have been developed, and books have been written, on each of these topics. The objective of this section is to create awareness of the necessity for acquisition and application of each of these skills and to motivate you to explore each topic further.

Empathy

The ability to virtually project yourself inside another person and understand how he feels is what I call *empathy*. You may have another definition, and if that works for you, that's great. In a world wherein many people are self-absorbed, empathy is a rare commodity. Community Leaders 4.0 understand the importance of perceiving the feelings and motives of other people. Until you can understand where another person is coming from, it is difficult to relate to that other person. If your mind is constantly on yourself, it is difficult to shift it to others.

Understanding and then responding to other people is like playing chess. The other person makes a move, and in response you make a move.

So the game progresses. All the time, you are strategically working. And, make no mistake about it, interpersonal relations do involve strategy. Without empathy, the first phase of your interpersonal relations plan will not work.

Understanding Personalities

There are numerous instruments designed to identify people's personalities. Some are more scientifically tested than others. In a general sense, these tools are very helpful. Great community leaders constantly make an effort to understand people. When you master the art of identifying people's personalities, you will have accomplished much in the area of interpersonal relations. I recommend that Community Leaders 4.0 take a class in personal behavioral styles and learn to identify people's styles by their verbal and nonverbal communication as well as their personal interests and preferences—among other things that you can observe and inquire about them.

People are products of their heritage, culture, environment, and experiences. Plus they are hardwired with a tendency toward a particular personality. All these ingredients must be considered when tagging the individuality of a person. I am not recommending that leaders deal in stereotypes, but that they make the study of people a habit that they are continually perfecting. It is helpful for leaders to know when to use emotion, facts, encouragement, verbosity, clarifying descriptive language, and direct versus softer styles of communication. Astute leaders decide when to hold informal dialogue as opposed to formal presentation of data and facts.

Rather than writing off difficult people, try to understand their inner motives. Perhaps they are having a hard day. Maybe there is an issue at work or home. Often, difficult people have poor relational skills and find it hard to express their opinions and feelings. More often than not, they also suffer from lack of good self-esteem.

Understanding people's personalities involves hard work and targeted effort. You also need to be aware that you may not be able to relate well to all people. You may never experience a 100 percent success rate. But it is to your advantage to try to understand as many people as possible so that you can successfully relate to them. By operating from empathy of the personalities of others rather than expecting everyone to adapt to your own style, you will be better able to have productive interpersonal relations.

Teamwork

In today's complex environment, it is difficult, if not impossible, to accomplish anything alone. Success demands teamwork in most cases. Those who have participated in team sports have already experienced, and most likely developed, the skills necessary for teamwork: generosity balanced with seeking help; sacrifice poised with reward; and sharing goals, dreams, and successes. These factors are all part of teamwork. To promote community collaboration, Community Leaders 4.0 help people identify their common dreams and ask each person to commit his special strengths to helping achieve that dream. Instead of focusing on differences, of which there are many in a world gone wiki, leaders help people to focus on their commonalities. When each person or entity on the team takes responsibility for a deliverable, then those dreams can become realities.

Collaboration requires humility. When people vie for personal attention, glory, or the role of hero, teamwork can break down. In working toward a community goal, strength results from unity. Community Leaders 4.0 can structure their leadership strategy for promoting concurrence, not discord. Some hints for promoting unity include avoiding participation in gossip, encouraging all people involved to use their strengths, offering compliments and encouragement to each member of the team, and making positive comments to constantly bolster team spirit.

Verbal Communication

Community Leaders 4.0 who master verbal communication will increase their influence tremendously. Tone, pitch, and choice of words are important in interpersonal relations. By understanding the other person, you can choose the appropriate form of communication. Dr. Frank Luntz's book, *Words That Work* (2007), explains how your choice of words can motivate, clarify, and transform. It further indicates that it's not what you say that impacts relationships, but what the other person perceives that you are saying that creates the ultimate result. I highly recommend the reading of Luntz's book for making wise choices of verbal communication tools.

Tone of voice and speed of speech also have an effect on communication. Screaming and yelling avail little. Word emphasis, talking slowly to emphasize points, lowering your voice at strategic times—all these techniques can express everything from seriousness of a situation to disapproval, depending on what you are trying to accomplish. Conversely, faster speech patterns, higher pitch, smiling while speaking, sweeping use of your hands—these tactics can be motivational and uplifting, thus promoting hope and promise.

Nonverbal Communication

What is observed about a person might be more important than what that person says. Often someone will express something in one way, but her facial expression says that her true feelings differ from the words she just used. Thus, when in the process of communicating with someone, it is vital to listen not only to the words, but also to watch hand movements, facial expressions, eye movements, body position, and other physical indicators—which can tell you more than words ever could.

Reading body language is both an art and a science, and it takes much practice to become proficient in that subject. In addition, different cultures have different ways of expressing body language. Because of the growth of diversity in all communities, unless you know the culture that the person represents, it will be easy to misread his body language. For example, in some cultures, men and women do not make eye contact. Doing so is considered disrespectful. In America, we like to observe direct eye contact as an indication of authentic, truthful, and caring behavior—no matter whether the interaction is between two men, two women, or between a man and a woman. Different cultures have different expectations, and leaders should be aware of that.

 споро

Community Leadership 4.0 Strategies

Understanding the stages of the Chaos Model can make a distinct difference in leadership effectiveness. Since some degree of chaos continually exists, leaders will be forced to confront it regularly.

1. Learn the stages of the Chaos Model in Figure 8.1.
2. Practice the skills necessary for moving people through chaos to the other side.
3. Be able to clarify your vision of the other side in order to provide hope and motivation to people for endurance of the chaos.
4. Learn to recognize the six markers of chaos and be able to pre-empt severe chaos by practicing the countering techniques for these six markers.
5. Apply cost calculations of chaos as mentioned in this chapter. Comprehend the penalties that failing to address chaos can have on a community system.
6. Appreciate the value of interpersonal insight. Set a goal to master the art and science of practicing the skills discussed in this chapter.

Questions for Contemplation

1. Are you experiencing any of the three stimulators of change (speed, rules, structure) at this time? If so, is that change introducing chaos in your community?
2. What are some signs of chaos that you are noticing in your community? Have you observed polarization taking place?
3. Are there plans in place to prevent the chaos from getting worse? If so, what are those plans?
4. Do you have a strategy for reducing the cost of chaos should severe chaos strike your community? If so, what is that strategy?
5. List the six markers of chaos. What techniques would you use to counter these markers?
6. In your role as a leader, have you exercised empathy in the past? If so, how did you do that? What was the outcome?
7. Do you feel that you are astute in recognizing personalities and behavior styles of people? If not, how do you plan to acquire that skill?
8. Are you accurate at reading people's body language?
9. Do you have plans (beyond those that you are applying today) for becoming more astute at harnessing chaos in your community? If so, what are they?

CHAPTER NINE

Manage Conflict

C HANGE INITIATES SOME degree of chaos. And chaos breeds varying levels of conflict. Proficiency in managing discord will be
required of Community Leaders 4.0. As a leader, you will either
be in conflicts yourself or you will be called on to mediate conflict situations. Mayors will intercede in city council conflicts. School superin-
tendents will mediate school board disputes. Members of boards and
commissions will experience argumentative people from time to time.
The mayor of one city will conflict with the mayor of another city over
an issue. The list is endless. Therefore, as we go through this discussion,
project yourself into the process both as a mediator and as a disputant—
because you will play both roles during your leadership life. This chapter discusses the 13 major elements that conflict managers will need to
address to deal with the disagreements over issues that are bound to arise.

Unless you are a professional conflict manager, perhaps with a legal
education, and/or have been certified for such practice through a repu-
table program, some situations may be too complex for you to address.
If you feel that these issues are beyond your level of expertise, please call
in a professional in the field of conflict management to help you. Community Leaders 4.0 must make a judgment concerning when to call for
legal counsel or a professional mediator. Sometimes a conflict should be

taken to arbitration—where the arbitrator solves the problem for the disputants. Please do not enter into conflict situations that are beyond your ability to handle.

In this chapter, I will be presenting principles for Community Leaders 4.0 to use in situations that are more direct and simple—those that are easier to handle and in which you will likely be involved.

Definition and Observations

But first, let's take a look at a definition of *conflict management*. I believe that conflict management is a process in which you work hard and make every reasonable effort to foster peace between, or among (if there are more than two), disputing parties. Achieving peace doesn't necessarily mean that resolution of the conflict is reached but that there is cessation of hostilities.

And second, let's consider some annotations about conflict itself. The word *conflict* can be frightening to some people. Many individuals try to avoid conflict if at all possible because they believe that involvement in conflict carries a negative connotation. This perception of fear at the first sign of conflict is not necessarily correct because conflict can be healthy and positive when managed constructively. I cannot imagine living in a community that is void of any conflict. To me, that would be boring and robotic. However, all the skills and wise techniques in the world cannot cause all conflicts to have positive outcomes. So Community Leaders 4.0 must be astute in conflict management to achieve as many positive outcomes as possible. Creativity and innovation can arise from conflict. Those thoughts bring us to the first observation: great leaders realize that diversity can breed conflict and that conflict can be beneficial when the leader is tuned in to needs of dissenting sides.

Another observation is that conflict resolution is not always possible. Sometimes, all sides represented must simply agree to disagree. If leaders believe that all disputes can be resolved, then they will be severely disappointed in many cases. There is a difference between *managing* conflict and *resolving* conflict. Managing a conflict deals with channeling the dispute to the best possible end; whereas resolving a conflict means stopping the discord by settling the dispute. Causing conflict to disappear may be impossible. Managing conflict is much more achievable.

As a third comment, it is important to view the community as a system. That concept was discussed in Chapter Three. When something changes in a system, it might cause the whole system to transform. It is possible for disputes within the community to alter the whole community. For example, the issue of undocumented immigrants is a hot socio-political topic among people in the United States. People are polarized over the subject. Conflict over the issue has caused states to dispute with other states as well as the federal government. This has affected community systems across America. In other words, one socio-political issue has affected the whole system. Conflicts over issues do not exist in isolation. They, instead, cause ripples throughout the entire social network. Smart Community Leaders 4.0 make an effort to become aware of unintended consequences throughout the whole system when they are endeavoring to manage conflict in just one area.

A fourth observation concerns the motives for a large amount of conflicts. I have informally explored the basis for most wars, local disputes, marital conflicts, and disputes between children and parents. It seems that the root cause relates to one side trying to trump the other side in demanding to be right; endeavoring to gain control over the other; or trying to secure power to force the other side to agree to do (or not do) something. Some disputants even go so far as to issue a threat with conditions for punishment and reward—depending on how the other side responds to the threat. For instance, specific nations might be disputing over the possession of nuclear weapons. One side is trying to gain control by enforcing sanctions to compel the other side to get rid of its nuclear weapons—whereas the side with the nuclear weapons is trying to trump the other side with the argument that it has the right to possess nuclear weapons. Major disputes can escalate over this critical global issue.

The final observation to consider is that intrapersonal insight and interpersonal skills are necessary for successful conflict management. Leaders must know themselves well and must be able to read the behaviors of others—as well as relate in a civil and tactful manner—to be effective in managing conflict. We have already discussed in previous chapters the significance of interpersonal and intrapersonal skills in becoming an effective Community Leader 4.0.

A Dozen and One Elements of Conflict Management

The following discussion of these elements can be somewhat complex and may even be a bit difficult to comprehend. I suggest that you review these topics for the major ideas and then read the case study at the end of the presentation of these 13 elements. As you interpret the case study and answer the accompanying questions, you can observe the practical application of these elements. While working through the case study, you may wish to reread the discussion of the 13 elements more carefully. By approaching this section in this manner, you may perceive conflict management with more clarity.

Identification

The first thing you will do when you recognize that you are in a conflict situation is to identify the players/disputants while doing your best to get a grip on what the problem really is. Learn who the players are by name if possible and, at least, by category if they are in groups. If a group is represented, identify the leader by name.

Research these players in all ways possible. Find out all you can about each one to uncover their true motives. It is amazing that, in many cases, the reasons that people indicate for the conflict are not the real reasons they are in the dispute. Deeper motives might include fear of losing control, greed, a sense of entitlement, a need to dominate—or sundry other reasons.

If you determine that one or all of the players have evil motives in mind and their motives are not negotiable, then you have a problem. Conflict management cannot happen. I define the word *evil* as the deliberate intention of one party to do harm to the other party. If a player is evil, then she is deliberately seeking to perpetrate damage—and probably there is little you can do to stop it. At this point, you probably will want to end the more formal conflict management process. However, you may wish to keep on talking, if the disputants agree, just to hang on to the lines of communication as much as possible. You will need to make a judgment call about this choice.

If you have determined that the motives are not evil and have a chance at resolution, do your best to uncover the real issue and be able to verbalize that issue. Discuss the issue with the disputants and get them to agree on the real motives involved before moving forward. Keep in mind that many disputants will not be able to define their actual motives because they truly aren't aware of them.

As you review the players involved in the friction, assess each one to see whether the player is rational—i.e., if he can operate with logic, good sense, and wisdom. If, for some reason, you determine that the player isn't rational, then you will discontinue the process. If you feel that the players need anger or other emotional identification and management, counseling, or deeper psychological help, you may suggest that avenue to them. Irrational people find it difficult to enter into the conflict management process. It's best not to proceed until you feel that all parties are rational (Rediger 1997).

Decision

In the beginning of the process (or anywhere along the way during the process), you will be constantly making decisions. Once you have determined that all parties to the dispute are rational, you will want to decide on a course of action. The ultimate failure of conflict management is war—a win/lose situation. In the end, one party dominates the other. That should be a last-resort decision.

Another choice open to the disputing parties is avoidance of the issue altogether; i.e., choosing to walk away. If you decide to leave the process, you should have decided to do so only after analyzing the long-term effects of your actions. If you walk away in appeasement and allow the conflict to escalate, that might not be the best decision in the long term.

Avoiding a situation out of fear—or even out of delusion—isn't a healthy response. However, walking away under some circumstances can be quite healthy. Maybe you are on a committee that is plagued by difficult people. Nothing ever gets done. Gridlock prevails. Special interests trump the organizational mission. You feel that you have tried hard to help your fellow committee members find unity—but to no avail. You may choose to resign from that committee and walk away.

The third choice is to truly negotiate a reasonable outcome. This can be done through dialogue. Before Lyndon B. Johnson became president of the United States, he served as U.S. vice-president under President John F. Kennedy—and before that, he was a U.S. senator. Just before the 1960 election, Senator Johnson was interviewed by the greatly-respected

CBS news correspondent, Walter Cronkite. That interview was broadcast on September 26, 1960, on the CBS television network and on September 27, 1960, over the CBS radio network (CBS News 1960). In that interview, Cronkite asked Senator Johnson about his leadership techniques in the U.S. Senate. Senator Johnson replied that he followed advice from the ancient prophet, Isaiah. He was referring to verse 18 of the first chapter of Isaiah in the Bible. It says: "Come, let us reason together . . . ." Senator Johnson was talking about dialoguing as a leadership skill. That's the definition for dialoguing that I like to use: reasoning together. And that is the definition that I will use throughout this discussion of conflict management. Logic tells us that only people operating in a rational state of mind can reason together.

A great book to study on dialoguing is *Dialogue and The Art of Thinking Together* by Dr. William Isaacs, who is a Senior Lecturer at MIT's Sloan School of Management and president of Dialogos, a consulting and leadership education firm located in Cambridge, Massachusetts. I recommend it as required reading before engaging in the conflict management process (Isaacs 1999).

If you have decided to employ the dialoguing choice, then you will want to engage the other elements necessary to conflict management.

Presentation and Listening

I am combining elements three and four because you will most likely be looping through both of these phases multiple times before moving forward. As a mediator, you will ask each side to present its case. Or if you are one of the disputants, you will see to it that each side presents its case. While the situation is being presented, the other disputants will listen intently without interruption. When one side has finished its presentation, the other disputants will present their side while the party that formerly presented listens intently without interruption. Both (or all) sides work at presentation and listening until clarity about the disputed issue has been achieved. One statement should be written that defines the issue. All parties agree that the issue has been defined and that they understand clearly what the parties are saying. At this point, the sides are not arguing or debating. The presentation and listening elements are designed for achieving clarity.

During the listening element, it is important to employ good listening skills. As I have mentioned, interruptions aren't allowed. Objective listening, without prejudice or mentally forming opinions while the other party is presenting, is valuable to the process. The parties involved must work hard at listening objectively while truly hearing what the other disputants have to say.

After you are satisfied that these two elements have achieved their purpose, and the parties have defined the issue in conflict, then you may wish to take a break—which may last several days or even weeks—so that you can lead a research effort which will allow each side to form a strategy.

Research

During this phase of conflict management, you will dig for indications about how the disputants really feel. You will continue to search for true motives for the dispute, including greed, feelings of entitlement, anger, retribution, misunderstandings, long-standing generational disputes that have been carried forward, money, fear, inability to accept change—and many other things that you may unearth. Finding the real root of the problem will go a long way in devising solutions in a later stage of this process.

You must be able to list the problems that are to be solved to resolve the conflict. At this point, you will determine any areas that you will not negotiate. For example, if part of the resolution requires you to do something that you consider immoral (based on your philosophy of life), you will most likely consider that non-negotiable.

After determining what you will not negotiate, you are then ready to set your goals for resolution—provided that your non-negotiables won't interfere with the process. Write out a statement concerning what a successful resolution of the conflict will look like. For example, if your community is disputing with you over applying eminent domain because the city wants to use part of your property for a thoroughfare—and you are wanting to preserve your property as it is without splitting it—your idea of resolution might be for the city to change its plans and move the thoroughfare location to the property a short distance away. You would then gather data that would support your case for meeting your goal and present information showing that the city's project would not suffer if it moved the street to your suggested location. You will also want to present data showing the harm that putting a thoroughfare through your property would cause.

Other research involved might include asking relevant questions of various people, seeking legal counsel and the advice of other professionals, studying such documentation as letters and electronically transmitted documents, and exploring the results of similar disputes that have occurred in the past in your community or in other communities. In other words, you are investigating any and all types of information that will help you achieve your goal.

In the first element, you identified the players in the conflict. In the research stage, you will go more deeply into acquiring as much information as is legally possible about the disputants so that you will be better able to determine their motives and understand their reasons for their entry into the conflict situation. Also, here you will apply your interpersonal skills. Doing your best to determine their personality type, you will be careful to use words that will help you achieve your goals while not aggravating the situation. Additionally, you will watch for body language which will indicate how the other parties feel about your proposals and statements. At all times, you will want to be tactful when communicating with the disputing parties.

Finally, in this phase Community Leaders 4.0 will perform self-assessment. Question yourself about how you have contributed to the dispute. Try to determine if you can offer a practical solution that will resolve the dispute. Assess your own motives. Could you be expressing greed, a sense of entitlement, anger, fear, or any of the qualities you have considered as possible motives of the other disputants? Self-assessment is difficult. At this point, you may wish to seek the advice of a professional counselor to help you reflect on your own personality and motives.

Strategy

After you have conducted adequate research and feel satisfied about your findings, you are ready to move forward. Developing your strategy is the next step. In effect, this is much like establishing a strategic plan for an organization. You will have a vision and mission statement, well-defined primary and secondary goals, and steps that you need to take to accomplish those goals in order to pursue your mission. You will want secondary goals because you will not always get what you want as your primary goal.

If you have ever negotiated the purchase of a new automobile, you probably have a price in mind you *want* to pay and a secondary goal for an offer that you are *willing* to accept (although reluctantly) if the salesperson won't agree on your first offer. Pre-planning your secondary goals helps establish a range of acceptability in your mind so that you can offer to sacrifice something in the process. In this simple example about a car purchase, your vision is to be driving a safe, comfortable car in your personal and work life for the next five years. Your mission is to purchase a car that can help you attain your vision. Your primary and secondary goals establish your price range. These same principles work in negotiation of complex peace treaties, United Nations agreements, disputes between communities, and in family disagreements.

To formulate your strategy, you will continue to ask questions; conduct surveys; talk with relevant, helpful resources; seek professional counsel; and assess your intrapersonal motives, fears, and needs. The continual seeking of this information helps support your case as the process progresses.

The last part of the strategy stage is the subject of forgiveness, which I will use in this context to mean dropping the blame-game and giving up thoughts of revenge. Forgiveness begins with a decision to change your way of thinking about another person or situation. During this phase, while working through your mission and formulating your goals and plans, it is important to the successful outcome of the process for you to forgive the other disputants. As anger builds during conflict, it is difficult to remain rational if you, in anger, seek personal revenge. Your personal forgiveness of disputants doesn't mean that that they won't suffer natural consequences for their actions. And, if there are legal consequences to be applied as a result of the disputants' actions, it is the responsibility of the legal authorities to seek justice and designate suitable consequences. In this section, I am merely talking about personal forgiveness on your part—i.e., giving up the need to personally "get even" with the disputant.

You may not even be aware that you are seeking retribution. It may be so subtle that you are merely sabotaging the process through your use of words, tone of voice, or body language. Yet your anger can fuel the fires of the dispute. Lack of forgiveness can trump rationality and the attainment of resolution. Forgiveness allows disputants to save face—i.e., preserve their dignity—which helps in keeping the dialogue moving. Once dialogue blocks, it is difficult to start the flow again.

When Nelson Mandella, who later was elected president of South Africa, was released from prison in 1990 after having served a long sentence for his stand against South African apartheid, something big was about to happen. Sweeping change in South Africa's national consciousness was on the horizon. Years of oppression had damaged multi-generations. A wide gap existed between blacks and whites. Deep-seated anger abounded for lives restricted and opportunities lost.

Ethnic anger is painful to overcome. I have met people who have been victims of cruelty or whose ancestors suffered violent atrocities and yet have been able to forgive their offenders. These people realized that forgiveness is a choice.

Archbishop Desmond Tutu is known for his efforts to end apartheid in South Africa. For these struggles, he won the Nobel Peace Prize in 1984. In his book, *No Future Without Forgiveness* (Tutu 1999), the archbishop promotes healing of breached relationships. He was appointed by President Nelson Mandella to head the Truth and Reconciliation Commission created to look into all the violations committed under apartheid for the 34-year period ending in 1994. Rather than promoting revenge for wrongs, Archbishop Tutu advocated forgiveness based on his belief that God created humanity to live in peace and harmony (Corbin 2003).

The movie *Invictus*, released in 2009 and directed by Clint Eastwood, is the true story of how Nelson Mandella, during his first term as president of South Africa, inspired South Africa's rugby team to win the Rugby World Cup in 1995. The story also reveals how President Mandella carried the spirit of forgiveness for his long imprisonment into his presidency—even when he had the power to practice retaliation. He made a choice to forgive and move forward in peace.

Affirmation and Wholeness

After you have completed the elements of research and strategy, it is time to reassemble with the other players to engage in affirmation and wholeness. As I did with the discussion of the topics of presentation and listening, I have combined the elements of affirmation and wholeness.

When you are back with the disputants, you will make more progress if you are able to affirm them. First, indicate to them that you trust them—if, in fact, you do. If, by this stage of the conflict management process, you can't trust all disputants to be truthfully working toward an outcome for the common good, then this is a good place to stop and examine whether you want to continue the process. If you can't trust the other people, then you can keep on talking, but you will need to back up to some of the other steps in the process and repeat them. If you determine that dialoguing is bogging down, you may go all the way back to the decision stage, and choose another option—withdrawal or win/lose, i.e., flight or fight.

However, if by now—if you are a disputant—you can trust the other disputants to be honestly seeking an outcome that is best for all involved, then you should affirm that trust to them. Tell them that you trust them and wish to continue. Indicate to them that you respect their right to feel the way they do. You indicate that you have empathy and understanding for their reasons for framing their perceptions. You express that you continue to disagree with them on the issue, but that you are willing to work with them to find a solution. This stage validates the process and the players who are at the negotiation table.

At this point, you will direct the players to establish a position of unity. Each player will come to the table with a strategy. The parties must work out the disagreements on the strategies until unity is agreed upon. If resolution is to take place, there must be some things that they can agree on. Work on the strength that is produced by their coming together through agreement on some points. Work backward from these points of unity to try to resolve the points of disunity. This process may take several weeks to work through. On rare occasions, this process lasts a number of years. At the end of this phase, you will want to have established mutual goals on which the disputants agree to move forward.

Perception

In this element, disputants are directed to dialogue about their perceptions. In a dispute, there are nearly always things that are left over after the conflict is seemingly resolved that will continue to be points of agitation. Disputants should be honest with themselves and others by bringing up these lingering factors and honestly revealing their feelings about them. Once they are defined and discussed, the power of the left-overs is often mitigated.

In large international disputes, peace treaties may be signed. Yet remaining irritants keep popping up, and war breaks out again. Obviously the treaty is broken. For centuries, some countries have fought over things they were unable to forgive. Anger from the past continues to provoke agitation. As a result, their fight never ends.

While discussing perceptions, and seeking clarification from all involved parties, it is important to create a safe environment for dialogue. Disputants won't bring up their utmost concerns if they feel that they are going to be attacked physically or verbally. Expression must take place in a non-threatening atmosphere. After perceptions are dealt with, then the process of forgiveness must again be applied—as discussed in the preceding strategy section.

In community disputes, for example, disputants need to express what they hear the other parties saying. They should answer the following questions:

- Do they perceive ultimatums being given?
- Do they perceive threats being made?
- What do they think the other disputants are demanding of them?
- Do they feel that the other disputants are giving them a way to settle the dispute? If so, how do they envision their role in the solution?

Healing

Healing is also a choice—just like forgiveness. And the full process takes time and much effort. Mental and emotional work must take place among the disputants. Professional counselors may need to be called in to facilitate the process. Forgiveness is hard work. And healing cannot begin until forgiveness happens. If disputants continue to bring up unresolved issues from the past—as discussed in the preceding topic—healing cannot take place. And reconciliation can't happen without healing. In addressing this element, you should always keep in mind the ways you can maintain the dignity of the players. Even if you are right and the conflict is tilting in your favor, always let the other disputants save face.

During healing, emotional wounds must be addressed. Each disputant should express how they have been injured by the others. The presentation and listening elements must be employed. When someone is telling you how you have hurt them, it is tempting to interrupt and start defending yourself—or even worse, become angry and escalate the conflict. However, you should exercise discipline and wait to speak until the other disputant has finished expressing his pain. Then you can seek clarification and explain your motives and perceptions.

In this element, there is ample opportunity for apologies to be made by the disputants to one another. The conflict management process can move forward only if the apologies are sincere. You can conclude that the apologies are sincere if you sense a change in behavior and attitude over a period of time from the one who is apologizing. It is far easier to make verbal apologies than to demonstrate behaviors and attitudes consistent with that apology over time.

At this point, you might want to take a break for several days—or even several weeks—so that genuine healing can take place. During this timeframe, changes in attitudes and behaviors can be observed. This break will also provide the opportunity for disputants to work with professional counselors and do the hard work of healing.

Discovery

If all ten elements which have been heretofore discussed have worked properly, you are ready to pursue the discovery process. This involves listing the options for solution. Each disputant, by now, should be ready to seek resolution. In fact, they should be excited about the opportunity for reconciliation. If you are acting as the mediator, you will ask the players for their ideas concerning how the issues can be addressed so that a peaceful, satisfactory outcome can happen.

Contracting

This element contains the details of planning and execution. The disputants work together to define the ways success will be measured once they reach a point of unity in the affirmation and wholeness stages. In other words, what will resolution of the conflict look like? Can it be defined in words and numbers? For example, if two communities are arguing over the location of a new regional airport, they will eventually want to come to agreement over where the airport should be built. The location can be described explicitly both verbally and by the use of exact metrics. That would be the conflict's measure of success—defining the location of the airport on which the disputants can agree.

Additionally, a verification process should be defined. In other words, how will the disputants know that the others are living up to their responsibilities? The United Nations International Atomic Energy Agency sometimes serves as a verifier that agreements are being carried out. Historically, they have been in charge of seeing that weapons of mass destruction have been destroyed by nations who were asked to get rid of such weapons as a part of a dispute settlement. If these nations were found not to be meeting their responsibilities, then there were consequences according to those defined in a resolution or peace agreement.

Monitoring

After defining how success will be measured in the contracting stage, you are ready for the monitoring phase where progress is scrutinized. Each disputant will be accountable for carrying out tasks and meeting goals for which he has assumed responsibility. During the Cold War, former U.S. President Ronald Reagan was famous for the words: "trust, but verify." In the monitoring stage, formal verification that each party is holding up his end of the bargain, which he made in some sort of agreement with the disputants, will be established. Consequences or rewards—depending on results of the monitoring process—will be administered.

ᕷ

Practical Application of the 13 Conflict Management Elements

The best way to understand the 13 elements of conflict management is to work through a case study on the subject. To help you do this, I formulated a fictional story that might happen in your community. At the end of the story, I have listed questions that you should consider about the case in order to manage the ensuing conflict. All names and incidents in the story are fictitious, and any likenesses to circumstances, organizations, or persons are purely coincidental. This case study is constructed from my imagination while trying to use plausible circumstances.

Case Study: George's Dilemma

George moved into the area last year. He now lives in a city much smaller than the one he moved from. Already, he has begun to participate in community activities. He has been appointed to the board of trustees of a nonprofit organization. Having had lots of board experience in one of America's largest cities, he feels that he can be helpful as the city where he currently resides continues to grow. He is eager to help the nonprofit organization meet its expanding demands.

George spent several weeks observing the board meetings and the executive director (ED) in action upon his being elected to the board. It seems to George that the ED is friendly and is active throughout the community. The ED is well liked and is in social circles with many of the board members. He has been ED of the nonprofit organization for 15 years. The ED has also been very helpful to George—referring him to various potential clients for his computer company, helping his daughter find a good Girl Scout troop, and introducing George's wife to numerous job opportunities.

Knowing a lot about leadership, George quickly realizes that the ED is often busy, but George doesn't see great evidence of his productivity. During prosperous stock market years, the organization's funds grew nicely—and the ED got the credit for that. Some major donors had given sizable funds, but mostly due to board members' efforts. Yet the ED took the credit. George has determined that much of the growth was due to a great return on investments. He quickly calculated the ED's funds that he had personally raised in the past 15 years. They were not too bountiful when computed over the period of time that the ED had been with the organization.

After several more weeks of observing the ED's abilities in handling his job, George has determined that the ED cannot take the organization to the next level. And the organization must move to the next level to survive in a slower economy and with increased demands in a growing city. The ED seems to always have an excuse for lost donors and failed efforts. He simply does not have the experience necessary in heated competition for the donor dollar. The other board members do not seem to be too concerned about the situation.

George is in a dilemma. He is new to the city. He doesn't know all the board members well. The board members seem to like the ED and appear to be satisfied with his work. George recognizes that the board members are also not ready for the more sophisticated efforts that the organization must make to compete for the donor dollar. The ED has helped George and his family become involved in the community, and George really likes him. Yet, George is serious about his board responsibilities and feels that he must bring some 21st century expertise to the table.

George decides to approach the ED with his observations. When he does so, the ED immediately becomes defensive and states that rather than being criticized for how he executes his duties, he really deserves a raise. In fact, the ED tells George that he is already devising a plan to request that the board conduct a salary survey of EDs heading up similar organizations with similar responsibilities. The ED says that he wants his salary equalized. The ED feels certain that the board will discover that he is underpaid. The ED further states that he feels confident that the board is very happy with his work. He claims that he has heard no one complain about how he does his job.

George then politely tells the ED that he knows he is very busy, but that perhaps the ED might want to review his responsibilities with the board and determine ways in which the ED could become more productive with his time in order to raise more funds. George then projects the future funds needed in the endowment to successfully meet organizational goals five years into the future and indicates that he feels the ED is not on target to meet those critical needs. He shows the ED how he has calculated future needs versus projected actual endowment funds. The ED then tells George that he will review the funding requirements and see what he can do.

When George leaves the meeting, he doesn't feel comfortable. To be fair, George wants to give the ED some time to become more productive. In his mind, George decides to wait two more months—through two more board meetings.

The ED has a plan of his own. Unknown to George, the ED calls on five key members of the nine-member board and tells them that George is a trouble maker. He indicates that George is getting ready to try to exert his power to secure a leadership position on the board. He paints George as divisive and self-absorbed, looking out only for himself. The ED indicates that George is certainly not a team player with the common good of the organization in mind. The five board members are easily persuaded and begin to perceive George as a man with ulterior motives.

George, meanwhile, is waiting out the two months to see what the board does about the salary survey and seeing if the ED changes any of his behaviors in the fund-raising arena. At the next board meeting, the ED asks for the salary survey. Everyone on the board except George casts a vote of approval. At the second meeting, the board notes that the ED is indeed underpaid and that a raise is due. A 20 percent raise passes with everyone on the board voting "yes" except for George. After the ED receives the raise, George, however, sees no indications of increased fund-raising activity. In fact, the ED seems to be doing less—not more.

George then returns to the ED to tell him that he sees no indication that there will be additional fund-raising activity in the future and that he has no alternative but to contact the board members with his concerns. The ED, no longer defensive, tells him to feel free to bring the subject up to the board.

George does just that at the next board meeting. All the other members of the board tell George that they are happy with the ED and that they feel he is doing a fine job. The economy is down a bit and money is tight in this growing community, so they don't expect much more from the ED than he already provides.

George is shocked! A board without lofty goals! Satisfied with the status quo! Unbelievable! And George politely tells them how he feels. He further states that he would like to see the endowment grow by 10 percent per year for the next five years. The other board members agree that this goal is too lofty and that such growth is impossible. Frustrated, George decides to wait longer since the remainder of the board doesn't seem to agree with his concerns. After all, George is the new man in town and needs to build trust. George realizes that.

Three months later, George is visited by two of the board members stating that they are beginning to realize that George might have made some accurate observations. Funds aren't growing. One of the ladies who is visiting indicates that she has reason to believe that the ED is taking his children to the optometrist, other doctors' appointments, and attending the children's soccer games when he indicates to his administrative assistant that he is calling on prospects. Sometimes, he is even leaving town for a family trip when the office staff thinks he is out fund-raising. Interesting information!

The three board members (including George) decide to confront the ED. The ED becomes livid and accuses them of a power move in an effort to take over the board leadership. He then declares that the other six board members are on his side, and that he is intending to present the whole situation at the next board meeting. He further states that the three board members who are gossiping behind his back and trying to ruin his good reputation will be dealt with at the next board meeting.

At the next board meeting, that is exactly what happens. The ED indicates to the board members that George has been talking behind his back and is trying to recruit people to George's side to divide the board and cause trouble. The ED further tells the board that he feels that all of them should work together to resolve the problem before the situation polarizes the board.

Ah, the beginning of a conflict!

℘

Now that you have studied the case about George, pretend that you are George. How would you handle the situation? Use the information from the discussion in this chapter plus any other knowledge you have on conflict management to make your decisions. Then, from your perception of George's role in the conflict, take this conflict through all 13 elements. I have listed some questions that may be helpful to you. And you will have other queries, I'm sure, that you will want answered to try to resolve the conflict.

1. Who are the players?
2. Are the players all rational? How did you determine rationality/non-rationality?
3. Do any of the players have evil intent? If so, justify your position.
4. What is the major issue involved in the conflict?
5. What could the possible motives be?

6. Should the approach to the conflict be avoidance, win/lose (fight), or dialogue? Why?

7. How should George present his case?

8. What communication skills should George exercise?

9. What types of research options should George use?

10. What strategies should George take into consideration? Which ones would you employ if you were in George's situation? Why?

11. What kinds of affirmation statements might George use?

12. What point of unity should George, the ED, and the board agree on?

13. What are some goals/outcomes the players should set as indicators of success?

14. What points of agitation from the past must be disposed of?

15. George may have to provide an ultimatum. How should he state the ultimatum? How should he state the negative and positive consequences that he will apply if the ultimatum is not honored?

16. List some healing techniques that might be used among the players. What are some things George can do and say that will allow all players to save face—i.e., maintain their dignity?

17. Suggest the following options for managing the conflict:
    - Responsibilities each player should assume
    - How to measure success of outcomes
    - Ways to monitor progress and consequences if success is not achieved.

⌇

For Further Learning

There are a number of outstanding resources to explore for enhancing your skills in conflict management. These are excellent for group discussion. Here are a few of them:

1. Blake, R. R., and J. S. Mouton. (1984). "Overcoming Group Warfare." In *Harvard Business Review on Negotiation and Conflict Resolution.* (2000, pp. 57-86). Boston, MA: Harvard Business School Press.

2. Cullinan, G., J. LeRoux, and R. Weddigen. (2004, April). "When to Walk Away from a Deal." *Harvard Business Review*, 82, 4, 97-104.

3. Dana, Daniel: *Conflict Resolution*. New York, NY: McGraw-Hill, 2001.

4. Ertel, D. (1999). "Turning Negotiation into a Corporate Capability." In *Harvard Business Review on Negotiation and Conflict Resolution*. (2000, pp.101-127). Boston, MA: Harvard Business School Press.

5. Fisher, Roger, Elizabeth Kopelman, and Andrea Kipfer Schneider. *Beyond Machiavelli: Tools for Coping with Conflict*. Cambridge, MA: Harvard University Press, 1994.

6. Fisher, Roger, and William Ury. *Getting to Yes*. New York, NY: Penguin Books, 1981, 1991.

7. Lombard Mennonite Peace Center. Lombard, Illinois. For more information on training offered and contact information, see website http://www.lmpeacecenter.org.

8. Schmidt, W. H., and R. Tannenbaum. (1960). "Management of Differences." In *Harvard Business Review on Negotiation and Conflict Resolution*. (2000, pp.1-26). Boston, MA: Harvard Business School Press.

Community Leadership 4.0 Strategies

Conflict management is one of the most important tasks you will perform as a Community Leader 4.0. With all the diversity that exists and all the special interests that are vying for gratification in our communities, conflict will continue to escalate and will be constantly on a leader's radar. Astuteness in conflict management will be a necessary 21st century community skill.

1. Please review the observations concerning conflict management. Each point is important. Add some of your own observations to this list if you have had experience in managing conflict.

2. Not all conflicts can be resolved. Many dissenting groups or individual citizens must do life together agreeing to disagree.

3. The three choices for handling conflict are avoidance, win/lose, or dialoguing. There is a time and place for the application of each choice.

4. Dialoguing is an effective way to manage conflict and, hopefully, reach resolution.

5. Conflict management is both an art and a science. It takes much practice to be an effective conflict manager.

Questions for Contemplation

1. Have you ever been in a conflict situation? How did you handle it?

2. Have you ever let others save face in a conflict? How did you do that?

3. Have you ever had to live with a situation in which the conflict was not resolved? What was the outcome?

4. Do you feel that you can agree to disagree and live in the same community comfortably and peacefully with the disagreeing party or parties?

5. Did you project yourself into George's place in the case study in this chapter? Do you feel that you answered the questions completely and spent your time thoroughly developing your answers?

6. Have you used the case about George as a group exercise and as a training opportunity?

7. Do you feel the need to acquire professional training in conflict management? If so, when, where, and how do you intend to pursue that training?

SECTION FOUR

Putting It All Together

CHAPTER TEN

Leading Legacies

A s I've journeyed through the process of writing this book, I've encountered some awesome people and experiences. It was a tremendous opportunity for me to explore the Community 4.0 phase into which many towns, cities, and villages will be required to reposition for survival in the 21st century. As we've discussed multiple times throughout this work: some communities have several qualities of Community 4.0 status, but no place has all the characteristics of Community 4.0 which I have described. This status is relatively new. Cities, towns, and villages are just beginning to comprehend the need to shift to this phase. Most communities are still classified as 3.0.

As I approach the end of a project, I always review it to see what I've learned. In this work—besides the obvious conclusions from research I have indicated throughout—there are some general principles that I've garnered. They are as follows:

- Many Community Leaders 4.0 are ordinary people who aspire to accomplishing extraordinary things.
- Community 4.0 leaders don't personally possess all the skills necessary for becoming a Community Leader 4.0. However, they know how to find and ask for help from other people who do

have the skills they lack. In one way or another, these leaders know how to obtain the resources necessary for leading Community 4.0.

- There is no one-size-fits-all, cookie-cutter paradigm for becoming a Community Leader 4.0. Different people with a multiplicity of experiences approach the leadership of Community 4.0 in different ways. Each leader contributes a unique approach and philosophy. Yet the elements of great leadership prevail.

In the remainder of this chapter, I want to introduce you to two Community 4.0 leaders who are ordinary people doing extraordinary things. Their backgrounds differ. Their dreams and goals fall into distinctly different categories. Yet both are driven by their passions. They are operating with a people-to-people philosophy. They both have had outstanding achievements. And they are both true Community Leaders 4.0.

Sharon Tennison
Founder and President, Center for Citizen Initiatives

By the time the general public begins to pay attention to most current issues, that recognition has normally been preceded by several years of quietly percolating events on the horizon. The emergence of Community Leaders 4.0 began to be noticed in the late 1980s and early 1990s. However, many grassroots leaders were active several years before their efforts received any public attention. Sharon Tennison was one of those early 4.0 leaders.

Passion for Her Dream

In 1983 at the peak of the Cold War, when relations between the superpowers were at a standoff, an ordinary American citizen, Sharon Tennison, made the decision to try her hand at international diplomacy. She took a group of business and professional people, along with a film crew of four, on an investigative trip to the USSR. This adventure was designed to try to understand the Soviet world by walking the streets, mingling with them in market places, meeting with teachers and students in schools, and visiting Soviets in their homes—all for the purpose of promoting goodwill between the two enemy countries.

The stakes were high. Thousands of nuclear weapons were on launch pads and aimed at each country. If even 10 percent of the weapons were detonated, according to scientists, the entire planet would be rendered inert. Following their 1983 trip, the travelers were determined to educate ordinary American citizens regarding the dangerous standoff between the United States and the USSR. To carry out their work, the Center for U.S.-USSR Initiatives (CUUI) was established. When the Soviet Union imploded in 1990, the organization's name was changed to the Center for Citizen Initiatives (CCI).

From the San Francisco headquarters and partner offices in Russia, Tennison and her team implemented programs to help Soviet citizens with critical issues they were facing as their country was heading toward collapse. The first problem Russian citizens requested help with was alcoholism. By April 1986, CUUI organized the first Alcoholics Anonymous (AA) meeting in Kiev, Ukraine, with behind-the-scenes approval of the USSR's new party general secretary, Mikhail Gorbachev. This started the establishing of AA in the Soviet Union.

By 1988, "Soviets Meet Middle America!" (SMMA) program was developed. This effort brought non-official Soviet citizens of CUUI's choice to the U.S. to meet and interact for the first time with American citizens. Soviet citizens, in small groups of four persons, traveled to 265 American cities and stayed in private homes. They returned to the USSR and spread the word about how wonderfully U.S. citizens treated them and how impressed they were with the American way of life. These trips also began to open the minds of American people about Soviet citizens.

In 1989, CUUI designed early environmental projects in the USSR. In addition, the U.S. agricultural extension model was transplanted to Russian soil in 1990. After the dissolution of the USSR, Russia's agricultural system was is complete disarray. The extension service gave much needed up-to-date information to Russian farmers as they privatized land and developed private farms.

CUUI began business training for Soviet entrepreneurs in 1989, through a new program called the Economic Development Program (EDP). It was the first step toward CCI's Productivity Enhancement Program (PEP), which began in 1994. PEP was designed for non-English-speaking entrepreneurs and became the largest business management training program between the two countries. For 15 years, PEP trained Russian entrepreneurs in American companies with the help of over 500 American Rotary Clubs. Other partners included Kiwanis, Optimist, Soroptimist, and Lions clubs. Some 7,000 Russian entrepreneurs came to American firms to learn how to run small and medium-size businesses.

The PEP program was funded by the U.S. State Department. Previously CCI programs had also been funded by the United States Information Agency (USIA) and the United States Agency for International Development (USAID). American foundations, philanthropists, and CCI memberships provided additional funds. CCI's annual budget from the U.S. government was about $5 million. In-kind contributions of about $2.5 million came from Rotarians and Kiwanians. Russian participants collectively paid approximately $1 million a year to the program, bringing CCI's total annual budget to about $9 million (Corbin 2000). Other CCI contributors over the years have been various philanthropists, the C.S. Mott Foundation, and numerous smaller foundations.

In 2004, U.S. State Department funds to CCI were terminated, and Russian entrepreneurs took full financial responsibility for PEP training and operations costs. CCI began austerity programs to save PEP. However, the global financial crisis of 2008 hit Russia hard, and their entrepreneurs began canceling 2009 training. Without revenues coming in, the PEP program was forced to close.

Today CCI operates a blog entitled *Russia: Other Points of View*, which can be found at website http://russiaotherpointsofview.com. The blog's goal is to promote more accurate U.S. press coverage of Russia. Another connected project, CCI's *Russia Media Watch*, analyzes Western media coverage of Russia based on 17 objective criteria and journalistic standards. Recipients of this report are members of U.S. Congress, think tanks, business and civic leaders, and the journalists and publishers of the analyzed articles.

Additionally, CCI runs The Nika Thayer Angels Program which installs and runs computer labs in Russian orphanages to provide skills for orphans between ages 12 and 17. This was created by Ms. Thayer to give Russian orphans a way to earn a living once they are on their own at age 17 (Center for Citizen Initiatives 2010).

CCI continues to work with U.S. Congressional members by providing information to them on Russian foreign policy issues. Tennison consults with individuals and corporations interested in working in the Russian marketplace. She also assists thousands of CCI volunteers who need help with Russian adoptions, student exchange programs, and other special requests. Tennison is helping organize the first-ever Russian lobby in the United States.

Today CCI has 30,000 volunteers in its databases. They are in 45 states and in over 500 cities across America. These volunteers participate in CCI's mission because they have a passion for making a difference in international relations. CCI continues to evolve as its mission is updated to adapt to global conditions. More information about CCI is available on its website at www.ccisf.org. Up-to-date status reports on Tennison's work can be found by clicking "President's Report" on the homepage.

When I first saw these accomplishments of an organization started by an ordinary American citizen who was concerned about the growing missile race, I contacted Sharon Tennison to investigate what drives her. I found a fascinating, dynamic, passionate, humble, and very intelligent leader. When I asked her what leadership skills served her best in starting CCI, she stated: "I had no leadership skills. They had to be developed in the process. It was hard because I had always just taken care of my own interests. However, I found that in a nonprofit organization, the person who is the "vision holder" automatically becomes the leader—and then one must learn how to work with others in order to get the mission carried out."

There were barriers along the way, Tennison indicates. Year after year, she worked 80-hour weeks, while staying on a 45-degree learning incline. In the beginning she had no knowledge of U.S.-Russian relations, no knowledge of the Russian language, and no experience in fundraising. I asked her how she overcame all of these obstacles. She answered: "By hard work—sheer hard work. Whatever I didn't know, I found people to teach or mentor me. I threw myself into learning everything as it came up. I always promoted "learning by doing" at CCI. We never waited until I knew precisely what to do. I just waded in, got my feet wet, and we all learned to swim in the process."

Tennison says that she is driven by the knowledge that what she is doing *must* be done. When she started CUUI, and later CCI, she felt that if she didn't do it, no one else would. She is authoring a book about her journey over the past three decades. "The book is about citizen diplomacy," maintains Tennison. "It is a testimony to what tens of thousands of ordinary people did to make a difference in our world. International citizen diplomacy had not been tried before the 1980s—fortunately, together we created amazing differences in hundreds of thousands of lives. All of this has produced ripple effects that will never end—as one generation influences another."

Walking Her Talk

Tennison doesn't just manage her relationship with Russia from afar. She chooses to spend half of her year residing in the United States and the other half living in Russia. The dual cities she inhabits are San Francisco and St. Petersburg. "I love both cities," she told me, "so probably all my life, I will maintain residences in two places. I feel completely at home in each." She is attracted to St. Petersburg because of the great classical culture the city provides. She is delighted that ballet and opera are attended by all ages and economic strata there——whereas, in the United States, she feels that classical culture is supported mostly by the wealthy, older generations.

St. Petersburg is the most Western of all Russian cities. Tennison says that it is a progressive international city: "Business, housing, production——everything is privatized. It looks like a normal European capital city. Churches have been returned to the Orthodox faith. They gleam in nearly every corner of St. Petersburg, as in other Russian cities. Other religions are also present—Buddhist centers, Muslim mosques, a few Protestant churches, and a rare Catholic church."

Since Tennison experiences St. Petersburg as home several months per year, she knows the essence of the city. She says it now has the conveniences of the West, less street crime, good public transportation, and more people on the streets day and night. Over the past ten years, she reports that St. Petersburg and other Russian cities have made huge improvements. Generally, Russian cities of over 150,000 population have made great progress, whereas the small towns and villages still look like they did during the Soviet era.

I asked how St. Petersburg compares with Moscow. Tennison feels that it is more like San Francisco whereas Moscow, which is over twice the size of St. Petersburg, is more like New York City. Additionally, she says that Russia as a whole, is more focused now on rebuilding the country after the decades of communism, rather than competing internationally. In terms of production, Russia is definitely behind; on the other hand, they have a wealth of oil, gas, metals, jewels, and other extractive products to tide them over during their redevelopment phase.

In closing, Tennison pondered: "Will I continue to stay in the U.S.-Russia interface? Yes, most likely for the rest of my life. Few, if any, have had the bi-cultural experience at Russia's grassroots that I have had. I've watched with fascination as Russians moved from communism, through their criminal '90s under Yeltsin and the oligarchs, and into the 2000s with Putin and now Medvedev. I operate as somewhat of a bi-cultural translator. To me, Russia is the most intriguing country in the world given her history and culture. Russia developed in isolation from the European nations––and her citizens have quite different conditioning and behaviors from the people of Europe and America. Russians today are trying to fit into the world of the 21st century, and at the same time, trying to keep their very rich cultural heritage alive. It's not easy––and at times the differences cause international misunderstandings. I am somewhat of a "corpus callosum" between Russia and the West, which operate so differently from each other. America seems to me to operate primarily from left brain consciousness—while Russia is at home with right brain consciousness. Both have major deficits—and both have enormous gifts to share with each other––and to give to the rest of the world. I'm blessed to be functioning, and hopefully assisting, at this interface" (Tennison 2010).

❧

Bob Dixson
Mayor, Greensburg, Kansas

You read about the courage of the leaders and citizens of Greensburg, Kansas, in Chapter Five. Before reading this part, you may wish to return to that chapter and review the details. After writing that piece, I continued to follow the progress of the brave rural town positioned on the plains of Kansas. There is an abundance of information available on the Internet simply by "Googling" the name of the town. As I reviewed the information, I was motivated to drive to Kansas from Texas and visit the place that was in the process of becoming the greenest town in America. I wanted to experience the positive attitude of the townspeople and interview the mayor personally. I had talked with him on the telephone and knew that he possessed unique leadership skills.

The day I spent in Greensburg, the county seat of Kiowa County, was truly an inspirational experience. I don't see how a person can visit there without undergoing a changed attitude about life. For me, it was the realization of how I, as well as many other Americans, cling too tightly to our material possessions. On May 4, 2007, in a period of 15 minutes, 95 percent of the population of Greensburg had lost almost every material possession they owned. Eleven people tragically lost their lives. Mayor Dixson told me that in the aftermath of the storm when people began to dig their way out of the rubble that had fallen around them, there were suddenly no differences among the people. No ethnic differences, no differences in financial position, no differences in power. Everyone had lost almost everything classified as material. They all stood as equals. A community came together that Friday evening to rise to the challenge of seeking a second chance—and today is still working hard to carve out a distinctive future.

Three years after the powerful tornado, the town's streets are new and landscaped with native plants to conserve water, the lots are cleared, and many energy-efficient houses have been built to replace the homes which were lost. The community is buzzing with activity on construction sites. Downtown buildings have been replaced; the city hall structure reflects high-level energy efficiency; the hospital is a state-of-the art green building; and the new high-performance K-12 school opened in the fall of 2010. It houses students from three school districts which consolidated to use the contemporary facility after the tornado. The first LEED Platinum building to be completed was the arts center. Many other green buildings dot the landscape. Touring this town is an awesome experience. All new city buildings larger than 4,000 square feet are required by a resolution of the Greensburg City Council to meet LEED Platinum certification and have energy consumption that is 42 percent less than that of standard buildings.

The Greensburg community has had willing, generous, and creative partners in this quest to be the greenest town in America. It has the involvement of state agencies and nonprofit organizations. Innovation has also come from the help of commercial businesses, the U.S. Department of Energy, the U.S. Department of Agriculture, and the Federal Emergency Management Agency (FEMA)—as well as other federal agencies. This is definitely a national community effort.

Driving into Greensburg, I saw the wind turbines—with their blades gracefully turning— poised against the horizon. This is a visible sign that the town has no intention of generating electricity from fossil fuels. It will use renewable energy from wind, hydro, and other renewable electricity generation sources. Greensburg is the first city in the world to resolve to reach this level of sustainability.

The John Deere Dealership and Service Shop has become the model for all green John Deere dealerships and service shops. Greensburg's homes are energy efficient. In fact, Greensburg GreenTown—a nonprofit organization whose mission is to educate people about green building, create eco-tourism in Greensburg, and showcase the latest green technology—has an eco-home project built around a silo-shaped core. The idea came from noticing that the only building left standing, and receiving minimal damage from the greater than 200 miles-per-hour winds, was the local silo. Tourists can stay in this, and later in other eco-homes which will be built, while they are visiting and touring in Greensburg.

The first building to be constructed and opened was the Kiowa County Care-n-Share, which is a thrift shop and food bank sponsored by the Kiowa County Ministerial Alliance. Dixson explained that since almost everything was lost in the storm, the people immediately needed clothes and food. When we drove up to the building, I noticed that the words *Sharing Christ with Everyone* were artfully and prominently inscribed on the window. Throughout Greensburg, the attitudes and conversations of the people reflect a place housing deep spiritual convictions.

In the reconstruction process, Greensburg was careful to save as much of the physical evidence of its heritage as possible. Bricks and stones that were rescued from demolished buildings are incorporated into the architecture of the contemporary buildings now lining the streets. Long known as the town with the world's largest hand-dug well (completed in

1888), Greensburg showcases that site as a masterpiece of pioneer engineering. After much searching, people recovered the Space Wanderer, the largest pallasite meteorite ever uncovered and weighing 1000 pounds. It will be housed in the new museum. In fact, in April of 2010, the groundbreaking ceremony for the Kiowa County Commons was held. This 21st century LEED Platinum facility will accommodate the Kiowa County Library, Historical Museum, Extension Office, and the Media Center.

The 95-year-old Kiowa County courthouse wasn't totally demolished, yet it sustained substantial damage. It is being renovated to meet LEED Gold standards. For such a sustainability project involving an old building being renovated rather than replaced, this is quite a challenge. However, the people of Greensburg, and Kiowa County, feel that they are up to the challenges that lie in creating the greenest city in America—and perhaps the world.

As the first community in the United States to use LED (light emitting diode) lamps for 100 percent of its street lighting, Greensburg has improved outdoor lighting energy efficiency by 40 percent. As compared to sodium vapor lights—used by many communities—Greensburg has reduced energy and maintenance costs by approximately 70 percent (U.S. Department of Energy 2010).

Faith, Family, and Friends

On my search for the leadership qualities that are catapulting Greensburg from devastation to becoming the greenest town in America, I asked Mayor Bob Dixson the secret behind the positive enthusiasm of the townspeople. He told me that the answer is "faith, family, and friends." He feels that these are the highest-priority features of rebuilding. "When virtually every material thing you have is gone, you have God, your family, and your friends left to help." He continued: "Our community grew to include nationwide help. We met people from all over America who either helped from their homes across the nation or who actually came to Greensburg to help serve meals and provide clothing. FEMA was immediately responsive with trailers for us to live in. They were set up in a group so that we could establish residency there while we worked to clean off our lots and supervise the building of our new homes."

The mayor gave my husband and me a tour of Greensburg then took us to meet his wife, Ann, who is a Kansas Magistrate Judge. Both of them reiterated what I had heard throughout the morning in Greensburg: there is a feeling of responsibility to build back greener and better. Dixson told me that Greensburg was named for Donald R. Green who owned and operated the Cannonball Stageline. The town began in the late 1880s and was meant to be sustained by future generations. He indicated that the citizens of Greensburg feel responsible for continuing the legacy of hard work, responsibility, and accountability to the land that was established by their ancestors. "With the word *green* as part of our town's name, it seemed natural to go green. And most of us are involved, or have been involved, in agriculture as a way of life. As farmers and ranchers, we learned early that we have a responsibility to be good stewards of God's resources that He has provided for us. In the *Holy Bible*— in the book of Genesis—we read that God created everything we need. The idea of "going green" is as old as life itself. Many of the techniques for saving energy and reducing our carbon footprint are not new. The technology may be new, but we have always tried to preserve, to the best of our ability, what God has given us."

Quick to give credit to a leadership team, Dixson stresses the importance of listening to the people and not trying to create a top-down leadership culture. Upon hearing many of the mayor's statements about leadership, I began to think he had already read this book manuscript. He is instinctively, naturally leading with Community Leadership 4.0 skills. Dixson understands the "world gone wiki" philosophy. "People want to be a part of the solution. They want leaders to listen to them. They want to be heard," he claims with depth of understanding.

"The people of Greensburg are doers. They want to take responsibility for rebuilding their town. They are not entitlement-oriented. They are willing to do the hard work of rebuilding," the mayor continued. As I talked with various people in the town, I heard the word *hard* used multiple times—not in a negative way, but in a fashion which expressed that this enormous task of rebuilding isn't easy, but it is worth the massive effort.

Another Community Leadership 4.0 skill that Dixson possesses is that of vision. He understands the necessity of keeping the people's eyes and hearts focused on the way things will be in the future. In the chaos of overcoming disaster, a great leader focuses the attention of the community on the advantages of reaching the other side—of walking through the hard times into the bright future that awaits. Dixson is astute at projecting a big picture view of what Greensburg will be able to achieve. "When things are down," he comments, "it's time to be bold. We must think out of the box because the box we would have normally thought out of is gone. We must create a new box—a new vision." The mayor explained to me that one of the first things to be rebuilt was the very tall water tower. "That became a symbol of hope," he said. "When approaching Greensburg, that water tower could be seen in the distance. It created optimism in the minds of the people." Water is as necessary for life as air. That tower was a metaphor for sustainability and vitality. "Leadership," he proposed "is all about relationships—all about people."

Everyone Leads

There's a sense of excitement as Greensburg moves forward. Dixson indicates that everyone in town is a leader. The people have invested their life savings in rebuilding. "They are invested emotionally, spiritually, physically, and financially," he points out. About half of the town moved away after the tornado for one reason or another. Some left to live with relatives. Others left to secure jobs. Now some of those who left are returning. And new people are moving into the town.

Each person who lives in the community has taken on a responsibility as an individual leader. Each one has a task to help move Greensburg forward for future generations. Dixson believes that people desire three things no matter where they live, and he is trying to see that people living in Greensburg have them: (1) hope; (2) good news; and (3) sense of community. He believes that people want an awareness of their identity and firm roots. He acknowledges that people aspire to be a part of something greater then themselves. As mayor, he leads the citizens in a way that causes them to feel that they are making a great difference.

As a leader, Dixson enables people to perform difficult tasks. He believes that people can be self-directed leaders and only need to be facilitated—and not coerced— by his efforts. In setting priorities for the green movement, he concentrates on what the citizens care about. Together the townspeople set priorities. They rank-order the priorities, create a plan, and then execute the plan. Each person—including school students—has a responsibility to carry out. All people are an integral part of the whole community.

Life's Preparation For Such a Time as This

In leading Greensburg, Dixson calls on the skills he learned while growing up on a farm. "When you live 17 miles from town, you learn to innovate when you have a problem or a piece of farm equipment breaks down," claims Dixson. "Farmers don't always have the luxury of going into town to find a fix for every dilemma. You need to find solutions yourself along with help from family and neighbors. On the farm, we learned to work hard to get results. We learned the principles of sowing and reaping—cause and effect—investment and results. When hard times came—e.g., someone was ill and couldn't work on the farm—the community pitched in and helped. We all helped one another."

Those principles garnered from farm life, his experiences while serving as postmaster in Greensburg and the neighboring town of Pratt, as well as his strong spiritual life have prepared Dixson for his mayoral job of leading Greensburg at this unique time in its history. He indicated to me that he is a humble servant with a vision of a brighter tomorrow. He said: "It's in the Bible (Proverbs 29:18). Without vision, people perish." He also believes the opposite is true: where there is vision, the people have vitality. He shared with me a truth he's discovered: "You can't let the realities of today cloud your vision of tomorrow."

A Living Laboratory

As Greensburg continues to rebuild, the people are working hard to realize their dreams. Mayor Bob Dixson is leading a unique effort. "We see new opportunities, new horizons, and new alternatives," he pronounces with conviction. "We want Greensburg to be a living laboratory for the stewardship of God's resources—i.e., financial, social, and environmental sustainability. We have a tremendous opportunity to influence the world. Our community has a vision. Each person is taking responsibility for his/her part in making the vision a reality. It's amazing what happens when people work together unselfishly and don't care who gets the credit" (Dixson 2010).

∽

Defining Moment for Planet Earth

The global community is at a crossroads. Technology is enabling countries to establish alliances that were heretofore deemed impossible. The world really is shrinking when considering the warp speed of transactions and communications. We are indeed becoming a global village with all the predictable chaos leading to the potential melding of differences. We are entering an era that will produce events which have never been faced by anyone on the planet. While moving into Community 4.0, leaders will be required to guide people through experiences they themselves have never had. That's a tough assignment. This is indeed a unique time in history—and the future. By applying the principles we've discussed throughout this book, leaders will have a strong start toward creating a totally new world with restructured relationships and tremendous opportunities.

This is an exciting time to be alive! Moreover, it is an exhilarating time to be a Community Leader 4.0!

∽

Community Leadership 4.0 Strategies

Extraordinary things are done by ordinary people with a passion for activating their dreams. Community Leaders 4.0 probably don't possess all the necessary skills themselves. However, they know how to find the resources that can help complement their skills in leading their communities forward.

1. After reading the stories about Sharon Tennison and Mayor Bob Dixson, what Community 4.0 efforts do you feel that you can initiate?

2. Consider both stories. What were the elements of each story that inspired you most?

3. List the steps you will take to develop your Community Leadership 4.0 skills.

4. List the resources you can call on to complement your Community Leadership 4.0 skills.

Questions for Contemplation

1. What makes an ordinary person do extraordinary things?

2. Have you ever been faced with leading people to seeking a second chance after a devastating event? If so, how did you handle your leadership role?

3. Think about the history of your country. Who rose from being an ordinary citizen to having great accomplishments?

4. In our changing world, what will be required for countries to live in peace with one another?

5. How can you lead your community into Community 4.0 status to keep it competitive in the global marketplace?

REFERENCES AND NOTES

Ali-Dinar, Ali B., Ph.D., Page Editor. "Letter from a Birmingham Jail [King, Jr.]." African Studies Center, University of Pennsylvania. Extracted from website http://www.africa.upenn.edu/Articles_Gen/Letter_Birmingham.html on November 23, 2009.

Amsterdam.nl, Amsterdam's Innovation Motor. Extracted from website http://www.topstad.amsterdam.nl/english/projects/optimising_it/amsterdam's on October 22, 2009.

_____, Working Together. Extracted from website http://www.topstad.amsterdam.nl/english/working_together?media=print on October 22, 2009.

Anissimov, Michael. "What is the Prefrontal Cortex?" Extracted from website http://www.wisegeek.com/what-is-the-prefrontal-cortex.htm on March 20, 2010. Website copyright 2003-2010.

Augustine, Norman R. "Reshaping an Industry: Lockheed Martin's Survival Story." *Harvard Business Review*, May-June 1997, 83.

Butler, Kent, Sara Hammerschmidt, Frederick Steiner, and Zhang, Ming. *Reinventing the Texas Triangle: Solutions for Growing Challenges.* Center for Sustainable Development, The University of Texas at Austin School of Architecture. Austin, Texas: 2009.

CBS News. *Presidential Countdown: "Mr. Johnson: A Profile."* CBS News interview—Walter Cronkite with Senator Lyndon B. Johnson, September 26, 1960. Retrieved from website http://www.jfklink.com/speeches/joint/joint260960_johnsonprofile.html on June 5, 2009.

Center for Citizen Initiatives. Retrieved from http://en.wikipedia.org/wiki/Center_for_Citizen_Initiatives on May 15, 2010. Article last updated on May 6, 2010. Material retrieved also confirmed with Sharon Tennison, president of Center for Citizen Initiatives.

Corbin, Carolyn. *A Promise to America.* Austin, Texas: PenPoint Press (an imprint of Eakin Press), 2003, 81-82.

_____. *Conquering Corporate Codependence: Lifeskills for Making It Within or Without the Corporation.* Englewood Cliffs, New Jersey: Prentice Hall, 1993, 159-194.

_____. *Great Leaders See the Future First: Taking Your Organization to the Top in Five Revolutionary Steps.* Chicago: Dearborn, 2000, 127.

_____. *Strategies 2000: Declare Your Independence from the Uncertainties of Tomorrow.* Austin, Texas: Eakin Press, 1986, 38-45.

Cornish, Edward. "Foresight Conquers Fear of the Future." *The Futurist*, January-February 2010, 51.

_____. *Futuring: The Exploration of the Future.* Bethesda, Maryland: World Future Society, 2004.

Coster, Helen. "Affordable Places To Weather The Downturn." Forbes. com, November 12, 2008. Extracted from website http://www.forbes.com/2008/11/12/cheap-cities-affordable-forbeslife-cx_hc_1112realestate.html on May 24, 2010.

Council on Competitiveness. *Compete: New Challenges, New Answers.* Council on Competitiveness, 1500 K Street NW, Washington DC 20005 (Telephone 202-682-4292), November 2008. Retrieved from website http://www.compete.org/publications/detail/606/compete1, December 11, 2009.

Dixson, Bob. Interview with Carolyn Corbin took place on June 24, 2010 in Greensburg, Kansas. Mayor Dixson can be contacted by telephone at 620-546-3630 or by email at gbgdixsons@yahoo.com.

Florida, Richard. *Who's Your City? How the Creative Economy Is Making Where to Live the Most Important Decision of Your Life.* New York: Basic Books, 2008, 5.

Friedman, Thomas L. The *World Is Flat: A Brief History of the Twenty-First Century.* New York: Farrar, Straus, and Giroux, 2005, 324-329.

Gladwell, Malcolm. *Blink: The Power of Thinking Without Thinking.* New York: Little, Brown, and Company, 2005.

Goleman, Daniel. *Emotional Intelligence: Why It Can Matter More Than IQ.* New York: Bantam Books, 1995.

_____. *Social Intelligence: Beyond IQ, Beyond Emotional Intelligence.* New York: Bantam Books, 2006.

Gordon, Edward. "The Global Talent Crisis." *The Futurist,* September-October 2009, 35.

Greensburg, Kansas: A Better, Greener Place to Live. Extracted from website http://apps1.eere.energy.gov/buildings/publications/pdfs/corporate/45086.pdf on July 1, 2010.

Hangar 25 Air Museum. Extracted from website www.hangar25airmuseum.com on April 5, 2010.

Hart, Eloise. Extracted from website
http://www.theosophy-nw.org/theosnw/world/med/me-elo.htm on August
25, 2009. Website article is from *Sunrise* magazine, October/November
1985, Pasadena, California, Theosophical University Press.

Haskew, Ben. Interview took place with Carolyn Corbin on May 17, 2010.
For more information, contact Ben Haskew, president and CEO of the
Greater Greenville (South Carolina) Chamber of Commerce, 24 Cleve-
land Street, Greenville, South Carolina, 29601. Telephone: 864-242-1050.
Website: www.greenvillechamber.org.

Hayes, Tom, and Michael S. Malone. "The Ten-Year Century." *The Wall
Street Journal*, August 10, 2009. Extracted from website http://online.wsj.
com on August 11, 2009.

Institute for Innovation in Social Policy website http://iisp.vassar.edu/ish.
html. Vassar College, Box 529, Poughkeepsie, New York 12604. Director:
Marque-Luisa Miringoff, Ph.D. Extracted September 12, 2009.

Isaacs, William. *Dialogue and the Art of Thinking Together*. New York:
Currency, published by Doubleday, 1999.

Kanter, Rosabeth Moss. "Thriving Locally in the Global Economy." *Harvard Business Review*, August 2003, 119-127.

Kidder, Rushworth M. *How Good People Make Tough Choices*. New York:
William Morrow and Company, Inc., 1995, 90.

LaFreniere, Jodi Ann. Interview took place with Carolyn Corbin on January 8, 2010. For more information, contact Jodi Ann LaFreniere, president of the McKinney Chamber of Commerce, 2150 S. Central Express-
way, Ste. 150, McKinney, Texas, 75070. Telephone 972-542-0163. Website:
www.mckinneychamber.com.

Legatum Institute. *Legatum Prosperity Index*[TM]. Legatum Institute, 11
Charles Street, Mayfair, London, W1J5DW, United Kingdom (Telephone

+44 207 148 5400), 2009. Retrieved from website www.prosperity.com/rankings.aspx on October 31, 2009.

Luntz, Dr. Frank. *Words That Work: It's Not What You Say, It's What People Hear.* New York: Hyperion, 2007.

Maloney, Stephen. "More Jobs Created in Historic Restoration." *City-Business*, November 9, 2009. Extracted from website http://www.neworleanscitybusiness.com/viewStory.cfm?recID=34398 on December 8, 2009.

Manpower, Inc. Press release issued May 28, 2009. Milwaukee, Wisconsin. Extracted from website http://www.manpower.com/investors/releasedetail.cfm?ReleaseID=386282 on September 9, 2010.

Maslow, Abraham. "A Theory of Human Motivation." *Psychological Review*, Volume 50, Number 4, 1943, 370-396. Retrieved from website http://psychclassics.yorku.ca/Maslow/motivation.htm entitled *Classics in the History of Psychology*, an Internet resource developed by Christopher D. Green, York University, Toronto, Ontario, Canada, ISSN 1492-3713. Retrieved on January 17, 2010.

Mauboussin, Michael J. "Smart People, Dumb Decisions." *The Futurist*, March-April 2010, 24-30.

McCaleb, Gary D. *The Gift of Community: Reflections on the Way We Live and Work Together.* Abilene, Texas: Center for Building Community, 2001, paperback printing, revised and expanded edition, 2010.

McDonald, Gloria. Interview with Carolyn Corbin on April 3, 2010.

McKinney Education Foundation. Story from Carolyn Corbin's own personal experience. Recent data confirmed by Melanie Perkins, Executive Director, on June 8, 2010. More information about the McKinney Education Foundation can be found at website http://www.mmeeff.com.

Michener, James A. *Texas.* New York: Random House, 1985.

Myers, Courtney Boyd. "Two Hundred And Fifty Pills To Immortality." Forbes.com, May 27, 2009. Extracted from website http://www.forbes.com/2009/05/26/ray-kurzweil-immortality-live   forever-opinions-book-review-transcend.html on September 7, 2009.

Odugbemi, Sina. "Theodore Roosevelt, Quote of the Week." blogs.worldbank.org, December 28, 2009. Extracted from website http://blogs.worldbank.org/publicsphere/category/tags/man-arena on January 18, 2010. This quote of Theodore Roosevelt is in the public domain.

Paschal, Don. Carolyn Corbin interviewed Paschal on March 24, 2010. For more information, Don Paschal can be contacted by telephone at 972-529-1325 and by email at don@paschalconsulting.com.

Porter, Eduardo. "Marc L. Miringoff, 58, Dies; Measurer of Social Health," *nytimes.com*, March 6, 2004. Extracted from website http://www.nytimes.com/2004/03/06/nyregion/marc-1 miringoff-58-dies-measurer-of-social-health.html on September 12, 2009.

Putnam, Robert D. *Bowling Alone: The Collapse and Revival of American Community*. New York: Simon & Schuster, 2000.

Rediger, G. Lloyd. *Clergy Killers: Guidance for Pastors and Congregations Under Attack*. Louisville, Kentucky: Westminster John Knox Press, 1997.

Saelinger, Tracy. "Debunking the '54 Home Computer Hoax." *Popular Mechanics*, December, 2004. Extracted from website http://www.popularmechanics.com/technology/upgrade/1303271.html on January 31, 2010.

Scott, Mark. "Amsterdam as Smart City: Going Green, Fast." *BusinessWeek*, March 13, 2009.
Extracted from website http://www.businessweek.com/print/globalbiz/content/mar2009/gb20090313_662708.htm on October 20, 2009.

Seneca Meadows Landfill. "Landfill Expands Job Market," Press conference March 11, 2005.
Extracted from website http://www.senecameadows.com/Renewable.html on November 14, 2009.

_____. Marketing materials furnished by Terri Ricketts, Public Affairs Manager, Texas Region, IESI. Contact information: Telephone 469-452-8008, Email tricketts@iesi.com. Information received October 2009.

_____ "Working for a Cleaner Environment." Extracted from Seneca Meadows Landfill website
http://www.senecameadows.com on May 9, 2010.

Smith, M.K. "Social Capital." *the encyclopedia of informal education.* www.infed.org/biblio/social_capital.htm, 2000-2009. Extracted from http://www.infed.org/biblio/social_capital.htm on October 17, 2009.

Stein, Garth. "Seattle Grace." *Fast Company*, May 2009, 93-96.

Tennison, Sharon. Carolyn Corbin interviewed Sharon Tennison on April 16, 2010. More information about the Center for Citizen Initiatives can be found on website www.ccisf.org. On the homepage, click "President's Report" for updates on Tennison's work.

The Daily Beast. "America's Smartest Cities—From First to Worst." Extracted from website
http://www.thedailybeast.com/blogs-and-stories/2009-10-04/americas-smartest-cities---from-first-to-worst/?cid=hp:beastoriginalsR6 on October 17, 2009.

The National Commission on Terrorist Attacks Upon the United States, Kean, Thomas H., Chair and Hamilton, Lee H., Vice Chair. *The 9/11 Report.* New York: St. Martins Press, 2004. Reporting and analysis, *The New York Times*, 2004.

The Research Triangle Park. "Quick Facts: RTP Companies." Extracted from website http://www.rtp.org/main/index.php?pid=234&sec=1 on October 22, 2009.

The Saguaro Seminar: Civic Engagement in America. *Social Capital Community Benchmark Survey Executive Summary.* John F. Kennedy School of Government, Harvard University, 2000.

Tichy, Noel M., and Warren G. Bennis. *Judgment.* New York: Portfolio, 2007, 3.

Tutu, Desmond. *No Future Without Forgiveness.* New York: An Image Book published by Doubleday, 1999.

U.S. Department of Energy. *Greensburg, Kansas: A Better, Greener Place to Live.* Extracted from website http://apps1.eere.energy.gov/buildings/publications/pdfs/corporate/45086.pdf on July 1, 2010.

Wachtel, Paul L. *The Poverty of Affluence: A Psychological Portrait of the American Way of Life.* New York: The Free Press, 1983.

Wilson, Timothy D. "Know Thyself." *Perspectives on Psychological Science*, Volume 4, Number 4, 384-389: Association for Psychological Sciences, 2009. Extracted from website http://www.psychologicalscience.org/journals/pps/4_4_pdfs/wilson.pdf on January 10, 2010.

Wikipedia, website last updated July 29, 2009 at 17:03, is the source of information. Extracted August 5, 2009 from http://en.wikipedia.org/wiki/Wiki, Wikimedia Foundation, Inc.

ABOUT THE AUTHOR

CAROLYN CORBIN IS president of the Center for the 21st Century (C21C), a socioeconomic think tank providing executive briefings, organizational training, consulting, and research for the business, government, and nonprofit sectors. C21C helps organizations and communities identify critical 21st century issues and formulate actionable plans for future success.

As an internationally renowned author, speaker, socioeconomic futurist, and consultant, Corbin has been spotlighted in hundreds of TV, radio, Internet, and periodical interviews reaching people on every major continent. Her work holds a reputation for being accurate and decisive. Corbin's client base includes a virtual "Who's Who" of global organizations—including communities, corporations, professional associations, universities, governments, religious organizations, and nonprofit agencies.

She is active in her local community of McKinney, Texas, serving on multiple education, civic, religious, and historic boards and committees. During her career, she has received numerous professional honors and awards including Distinguished Alumna of the University of North Texas, Most Impressive American named by the Toastmasters of Peru, Texas Role Model for Entrepreneurial Women selected by Business & Professional Women's Clubs, Inc., and American Society for Training and Development's Regional Professional of the Year.

Other books by Corbin have received wide acclaim in their specialized fields. *Strategies 2000* (Eakin Press, 1986; 1990) was a #1 business bestseller and was cited by *The Kiplinger Washington Letter* (now known as *The Kiplinger Letter*) as one of the best business books of 1986. *Conquering Corporate Codependence* (Paramount/Prentice-Hall, 1993) was named as the esteemed Newbridge (formerly known as MacMillan) Book Clubs' Executive Program main selection.

Great Leaders See the Future First is published in three languages—English, Chinese, and Korean. It debuted as #1 on *The Dallas Morning News* bestseller list and has been ranked in the top five of The Business Success Store's current "best of the best" *Million $ [Dollar] Leadership Books* from Amazon.com by The Empowered Business. The book was also selected by *The Business Book Bookstore & Review* as one of the "100 Best Business Books for 2007 from Amazon.com." *Great Leaders See the Future First* was named by AchieveMax, Inc. to its *Top 10 Books—4*[th] *Edition*, which includes the best books in the business/personal categories.

Contact Information

For more details about the Center for the 21st Century, sample topics for speeches and presentations, list of clients, blogs, expanded profile of Carolyn Corbin, and information on her other four books, see website www.c21c.com.

Corbin can be reached for speaking engagements by email at carolyncorbin@c21c.com or by telephone at 214.802.5212.

INDEX

Made in the USA
San Bernardino, CA
18 March 2014